TOSCANINI

BOOKS BY GEORGE R. MAREK

Toscanini (1975)

The Eagles Die: Franz Joseph, Elisabeth,
and Their Austria (1974)

Gentle Genius: The Story of Felix Mendelssohn (1972)

Beethoven: Biography of a Genius (1969)

Richard Strauss: The Life of a Non-Hero (1967)

Opera as Theater (1962)

The World Treasury of Grand Opera (1957)

Puccini: A Biography (1951)

A Front Seat at the Opera (1948)

GEORGE R. MAREK

TOSCANINI

New York ATHENEUM *1975*

TO MURIEL

FOREWORD

Toscanini said to Walter, his son, "Walter, if after my death you write my biography, I'll come and haunt you." Then Walter asked me to do it; I felt I couldn't.

I felt I couldn't because I loved him very much and I feared that what I had to say would turn out to be a monophonic paean. Time had to elapse before, severed from that fulgent and flaming personality, one could arrive at some sort of balanced judgment. Time has now elapsed, more than a decade since his last concert, and I have attempted to gain a clearer retrospective view. One sees a conflagration better at a distance; one can measure its effect after it has ceased to burn. Still, I am not sure I have succeeded in assuming the calm observer's stance, the stance of the "impartial" biographer. It may be that even now I am too much the captive, that even now he seems to me so bright a taper of music that I cannot record the shadows correctly. At any rate, I have tried.

Though I was associated with him in his work from 1950 to 1954, though I frequently went to his house, and though occasionally he came to our house, other people knew him more intimately than I. Few, I think, heard more Toscanini performances than I. Long before I had any professional connection with musical activity, and before I began to work for RCA, neither distance, nor expense (important to me in those days), nor flu nor flood would keep me from one of his concerts. I remember I went to one of them with a fever of 101° and by the time I got home I had perspired so profusely that I was completely cured. My wife and I used to save up what money we could to go to Europe every second year, and the question which determined our itinerary was always: "Where is he?" We heard him in Vienna, Bayreuth, Salzburg, Milan, Lucerne, in addition to the New York concerts with the Philharmonic, the Philadelphia, and the NBC orchestras.

The book contains many of my personal recollections. It presents as well the talks I had—long talks, sometimes lasting far into the night—with singers, players, engineers, some of Toscanini's friends, and one or two of his detractors (they were hard to find, but the composer Varèse was one of them). I owe many thanks to:

Licia Albanese, Edwin Bachmann, Rose Bampton, Leonard Bernstein, David Bicknell, Kenneth Bilby, Hugo Burghauser, John Corbett, Samuel Chotzinoff, Ania Dorfman, Richard Gardner, Charles Gerhardt, Constance Hope, Dorle Jarmel, Milton Katims, Leo Lerman, Leonard Meyers, Nicholas Moldavan, Wilfred Pelletier, Ezio Pinza, Leonard Warren, Ed Waters, and the staff of the Music Division of the Library of Congress. Walter Toscanini was one of my good friends. Wally and Wanda, his daughters, still are.

I believe I have read just about everything which has been written about Toscanini, both in English and Italian, and I have used such material extensively, though trying to separate facts from legend. Samuel Antek's *This Was Toscanini* is the most sympathetic and warm-hearted of the books about him; unfortunately Antek died before completing the manuscript, and its last chapter assumed that the reader is able to decipher a musical score. All the same, it is a rewarding appreciation, and though written from the musician's point of view, is comprehensible to the layman. Other books on which I have drawn, such as the Italian biography by Andrea Della Corte, are listed in the bibliography. No doubt I have repeated a few familiar anecdotes; it is impossible not to do so when one writes about a man as much exposed to public gaze and conversation as he was. I hope I have dug out sufficient fresh material to shed new light on him as man, artist, and music's representative. Letters, documents, and excerpts from foreign-language reviews have been freshly translated by me. I own some of this material and would be glad to make it available to other writers; I am certain that no book about Toscanini can be considered "definitive" and that his contribution to the art of interpretation will from time to time be newly evaluated.

Toscanini told his son that he wanted no adulatory epitaph. Nevertheless, let Shakespeare give him one:

> *In framing an artist, art hath thus decreed,*
> *To make some good, but others to exceed.*

New York, 1974   *George R. Marek*

CONTENTS

ILLUSTRATIONS

(Preceding the Text)

———

Arturo as a little boy, with his sister Narcisa, and his aunt Esterina.

Carla and Arturo, photographed at the time of their marriage in 1897.

Toscanini conducting at Verdi's funeral.

The young father with Walter.

Giuseppe De Luca and Rosina Storchio in a scene from Don Pasquale.

Program of Toscanini's debut at the Metropolitan Opera.

Toscanini and Gatti-Casazza at the time they began working together.

Enrico Caruso in the role of Radames.

Geraldine Farrar as Cio-Cio-San.

Toscanini, Farrar and Gatti-Casazza.

Puccini, in his garden in Viareggio.

A Golden Age of conductors: Bruno Walter, Toscanini, Erich Kleiber, Otto Klemperer, Wilhelm Furtwängler (Berlin, 1932).

[*Illustrations*]

Members of La Scala wave farewell to a crowd of admirers in Berlin, 1929.

In Bayreuth. Toscanini, Nanny Larsen-Todson, Lauritz Melchior, Rudolf Bockelman, and Anny Helm.

Toscanini in Palestine.

A rehearsal of Fidelio *in Salzburg with Lotte Lehmann.*

David Sarnoff addressing the audience at NBC, Studio 8H, just before the first broadcast on Christmas night, 1937.

Toscanini conducting. Photographs copyright © by Robert Hupka.

A photograph taken near the Isolino, 1949.

Wanda, Wally, Toscanini and Al Walker at the beginning of the transcontinental tour in 1950.

A Christmas card; Toscanini and Wally.

At the last concert.

In Riverdale; four musicians come to visit and play for him.

At a New Year's party in Riverdale in 1957 with Rose Bampton.

TOSCANINI

Arturo as a little boy, with his sister Narcisa,
who died young, and his aunt Esterina.

Carla and Arturo, photographed at the time of their marriage in 1897.

Toscanini conducting at Verdi's funeral

The young father with Walter.

Giuseppe De Luca and Rosina Storchio in a scene from *Don Pasquale*.
Storchio, a beautiful woman and a fine artist, was one of Toscanini's early loves.

Metropolitan Opera House.

METROPOLITAN OPERA CO., Lessee.

GRAND OPERA
SEASON 1908-1909

GIULIO GATTI-CASAZZA
GENERAL MANAGER.

ANDREAS DIPPEL
ADMINISTRATIVE MANAGER.

LOUISE HOMER

ENRICO CARUSO

OPENING NIGHT
OF THE REGULAR SEASON.

MONDAY EVENING, NOVEMBER 16, 1908,
at 8 o'clock

EMMY DESTINN

ANTONIO SCOTTI

AÏDA

OPERA IN FOUR ACTS
AND SEVEN SCENES.

MUSIC by GIUSEPPE VERDI
Book by A. Ghislanzoni.

ARTURO TOSCANINI

GIULIO GATTI-CASAZZA

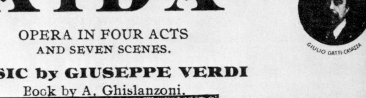

AÏDA . . . . EMMY DESTINN
(Her first appearance.)

AMNERIS . . . . LOUISE HOMER
UNA SACERDOTESSA . . . . . . LENORA SPARKES
(Her first appearance.)

RADAMES . . . . ENRICO CARUSO
AMONASRO . . . . ANTONIO SCOTTI
RAMFIS . . . . ADAMO DIDUR
(His first appearance.)

IL RE . . . . GIULIO ROSSI
(His first appearance.)

MESSAGGIERO . . . . ANGELO BADA
(His first appearance.)

CONDUCTOR . . . . ARTURO TOSCANINI
(His first appearance)

STAGE MANAGER . . . . JULES SPECK
CHORUS MASTER . . . . GIULIO SETTI

Toscanini and Gatti-Casazza at the time they began working together.

Program of Toscanini's
debut at the
Metropolitan Opera.

Enrico Caruso in the role
of Radames.

Puccini, from an unpublished photograph taken in his garden in Viareggio.

Toscanini (looking a little like Chaplin), Farrar and
Gatti-Casazza in heavy conference.

A Golden Age of conductors: Bruno Walter, Toscanini, Erich Kleiber, Otto Klemperer, Wilhelm Furtwängler (Berlin, 1932).

Members of La Scala wave farewell to a crowd of admirers in Berlin, 1929.

In Bayreuth. Standing at Toscanini's left: Nanny Larsen-Todson, Lauritz Melchior, Rudolf Bockelman, and Anny Helm.

…scanini in Palestine.

Candid camera photographs of a rehearsal of *Fidelio* in Salzburg with Lotte Lehmann.

David Sarnoff addressing the audience at NBC, Studio 8H, just before the first broadcast on Christmas night, 1937.

Toscanini conducting. Photographs by Robert Hupka, Copyright © by Robert Hupka.

A photograph taken near the Isolino, 1949.

Wanda, Wally, Toscanini and Al Walker seen through a train window as the train was leaving on the transcontinental tour in 1950. (Courtesy NBC)

A Christmas card, received and sent. Wally is with him.

At the last concert.

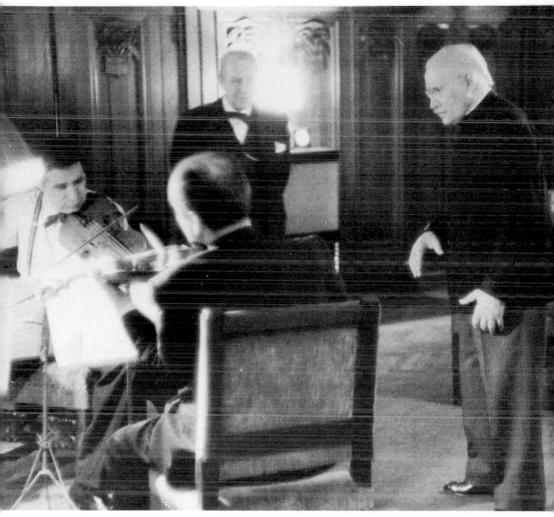

In Riverdale ; four musicians came to visit and play for him. Suddenly he arose, groped his way toward them, and began to "conduct." (The man standing is Wilfred Pelletier, to whom I am indebted for the photograph.)

At a New Year's party in Riverdale in 1957 Rose Bampton gave him a "good-luck kiss." He received it with a smile. (This is probably the last photograph taken of him; courtesy of Rose Bampton.)

LOVE

I NCIDENTS which spring unbidden into memory, like grass-hoppers jumping across a quiet path, are often recollections of regret, recalls of embarrassment, reflections of inanities we uttered, of words we should have said and did not, of things we failed to do and should have done. Fortunately we can summon other, more comfortable, memories to sweep the path. These restoratives we summon consciously. We call them our "unforgettable moments," which means that we forget them but can draw on them when we need them.

It happened long ago, more than forty years ago; yet no one who was in Carnegie Hall on the afternoon of April 2, 1933, could fail to remember the moment when Toscanini stepped on the stage. He was to conduct a concert in the regular subscription series of the New York Philharmonic, the second of a Beethoven cycle, a thrice-familiar program consisting of the Fourth and the *Eroica* symphonies.

He walked out with that mien sunk into itself which seemed to want to solve at the last second some unsolved riddle of the music. He walked out with his firm and yet unarrogant stride, mounted the podium without looking down, his myopia having long forced him to count the steps which would bring him to the right place, and was ready to begin. But he could not begin. The audience would not let him begin. An avalanche such as

3

"a breath draws down" descended from the top of the balcony to the first row of the orchestra, a churning flood of love, swirling away accustomed procedure. Toscanini was of course used to huge applause, to enthusiastic signs of approbation, and like any artist he enjoyed the appreciation tendered him, though unlike most artists he did nothing to promote it and much to cut short its excesses. (It was said that he hated applause, but that was not true.) But what now occurred was no longer applause, no longer enthusiasm, no longer approbation. The Athenians having just been told of the destruction of the Persian fleet could hardly have cheered louder. One man waved his arms so wildly that he tore the seams of his sleeves, an old man put his hat on top of his walking stick and waved it in the air, other men stamped their feet, women waved scarves, in the upper reaches people tore bits of paper from their programs and threw them like confetti, and a grey-haired lady, who one might guess would ordinarily behave with conservative decorum, cupped her hands to her face and uttered a jungle cry. The audience stood; they refused to sit down. The scene seemed almost like the one the Messenger relates in *Coriolanus:* "Matrons flung gloves, ladies and maids their scarfs and handkerchers." Toscanini stood, a light smile on his face, helpless, but for once patient.

Behind the demonstration lay a history of admiration and pleasure stretching over the eight years, off and on, he had been directing the Philharmonic. Yet the immediate cause of the onrush had an extramusical origin, or at least was triggered by a communal feeling in which the prospect of musical enjoyment was overswept by a torrent of thanks. It was due to an action by him which fused the artistic and the personal, and by which man and artist were no longer separable.

Two years before, he had gone to Bayreuth to conduct incandescent performances of *Tannhäuser* and *Tristan.* The year after, he conducted *Parsifal* in a way which had "bathed the score in the mystic light of Italian-Gothic cathedrals, an alternation of shadow and color . . . a Latin magic of sound which, however, introduced nothing not inherent in the music" (Paul Stefan). It was a performance in which "we heard the *Parsifal* of Wagner with new and unfilmed ears, recharged, magical, a thing of wonders and revelation" (Lawrence Gilman). This summer, the summer of 1933, which marked the fiftieth anniversary of Wagner's death, he was to give *Die Meistersinger* in addition to *Parsifal*, fulfilling a lifelong wish. To give the great comedy which he had introduced to Italy in his youth and to which he had devoted almost a lifetime of study, to set forth this spring night's revery at what he called the focus and shrine of the German genius, to expose it under festival conditions with a cast chosen by himself—it was the realization of a dream long dreamed.

At Bayreuth he had, as so often before, taken a work of art which had become an old story by being told too often, and had recharged it with the fullness of life it originally possessed. Rudolf Bockelman, the excellent baritone who sang Kurwenal, recalled, "The piano rehearsals were terribly fatiguing because he insisted on our singing in full voice. I have known many conductors of international reputation. Remembering them I now think that Toscanini was the most objective of them all; faithfulness to the work under consideration was for him the basis of performance. While wiping away all pedantry he did not tolerate the slightest rhythmic imperfection. Hitting the score with his baton or his hand, he used to say in German, '*Hier steht, hier steht*' ('It is written here'). He did not speak German, but those two words he knew. The singer who did not remember all his instructions was roughly treated. But when everything went well, when he was pleased with us, he used to chat amicably, tell us stories about Verdi, talk of Wagner. '*C'est mon grand maître,*' he would say, '*è il mio grande maestro.*' . . . We heard that he had returned his entire fee to Bayreuth. He said Bayreuth was the greatest experience of his life . . ."

When he was rehearsing the orchestra at the end of Act I of *Tristan*, he suddenly stopped and asked, "Where is the cymbal?" There was no cymbal crash marked in the score, there never had been. They showed him the part, but he could not be convinced. Finally they got out Wagner's manuscript: there was the cymbal crash. It had dropped out over the years.

This kind of re-creation, astonishing even those who knew every note of Wagner's music, was now to be repeated with

Die Meistersinger. Eva Chamberlain, daughter of Wagner and Cosima, who was then sixty-five years old but loved Toscanini with the adoration of a young girl, wrote to him:

Bayreuth, March 22, 1932

Dearest Maestro:

I wanted to greet you with a German telegram but thinking it would arrive all garbled and knowing you would be indulgent with my limited Italian, I decided to take the easy way and write to you. Yet my poor words are incapable of expressing the profound feelings which I carry in my heart for you, dear, blessed Maestro. No doubt you understand how to read the language of the soul—which now utters an ardent prayer: *"Oh, kehr' zurück Du kühner Sänger!"* ["Oh, return, brave singer," a quotation from *Tannhäuser.*]

Eva had given him a gift which he treasured so highly that he kept it on his night table. It was Wagner's manuscript of the so-called "Porazzi Theme," a melody of eight bars first jotted down for *Tristan* but never used. Wagner had come upon it accidentally years later, and it must have awakened old memories in him. He added six bars, made a clean copy of the whole, and presented it to Cosima the year before his death. It was an important gift, not easily detached from the Bayreuth archive.

But in the year before Toscanini was to conduct *Die Meistersinger,* Hitler had tricked, bludgeoned, and blackmailed his way toward dictatorship, the febrile Weimar Republic had expired, the Reichstag had been set afire by the Nazis and the arson blamed on a dim-witted Dutch Communist,* Stegerwald—the leader of the Catholic Trade Unions—had been severely beaten by the Brownshirts, the Jews excluded from the universities, the professions, music, and theater. On April 1, 1933, Hitler proclaimed a national boycott of Jewish shops.

---

* His name was Marinus van der Lubbe. Now forgotten, he became notorious (in the first tumultuous days of Hitlerism) and "a godsend to the Nazis," according to William Shirer in *The Rise and Fall of the Third Reich.* The fire took place the night of February 27, 1933. The whole truth of it, Shirer wrote, "will probably never be known. Nearly all those who knew it are now dead, most of them slain by Hitler in the months that followed."

Toscanini was in a deep depression. He had said frequently that he wanted no part of political battledore and shuttlecock, that art was, or should be, untouchable by politics, and he had even refused to meet senators and ambassadors, just because they were senators or ambassadors. In the last few months he had been restudying every bar of *Die Meistersinger* and he was so full of the music that he had an almost physical need to pour it out. Yet that need was asphyxiated by the pall that settled on him as he read the news of the degradations. He made his decision. On April 2 his name headed a cable sent by twelve conductors to Hitler, protesting against the measure exacted against Jewish musicians. Here too he broke a rule: he had never allied himself with other conductors. The cable appeared on the front page of the *New York Times* on Sunday, April 2, the morning of the concert.

It was this cable, then, which had unloosed the flash flood. No doubt there were in the audience of April 2 many Jews who had been offended to the quick, and there were some who feared for friends or relatives caught in a Germany which had become a field of gallows. No doubt there were some in the audience who, having no special concern with the Jewish problem, were sick at the confrontation with tyranny, though it was as yet far removed. No doubt there were some in whose hearts Toscanini's action had sounded a sound of idealism, buried under the everyday and now come to the fore, as a note sounded by an instrument suddenly liberates a forgotten thought, an obscured melody. No doubt there were some who simply took the occasion to express enthusiasm. And there may have been some who cheered for no better reason than that others cheered. Whatever the motives, there it was, a demonstration of love.

In those early days the real hardness of the flinty felons who were now governing Germany had not as yet been assayed, nor did we know how our own skies would be darkened by "the filthy and contagious clouds of heady murder, spoil and villainy." Some of Toscanini's friends felt that he was wrong, that he could do more good by returning to Bayreuth than by abstaining. Hitler wrote him a conciliatory letter:

7

Berlin, April 3, 1933

Very honored Maestro:
As an old friend of the house of Wahnfried I have always
regarded the Bayreuth Festival as the fulfillment of a high
artistic mission. I have experienced a profound joy when
you, honored Maestro, applied the force of your personality to this great task, even though my own hard fight for
existence unfortunately prevented me from being present
at the last performances.

Today, as Chancellor of the German Reich, I look forward
to the hour when I can personally thank you for your devotion to the work of the great genius of Bayreuth, you
who are a supreme representative of art and of a people
who feel friendly toward Germany.

In sincere admiration, Your devoted

Adolf Hitler

Toscanini answered in a letter which now seems all too respectfully couched:

New York, April 29, 1933

Honorable Excellency:
I wish to thank you sincerely for your cordial letter and
I am sorry not to have been able to answer it before this.

You know perfectly well how much I consider myself
bound to Bayreuth and what profound joy I feel to put
my small ability at the service of Wagner, whom I love
without limit.

Yet it would be for me a bitter disillusion if under the
present circumstances I were to take part in the coming
manifestations.

I only hope that my determination, which in the last
weeks has undergone severe trials, will remain steadfast.
With renewed thanks for your kind words, I remain Your
Excellency's

Arturo Toscanini

On May 10 Goering's police seized the buildings, newspapers, and properties of the Social Democratic party. Be-

fore long all parties—Democratic, Catholic, Center, Strese-
mann's People's Party, etc.—were dissolved. They all lay
down meekly on a road over which the Storm Troopers goose-
stepped. Paunchy and laughing SS men, as yet ill-equipped
with weapons, used their fists to hit Jewish children in the
mouth. They threatened children whose parents were known to
be "liberals." Children themselves were encouraged to inform
secretly on their parents. "I have often felt bitter grief"—
Goethe had written long ago—"at the thought of the German
people, so estimable in the individual and so wretched in the
generality." No hope was left for the generality of the hys-
terically deluded Germans, no hope that the "filthy and contagious cloud" would blow away. Toscanini knew that Winifred
Wagner, Richard's daughter-in-law and now the châtelaine of
Bayreuth, was one of Hitler's best friends; she had swallowed
the Nazi creed hook, line, and sinker.

On May 28 Toscanini wrote an open letter to Bayreuth:

The dolorous events which have offended my feelings as
man and artist have not undergone any change whatever
up to now, contrary to my hope. Therefore it is my duty
today to break the silence I have imposed on myself for
two months. For the sake of my own tranquility, yours and
everybody's, I wish to advise you not to count any longer
on my return to Bayreuth.
With unchangeable friendship and affection for the house
of Wagner
                              Your Arturo Toscanini

That was the draft; in the final version he crossed out "and
affection" and "your." The letter was published in the *Times*
on June 6.

When the missive arrived, Winifred phoned Hitler, who began to shout over the phone and at once ordered a smear campaign against Toscanini—"friend of vicious world Jewry"—
in the newspapers. Winifred, who did not want to give up,
sent her sister-in-law, Daniela Thode, one of Cosima's and
von Bülow's two daughters, to the Isolino in Lago Maggiore,
Toscanini's summer residence. Toscanini was fond of Daniela,
a lively and, though then seventy-three years old, still a pretty

woman; he admired the costumes she had designed for Bayreuth. But it was of no use. Daniela could not persuade him. He never returned to Bayreuth.

Toscanini's self-banishment, to him as severe a separation as that of the lover who walks away from his mistress at the very noon of love, represented a sacrifice which was understood by many.* The Philharmonic audience wished to recompense him for the loss he had sustained. They stood up when he entered because he had stood up for decency. They shouted their affection because he had demonstrated his disaffection with the shouts of savagery. Yet the noise was but a sign of an emotion which can be expressed in forms other than plangent praise and which connects a beloved artist to his public. The silence which used to descend on the audience as they waited for him to appear from the wings and which resembled Milton's "soft silence of the list'ning night" was just as certain an expression. Anticipating silence and enthusiastic noise— the before and after of performance—mark the frontiers of the affinity which exists between the audience and the artist.

2

Unlike happy families, successful artists are not all alike; rather our relationship to them is not the same. There are artists one respects, artists one admires, controversial artists for whose concerts one yet hastens to buy tickets—and there are artists one loves. Obviously, these categories blend into one another and the ultimate accolade, that of love, contains all the elements commingled, elements of respect, admiration, and popularity. Yet a separation is evident. Fritz Reiner was a superb

---

* One of those who understood was a German, Hans Paul von Wolzogen, the editor of the *Bayreuther Blätter*. He was then, in 1933, eighty-five years old and had been present at the opening of the Bayreuth house in 1876. He wrote Toscanini (in part): "Your decision is made—one which must be considered tragic. The victims are two: not only Bayreuth, but you yourself, Maestro and friend, hurt to the depth of your soul. . . . One understands your pain and one feels with it profoundly. All the same, we faithful ones in Wahnfried and on the hill of the Festspiele know that you will always remain linked to Bayreuth. Our artistic ideal—how great a measure do we owe you for its realization."

conductor and honed the Chicago Symphony into the flexible instrument which it now is, but people did not love Fritz Reiner, and he never achieved the popularity to which by sheer artistry he was entitled. George Szell was an ascetic spirit of the classic tradition, a lean and masterful marshal of notes, whose recordings may be placed on the top shelf, yet comparatively few bought those recordings, few went out to him with open arms, many thought him aloof or ill-tempered, causing a friend of mine who crossed his path to say that Szell has no fury like a conductor scorned. The hall floats in a pond of roseate waterlilies when Arthur Rubinstein plays Chopin: all is affection. When Schnabel played, he transformed the auditorium into a temple, himself the officiating priest, the audience a worshipful congregation; the ease which love produces was absent in so stern an atmosphere. Schnabel himself recognized this and said that the difference between his recitals and those of other pianists was that his recitals were boring even *after* the intermission. Heifetz seems like a character from Racine, Isaac Stern a character from Chekhov. With whom is it easier to form a relationship? One wept over Licia Albanese's Violetta; does one weep over Sutherland's, who is the stronger artist and surely has the greater voice? Gigli could sing like an angel—or like a pig. But his angelic singing went so surely to the heart that even the knowledgeable forgave the piggishness.

If we may believe the history of performance—an uncertain history to be sure, since the definition which Henry Irving applied to the actor, "a sculptor in snow," must also be applied to the musician—if we may believe past testimony, we must conclude that audiences of the nineteenth century held Mendelssohn as a conductor in greater affection than they did Wagner, who was the profounder interpreter. The people at the Munich Odeon who heard Bülow play and then Liszt—was not the difference in their response as marked as the calm sea from the wind-whipped ocean?

What traits must an artist possess to be able to open the guarded doors of emotion? When and how does he pass from stranger to friend? The listener who has nodded his head in thoughtful agreement—when does he sit up, his head and

11

hands hot, when does he stop being a spectator and become a participant, being dragged into the storm? This mutation cannot always occur: even the greatest artist fails some of the time and with some of the people. The spell cannot be laid on everybody. Once, at a Horowitz concert—and surely Horowitz is the most spellbinding of all pianists, in league with the devil and possibly the greatest interpreter of piano music since Liszt!—a man sat next to me who was so bored that he read every word in the program, including every word of every advertisement, and, having at last run out of reading matter, read his hatband. Yet to the right and left of that man sat men and women transported into an elation which only high art can produce and for which love is so helpful an ingredient. The difference between admiration and love is measurable in temperature.

Nobody has flamed the temperature higher than Toscanini. One or two conductors may well have equaled his interpretations of certain works, one or two conductors may have performed this or that composition in a juster concept (obviously he had limitations), yet no one rivaled him in the role of inspirator, as a trusted guide, as a teacher to whom we raised our faces. More than a teacher, to us who loved music, he was a father figure, though—ignoring years and white hair—he seemed a young father, agile and athletic and not in the least venerable.

How did he achieve this role? What were the qualities which formed him into the paradigm of the artist? How did he produce in us, by means neither circusy nor flirtatious, such ardor? What are the qualities which distinguish the artist who rises above mere approval? While artistry is undoubtedly the paramount consideration (barring a few anomalies), while finally it is the quality of the performance which counts, while the result must justify the means, there are personal characteristics which enter the purlieu of love. An artist who seems to us distant, walking weightlessly above the clouds, as do those angels in the Renaissance pictures whose bodies leave no impress—we can admire him, but we will not love him. The interpreter must give us a sense of being himself passionately involved, if we are to become involved. We felt about Toscanini that he was always involved, that he was forever in the thick of a fight.

Other, and quite earthy, considerations influenced our relationship. Toscanini was handsome, elegant, aristocratic in bearing. He was photogenic. He was enveloped—certainly by the time he became conductor of the New York Philharmonic—in a formidable reputation, and so many stories were circulated about his memory, his temper, his ear, his wit, most of them true, that he had become almost a fabled creature, a unicorn of music.

Yet he was a real creature and in a sense one of us. While he stood high, we could capture him within the lasso of companionship. While he was a wizard, he did not practice witchcraft; he was not a ghost who faded at the crowing of the cock. He did not hover above the human level so far as to lose contact. In this, I believe, one finds the definition of the beloved artist: an amalgam of the comprehensible and the incomprehensible, the familiar and the strange. That amalgam produces a warm and strong chemical reaction when it is present in the right proportion.

As to Toscanini's extraordinary musical ability—he showed this early, but of course he did not walk at once into the garden of the select. To understand him we should trace his career. We know that a man makes his career, but the career also shapes the man.

CHAPTER TWO

THE GIRL FROM THE MARKET PLACE

————

S<small>HE</small> is intriguing. She is beautiful. Yet many consider her features too regular for engrossing beauty, her mien too soft for enduring loveliness. She is eager as a child to give pleasure. Yet there are some who find that she is overeager and dispenses her favors a little too readily. She is capable of noble and composed emotion, of aristocratic behavior in the presence of sadness. Yet at other times and for not completely convincing reasons she becomes overwrought. Then she dashes with quick steps into all four corners of the room, she pulls her hair, she sobs and sheds thick, glossy tears, tears more sweet than salty. Her actions do not always make sense; often they seem unreasonable. Yet her behavior follows a logic of its own. She will renounce a good man who has committed only the slightest of discourtesies toward her and yet will be faithful to a lover who persists in offending her and who commits the most boorish infidelities. She is likely to swoon at a slight brawl, but she is also likely to look with equanimity on the sight of a gory battlefield. She is passionately fond of masquerades and adores dressing up in various costumes, being sure each time that she is not going to be recognized. She shares with other women a love for beautiful clothes, for stylish pageantry, and for jewels. She is not infallible in distinguishing diamonds from paste. She is almost always interested in love,

14

but she is by no means capable of sexual love only. She believes that all mothers are good, all white-haired people worthy of respect. She meditates on disease and is especially sympathetic to tubercular patients. But she can at once drive away her morbid thoughts and can smile and be gay. Her voice is her best feature. She has it under control at all times, she uses it with complete skill. She whispers adorably, she pleads irresistibly, she commands majestically, and she tells a story well. When she is in a tight situation, she uses that voice; it touches our hearts and we come to her aid. But once in a while that voice, so seraphic and so supple, rises to a shrillness and breaks out in accents of vulgarity which make us suspect that she has spent a considerable part of her life in the market place.

This is Italian opera.

It was—and is—as much a specialty of Parma as is Parma ham or Parmesan cheese.

In this ambience where what happens in the opera house often seems more real than what happens on the street, in a surrounding where the song the shoemaker sings is a snatch from Donizetti, amid a people who love the dramatic in thought and gesture, the child Toscanini was born. The girl from the market place stood at his cradle.

Toscanini was born in 1867 on March 25. The year marked the birth of some other men and women of talent: Pirandello, John Galsworthy, Emil Nolde, Käthe Kollwitz, Marie Curie. It was the year Maximilian, the Hapsburg Emperor of Mexico, was shot. Disraeli introduced his parliamentary reforms in Great Britain, the United States bought Alaska from Russia, Franz Joseph had to divide his realm into Austria-Hungary, Bismarck became Chancellor of the North German League, Alfred Nobel invented dynamite, Karl Marx published the first volume of *Das Kapital*, Ibsen produced *Peer Gynt*, Courbet and Manet held an exhibit of their work in Paris, heralding the beginning of Impressionism, Johann Strauss, Jr., composed the "Blue Danube Waltz," and Verdi *Don Carlo*.

Italy, as we know it, had been born six years previously when Victor Emmanuel was crowned as the country's first king. The struggle for independence, led by Camillo Cavour, had been

both fiery and crafty; both Brutus and Machiavelli inspired
the leaders in the great resurgence, the Risorgimento, which
wrested first North Italy from Austria, then Naples and Sicily
from the Bourbons. The battles of Magenta and Solferino had
been contentions of "blood-drinking hate." Even now, in the
year Toscanini was born, the unification was not completed,
Garibaldi making his second unsuccessful attempt to free Rome
of French soldiers. But finally men such as Cavour, Mazzini,
Garibaldi succeeded in driving the foreigners out and, what
was equally difficult, in unifying a people who, though they all
spoke Italian, had warred against one another for centuries and
in loud cockfights. The ideal was not to prove permanent. Soon
enough Italy, new-structured, was to show fatal cracks, the
flag-waving enthusiasm of a Garibaldi at odds with the lofty
vision of a Mazzini. Italy "might have become a beacon for all,
a thing of beauty," wrote the historian Giuseppe Borgese in
Goliath, the March of Fascism. "Why did it not happen?
Why was Italy so short-lived?"

Parma knew the taste of oppression as well as any city in
Italy. A conspiracy had killed the worst of its recent tyrants,
the Bourbon Charles III, the most dissolute of European
princes. Of him it was said that "no woman's honor and no
man's liberty nor any man's possession was safe," and he was
proud of that motto. His assassin was never tried; he was
spirited away by the people. The city is gentle, bathed in the
soft light of the Emilian landscape, its people are not. Aside
from Parmesan cheese it has given the world Correggio and
Parmigianino. Stendhal made it the scene of *La Chartreuse de
Parme* and Proust held it in special fondness.

Toscanini's father, Claudio, was a handsome man and he knew
it. He was a restless fellow, diffuse in ambition. He had left his
wife two days after their wedding to follow Garibaldi. He returned, having fought as well as the others, to the humdrum
and small life of a tailor, but he still wore a martial look and
dressed his hair in imitation of King Victor Emmanuel's,
straight back, an aggressive moustache and a small exclamation point of a beard dividing the chin. He reminisced about
the war with flashing glances and in a proud voice, hiding pres-

ent failure behind the recollection of past moments of excitement.

Arturo's mother, Paola, was an Italian mother dried out by the slow evaporation of disappointment. As compensation for her disappointment, she exacted respect from her children; she was religious, tight-lipped, kitchen-bound, ruling the family without smiles. Arturo was the firstborn, to be followed by two girls, Narcisa and Ada. Narcisa died as a child.

Claudio frequently went away, absenting himself from a house full of splinters and pursuing one scheme or another to make them rich; perhaps these were mere escapades with young women more flexible than the leathery Paola. He always returned, not a lira richer, to the bench where he sewed small-town clothes for small-town burghers. Paola pretended gentility. At least the children had respectable Sunday clothes (as shown in an early photograph of Arturo and Narcisa), perhaps pieced out from remnants of customers' material. Toscanini remembered his mother's stubborn pride: once, when he was six years old, he went to visit his aunt and Paola told him that he must not admit that he had not eaten. His aunt urged him to fall to, he refused weakly, but hungry as he was he finally could not resist the aroma of the sausages and he gobbled them up. When he got home and Paola questioned him, he confessed. Paola whipped him. Toscanini spoke only rarely of his parents, almost never of his mother. But once he said, "I cannot remember my mother ever having kissed me. Did she love me? I wonder." If she did she did not show it, and his children, Wally, Walter, and Wanda, remembered their grandmother as a martinet, one in whose presence one did not shout or crack jokes.

The poverty of the family, while real, has been sentimentally exaggerated. It was a poverty of decency, with the same napkin used over again, but folded neatly after every meal. The meal was often a sparse one, a soup in which bread had been dipped. It was not the poverty, it was the monotony of the struggle for a bare sufficiency, which drove the boy, by nature fiery and serious, to the street and the square where so much of Italian life is lived. He used to loiter at the bookstalls, trying to read as much of the book as was possible, sometimes peer-

17

ing between the uncut pages, till the inevitable moment when the proprietor emerged and chased him. He ran off, sadly and never knowing how the story ended. It was sad, not being able to buy books. Yet there were compensations: the lazy music of the river, the provocative noise the bees made in the sun—and once in a while, very once in a while, a visit to the gallery of the Parma Opera House. There was paradise. Neither parent showed any musical ability whatever—but when there was a little money to spare, they did go, equipped with bread and cheese, to hear the new soprano sing Lucia.

The inhabitants of that city are supposed to be exceptionally musical. "Music," wrote one historian, "flows in the Parma blood." Virtually every Italian singer will tell you that he fears the Parma audiences: they know their operas by heart and if they don't like what they hear or don't hear what they like, they are capable of shouting obscenities at the luckless Violetta or the scared Manrico. Catcalls are the order of the night. Everybody can relate an example, such as that of the baritone in *Aida*. "Then—you are—?" "Her father," he answers, "*Suo padre*." He held the first syllable of *padre* interminably, as most baritones do, and a voice from the gallery interrupted, shouting, "WHO?" Such were the stories the men told as they lounged before the white-and-black-veined walls of dwellings, forever in need of repair, which themselves looked like operatic scenery. To them opera was a sport and its house an arena. Yet their musical interests were limited: what they really liked was singing, or more precisely the tunes, swordclashing or sentimental, of nineteenth-century opera. Of Mozart or Handel they knew little, little even of their own Scarlatti or Cavalli. The country which has given us Monteverdi, Bellini, and Verdi is in some ways the most, in some ways the least musical of the European nations. Even today it possesses no first-class symphony orchestra, and while Milan does display its lordly Scala, Rome is as jejune musically as a sand pit.

Toscanini's passion for music showed itself early. It was evident that he was gifted, his ear sensitive, his memory astounding. In the second grade of school he experienced the good fortune which happens to most of us once in our youth: he had a warm-hearted and dedicated teacher, a Signora Vernoni, who sensed the spiritual hunger of the boy. He used to read all the poems she gave him, and having read them once or twice he knew them by heart. In her house there was a piano. She invited him to come, he stood before the miraculous instrument, he lunged at it, and at once he began to play with the soft fingers of a child the songs and the arias he had heard. Such talent merited support, she thought. Signora Vernoni called on the Toscaninis and in a family council she urged that Arturo be sent to the Royal Conservatory of Parma. As a musician, she said, the boy could make a living, as good a living as in any other profession. Some way or another they scraped up enough to pay for the tuition of the first two years, as well as for a few piano lessons given by a friend, a tuba player by the name of Bonini, lessons sufficient to let him pass the entrance exams. In the autumn of 1876 the nine-year-old boy was duly entered as a "resident student" in the Conservatory. He was delirious with a double happiness: to plunge into music and to escape home.

The Parma Conservatory, built originally as a Carmelite cloister, is a huge grey fortress, the walls broken as it were apologetically by tiny windows here and there. It was dank most of the year and in the winter it needed to be lighted by candles even when the sun shone outside. Inside the discipline was regimental: a set hour for rising, a set hour for retiring, a set hour for meals which, if they included an inordinate amount of fish and bread, these being the cheapest commodities one could provide, were at least regularly provided. The pupils wore dark-blue uniforms and once every fortnight were led for a walk through the city, like a cowed flock. Yet there was the warmth of music inside. Several of Arturo's teachers were intelligent and gifted men and most of the students leapt willingly from lesson to lesson. Each pupil was assigned the instrument he was to study; for Arturo it was the cello, because he was strong and had an exceptional ear. With that passionate concentration which was to become the essence of his being, he completed his assignments; but those were not enough for him. The best teacher in the Conservatory, he said in after years, was the library. There he sat and dug into the scores, attempting to fathom the meaning behind each note and dynamic sign. Even that was not enough. Once a week or once in ten days meat was served at the Conservatory, each pupil being issued a meat-coupon to make sure that each would get a share. Arturo would sell his coupon to a more prosperous fellow-student and buy scores with the money. In short, he was driven by an acolyte's desire to embrace the legend, a zealot's impatience to absorb the writ. He would ask to be excused from the city walks so that he could remain in the library. One summer, when the other pupils went home, he begged to be allowed to stay, a little boy alone save for an old caretaker and one or two workmen.

That intransigence in artistic demands which was to mark him later showed itself early: for weeks he had punctiliously practiced a cello sonata by Boccherini which he was to play at his final exam. Two or three days before the examination he went to his teacher and, standing stiff and straight, announced he would not play the piece. Why not? He could play it easily enough, but he felt that he did not really understand its meaning. His playing would be nothing if not superficial of music he thought beautiful. To him that was sacrilege. The teacher warned him that he would fail the exam, assured him that he could perform the sonata well enough, told him that Boccherini's spirit would forgive. In vain. Toscanini would not change his mind. What was to be done? asked the teacher, who obviously respected him. Well, he would be willing to play a Russian piece which was all bravura and which needed no great understanding, though he hadn't practiced it in a month. He stayed up the night before the exam, practiced the Russian music, and passed the exam.

In the nine years he spent at the Conservatory, in those years when his schoolmates nicknamed him (half-admiringly, half-mockingly) "Napoleon" and "the little genius," he accumulated an amount of musical knowledge, though obviously small when compared with later acquisition, of which the traces were indelible. When he was eighty-two he spoke of his school days, went to the piano, and suddenly played from memory a little Galuppi piece which he had not thought about since the Conservatory. The diploma of his graduation is extant, penned in the spidery handwriting of such documents: it reads that the student Arturo Toscanini absolved his studies "with high honor," the marks being 160 out of a possible 160 in Cello, 50 out of 50 in Piano, 50 out of 50 in Composition.

He was now ready to play professionally the instrument for which he received the mark of 160, and earn a living.

2

It has become common practice for the biographer to borrow the psychoanalyst's couch and to trace his subject's deficiencies or sources of power to early childhood. It is an easy line for the biographer to draw, since nobody can prove him wrong: he has the choice of arbitrary attribution. He can claim that Keats's looking into Chapman's Homer is an identity-transference, and who can gainsay it? Is it possible to explain Toscanini's lifelong continence in food and drink, his liking only simple dishes, in terms of regression? If the opposite were true, would that necessarily be a protest? As he grew old he liked, really liked, only soup. Was that because soup was what he had to eat in his parental home? If that were so, why did he detest any kind of fish, of which he had been served so much in the Conservatory? His mother was tall and strong. With one or two exceptions, he liked short women who were anything but stately. Was this a turning away from the image of the woman who had borne him? Did his legendary temper, did those wounded hoarse cries he uttered, have their roots in an early life which was largely loveless? Was his hatred of tyranny, his contempt for dictatorship, due to childhood suppression? These, let us confess, are but speculations, mere guesses. A dead man cannot be asked to lie down on the couch.

We move in a somewhat clearer light when we look at talent. The same signs occur frequently enough to allow us to make a few general observations. One of these, the most obvious one, is the early manifestation of talent. Musical talent especially shows itself almost invariably in the child. And certainly not in prodigies only, not alone in the wonder-boys or -girls, the

Menuhins, Heifetzes, Maazels, and those who, early blooming, early exploited, have early faded. Nor should we cite Mozart or Mendelssohn, infant geniuses—"genius is a secret unto itself," wrote Carlyle—because on the highest level we meet the total secret. Yet wherever we turn in musical biography, of composers or performers, we observe the early and unmistakable unfolding. At the age of seven the boy Verdi, son of a poor innkeeper, had shown such a desire for music that his father managed to procure a broken-down spinet for the boy. The instrument which Verdi kept all his life is now in the Scala museum; inside, a little plaque may be seen which reads, "These hammers were repaired and re-covered with leather by me, Stefano Cavaletti, . . . gratis, seeing the good disposition the young Verdi has shown for learning to play this instrument, which is sufficient for my complete satisfaction. Anno Domini 1821." Tchaikovsky, the son of a well-to-do government official, wept and pleaded when his parents and his governess decided that at four and a half years he was too young to receive piano instruction: his parents let the child have his way. Of Mahler his recent biographer, Henry-Louis de La Grange, wrote, "Even before he could stand, he would hum tunes he had heard." Liszt was a sickly child and when he began to study piano he did so with such an excess of zeal that he became seriously ill. Josef Hofmann, springing from a musical family—his father Casimir was a conductor at the Warsaw Opera—played the piano when he was three and a half years old, incredible as that seems. Pablo Casals's father was an organist; at six Pablo knew piano and organ music, at seven the violin. Marian Anderson made her first "professional" appearance at eight, singing in church and earning fifty cents. One is reminded of the old story (probably apocryphal) of Paderewski, who was asked by Edward VII how long he had been concertizing. "Since I was five, your majesty." . . . "And what did you do before then?" . . . "Before then I was a tramp."

The capacity is there, present in the young child. It is developed, rather it develops itself, in silence, while character "is formed in the flow of the world," to quote Goethe's beautiful line.* Goethe had something to say specifically about musical endowment: "It can show itself as the earliest [talent] because music is something you are born with, something interior which needs no great exterior nurture and requires no experience derived from living." **

Real talent nourishes itself with a strong instinct of preservation and acquisition. It can be aided. Perhaps it can be aborted, though the murder of talent is a rare crime. One suspects that the tales of talent stifled are based on an illusion, an alleviating illusion invented by those who do not have talent. In the complex of the Khmer temples of Cambodia the French explorers left one temple in the state they found it: through the massive stone floor the trees have forced their roots, twisting and growing so that the trunks resemble huge overfed snakes; they have burst through the roof as well. Stone could not stop the thrust of the jungle. "Thrust"—that is a characteristic of talent.

It quickly develops a tough hide. It must grow pachydermatous for self-protection. Man's most difficult task is to create, be that creation a painting which helps us to see something we could not see before, or a mathematical formula which helps us to reduce the complexity of the physical world. Yet the painter or physicist works without witnesses and may change his course and correct his errors. The performing artist's task is in some ways easier, in some ways harder than the creator's: he is given his material, but he is given no possibility to correct what he does with it. He steps out on the stage—and he conquers or fails. Then and there. And every time he steps on the stage he must give of himself, he appears so to speak in the nude, he must wear his heart on his sleeve for daws to peck at. Nobody can help him. He is alone. A man can be a mediocre bookkeeper and the strength of the organization will cover his weakness; he can go home at five o'clock to his wife and children in New Jersey, preserving his self-respect. An artist who has failed, whose contribution the audience has rejected, cannot preserve his self-respect. It is the difficulty of the

---

* *"Es bildet ein Talent sich in der Stille,*
   Sich ein Charakter in dem Strom der Welt." Torquato Tasso, Act I.
** Conversations with Eckermann, February 14, 1831.

task, then, which forces talent to grow obdurate. The artist is forever facing a rawer challenge than the man who works with others. Horowitz said that the longest walk in the world is the walk from the wings of Carnegie Hall to the piano stool; once you sit down it is not so bad.

A talented man or woman develops a highly selective digestion. Talent ingests what is useful to it and rejects the irrelevant. Dr. Watson is astonished when he discovers that Sherlock Holmes does not know that the earth is round. When he informs him of the fact, Holmes replies that he shall do his best to forget it. A strong musician will not only know the music itself, but all that surrounds and circumstances it, its place in history, the influence of previous work on it, the conditions under which it was composed and under which it was first performed, the opinions of other musicians on its execution, the reaction of various audiences to it. That learning is specialized; it is possible for an artist to be nescient of or uneducated in fields other than music, to ignore the fact that the world is round. The connection between talent and intellectualism, if it exists at all, is tenuous. Even the connection between talent and intelligence is not always easy to establish. There are signal exceptions, Toscanini being one of them. Arthur Rubinstein is a man of widest learning, responsive to art in many forms, whose reading has wandered into the literatures of past and present, who can recall as vividly the heroine of Ladislas Reymont's *The Peasants* as he can Balzac's César Grandet or Thomas Mann's Clavdia Chauchat or the gist of a Montaigne essay. He loved Vuillard and befriended Picasso—who later made a superb drawing of him—at a time when Picasso was still suspected of being a freak. He takes a deep interest in the political strife, his leanings being sensibly liberal. (With the result that his eldest son is a rabid reactionary.) His appreciation of fine food is enthusiastic, his knowledge of wines encyclopedic. In short, Rubinstein is open to life. Most artists are closed to life. Too deeply do they dig themselves into the musical score. Heifetz built a wall around himself. He sits on a hilltop in Hollywood, alone, twice divorced, censorious of a world he makes little effort to understand, his favorite solution for many ills being that the electric automobile ought to take the place of the gasoline motor. With the very few friends he admits, he likes to play cards, or show them magic tricks, the solution of which would not be difficult for a child of six to unravel. Secretive and precise to the point of fussiness, he will never tell his name when he telephones. You are expected to recognize his voice. He phoned me once in New York from Hollywood to say that a letter sent to him lacked sufficient postage—three cents—and what sort of orderliness was that? Nor will he tell you where he is going. The story is told of him that he called TWA to say that he wanted a ticket. "Where to?" asked the reservation desk. "That is my business." The early exploitation by his parents, his being forced to play too often, a childhood lit by footlights, have made him distrustful of even those who wish him well. He could repay loyalty with icy currency and be indifferent to the troubles of those near him. In what corner of that masked soul lies the nobility which emerges when he plays the Beethoven Concerto? Where does he hide the sense of beauty which he uses when he interprets Mozart? We know that talent does not shape or improve character, though we also know the obverse to be true, that character shapes talent. Living with Beethoven or Mozart does not necessarily ennoble a man.

The artist possesses to a remarkable degree the ability to lower a curtain at will. He can develop a selective deafness which fails to hear what he does not want to hear. His sense of sight, too, is selective, observing only what suits his purpose. He wraps a mantle around himself inside of which he dreams pictures which no ray of daylight is allowed to fade. It is a truism to say that most of us can make ourselves believe what we want to believe. The artist carries self-deception to the extreme.

A violinist I knew, Hyman Bress, had the idea of throwing onto a large screen placed behind him the score of some modern music he was playing in recital, so that those in the audience who could read music could follow the score. He was not a very good violinist and it was not a very good recital, but the idea was novel enough for *Time* magazine to report on it and to show his picture and the screen. What *Time* wrote was that as far as they were concerned, the device merely helped to show

25

that Mr. Bress played a number of wrong notes. It was a typical, snide *Time* remark. I knew that he would call me to bemoan his fate and pour out his bile. He did call me the first thing the next morning. I had thought of denying my presence but then I took the call—it was unavoidable. "George," he said, "have you seen *Time?*" I admitted I had. "Isn't it wonderful! They published my picture!" That was all.

The artist lives in a world of his own. Wide or narrow, it is an Eden, though not a quiet Eden, of his own planting. What goes on beyond the confines often seems incomprehensible to him, as it appears incomprehensible to us that he can be unaware of or unconcerned with the earthquake across the river. Such concentration may flatten the personality but it strengthens the force of the artist. My wife and I were very fond of Fritz Reiner. He lived in Westport and came to New York only when he had to. One afternoon he phoned, said that he was in town, and wondered what we were doing that night. My wife urged him to come for dinner—but after dinner we had to attend the preview of a film. He was welcome to come along, if he had nothing better to do. He came along. The film was *The Prince and the Showgirl*, with Olivier and Marilyn Monroe, a talky, noisy comedy, one of the least tasteful pictures ever filmed, Marilyn's monumental mistake. As it wended its interminably talkative way, my wife, sitting next to Reiner, thought to herself: here is this great man, he spends one evening in town, and *this* is what we offer him! She was suffused with a sense of guilt, a sense of failure as a hostess. At this moment Reiner turned to her and said, "Who is playing the bass cello?"

3

The conductor is music's paradox. He is both alone and part of a crowd. He makes music, but others play it for him. He executes his ideas not through one instrument but through eighty. He must by a democratic process get these eighty men and women to work together, but he can achieve his result only by autocratic oneness. Once he steps on his plinth he must be the sole commander, though obviously the widest variation is possible of how he absolves such leadership.

The ability to lead is not usually given to the very young; the conducting art belongs to the mature. Mature in years, anyway, not necessarily in mentality. The good fairy who stands at the conductor's cradle gives him the gifts of hearing, parsing, and understanding. Too often there is a wicked fairy present who lays on him the curse of coxcombry. It becomes an occupational malady, nursed by the very nature of his profession, his having to be the helmsman of the crew, and by the attitude of the public who look at him—"look" is the right word—as the witch doctor, the hypnotist, the Merlin of music. A hundred years ago Verdi foresaw the trend when he predicted that the conductor would take the place of the old-style prima donna. And just to show that abuse is as old as use, let me quote Ernest Newman, that wise music critic, who wrote a series of essays on conducting:

> As early as the sixteenth century we find one Philomathes waxing sarcastic at the expense of the conductor who not merely indicates the time but works himself up into a sort of dervish frenzy in his efforts to communicate his "reading," as we would call it today, of a piece of music; he beats the air, says our author, with both hands and arms as if he were taking part in a fight, tosses his head about, stamps his feet like a frantic horse, and so on. I should like to read the comments of Philomathes on some of the conductors of today.

Philomathes would have enjoyed the story of St. Peter, who calls on Freud and tells him that he is worried about God and that God evidently is in need of psychiatric help. "I should be glad to help, but tell me, what seem to be His symptoms?" asked Freud. "God thinks He is Karajan."

Precisely what Philomathes describes, Toscanini was *not*. "I am not pretty, I am not a genius, I am not a creator, I am a musician," he said. And several times he asserted, "It is easy to be a conductor. All you have to do is to play the notes that are written," that statement containing both a profound truth and a profound untruth. He formulated the tenets of this faith

27

even before he had the chance to raise the baton for the first time. Toscanini did not undergo a *Sturm und Drang* period: there were no musical sins of youth to be forgiven. Though he grew in artistic stature, he began young and was from the first sure as a commander, equally sure of being but a servant of the art, certain that it was unnecessary to beat the air with Punch-and-Judy gestures, always a student never an "expert," combining a scholar's tenderness for detail with a statesman's hold on the grand line, fantastically knowledgeable about the things he wanted to know and void of knowledge of the things he did not want to know.

The story of his debut as a conductor has become a legend and like most legends needs to be decrusted. The plain facts are amazing enough. An Italian impresario, one Carlo Rossi, who supplied operatic entertainment to theaters in São Paulo and Rio, engaged Toscanini as a cellist and assistant chorus master. Italian operas and integral groups to present them were then Italy's stable export article, as salable in Rio as in Cairo. Rossi's troupe consisted of a complement of singers (its tenor Nicola Figner became renowned), the nucleus of a choral group, the first-desk men of an orchestra, etc. The chorus and orchestra were to be filled out by locally hired talent. The chorusmaster, Venturi, was an Italian, as was the assistant conductor, Carlo Superti, but the chief conductor was a Brazilian, Leopoldo Miguez. No doubt that was a diplomatic move on Rossi's part.

One may easily imagine Toscanini's exultation when he got the job; now he could earn money, he could take a part however humble in operatic activity, and best of all he could travel to a distant land, he who had up to then ventured no farther than Lake Como. On the long sea voyage he was put to work rehearsing with the singers; they were impressed by the knowledge and sensibility of this earnest nineteen-year-old youth. The company performed successfully enough for two months at São Paulo, but as time went on trouble grew. The singers hated Miguez, judging him incompetent, inconsiderate, and overbearing. Once arrived at Rio, the intramural dissension broke into the open. After a performance of *Faust*, which was severely criticized, Miguez published an open letter in the news-

papers in which he defended himself by claiming that his efforts
had been sabotaged by the "foreign" singers. He announced
that he was forced to withdraw from further performances.
The letter appeared a few days before *Aida* was to be given.
Excitement boiled, the pro's and con's being as impassioned as
debates usually are in operatic circles. Miguez was a hometown
boy. Was his treatment to be interpreted as an insult to Brazil?

The night of the performance the assistant conductor, Superti, took his place. He must have felt like a fireman going
into a burning house without his helmet. Before he could raise
his baton, down came the crackling jeers, the thumping hoots,
the screeching whistles. The audience, which had paid for its
tickets, did not want the performance, much preferring the
turbulence, the fits of protest, a witches' sabbath of their own
creation. Rossi came before the curtain and was chased away.
Venturi, the chorusmaster, tried to take Superti's place and
was booed into silence. In the midst of the turmoil, Toscanini
slipped into his place in the cello section. He had planned to
play truant that night for a prospect more attractive, but at
the last moment his sense of duty had proved too strong, he
changed his mind and ran to the theater. He was late and he
hoped that in the confusion nobody would have noticed his
lateness. Indeed, complete confusion reigned in front and back
of the curtain. The members of the troupe knew that if this
and subsequent performances had to be called off they would
find themselves without money, left high and dry on operatic
shoals on the far side of the Atlantic. Several women burst into
tears, grotesquely streaking their Egyptian make-up. Suddenly somebody, some unknown whose name has been lost forever, pointed to Toscanini and screamed, "Let him try! He
knows the opera by heart." Rossi, the singers, the chorus people, all crowded in on the inconsequential cellist, begging him
to save them. It was the last chance. Perhaps the audience
would forgive, seeing one so young.

Legend has it that he was pushed to the podium, that he
took the score lying on the conductor's desk, closed it peremptorily, sat on it, and began. It is probable that he walked con-
fidently to the podium and it is impossible that he sat on the
score, since he never sat, not even at a rehearsal. "You sit when

you eat dinner," he said in later years. He may have closed
the score: he did know it by heart. Legend further has it that
at the first sounds the audience quieted and became enraptured.
That too is improbable: *Aida* begins with strings, pianissimo,
and if there was noise in the house it would have drowned out
the beginning. It is reasonable to conjecture that what happened was that Toscanini had luck. Timing came to the aid of
the master of time. When the slight figure appeared, the force
of the uproar had spent itself, the noise-makers were tired and
now willing to hear, or at least to tolerate, the third of the
candidates. The storm had abated, the performance could begin. As it proceeded, orchestra, singers, chorus, all strung to
the highest pitch of nervous tension, worked with the inspiration of desperation, while those deep dark concentrated eyes
seemed to look at every last man and woman individually and
the stick in his right hand moved as precisely as a comet's path.
Legend has it that he led *Aida* that night as masterfully as he
was to conduct the work in after years. That, too, is to be
doubted. He recalled that he made two mistakes and he recalled
as well precisely in what bars. In later years, whenever he came
to these two points of the score, he experienced a nervous
twinge. At the age of eighty-three he said that when he closed
his eyes he could, like Proust, remember the odor of the theater,
every detail of the performance, the looks of every singer, the
movement on the stage, the color of Amneris's mantle. Whatever may have been the true worth of that hectic night of June
25, 1886, it is certain that Toscanini led it securely to a triumph: the hissing changed to kissing and ended in general
jubilation. The newspaper *Paiz* reported that Senhor A. Toscanini "conducted marvelously the entire opera." An anonymous critic in the *Gazeta de Noticias* wrote, "Alert, dexterous,
enthusiastic and nervous, Mr. Toscanini turned out at the last
minute to be a full-fledged and reliable conductor. From the
applause and praise he received yesterday, the well known
phrase would seem to apply: *'le roi est mort, vive le roi!'* " He
slept soundly that night. When he awoke the next morning
he could not at once believe that what happened the evening
before really did happen, until the pain in his arms confirmed
the reality. Promptly Rossi promoted him to chief conductor—

without increasing his stipend—and he led sixteen other operas * before the season was over. At the last performance, *Faust*, he was showered with gifts by the cast and by his new Brazilian friends.

Returned to Italy, his newfound fame meant little or nothing. What did South Americans know about opera performances? Only one hometown paper carried a casual reference to it. And so for a time he resumed his post at the cellist's desk.

Not for long did he have to descend to the pit. The tenor Nicola Figner remembered him and recommended him to Giovannina Lucca, a lady who headed a music-publishing house in Milan. She was helping to prepare the Turin performance of *Edmea*, a new opera by a promising young composer, Alfredo Catalani. Toscanini was asked to come to Milan to meet Catalani. He tried to obtain a score of *Edmea* but could not find one. Unprepared, Toscanini entered the hotel room. A score of the opera was propped up on the piano rack, and he sat down and began to play it. A young man entered, Toscanini hardly noticing the opening of the door, and stood listening. After a while the newcomer asked, "Did you study this music before?" "No, it is the first time I see it." Thus began a friendship between the two men which lasted until Catalani's death from tuberculosis at the age of thirty-nine, seven years later. Catalani was a cultivated man and a liberal thinker whose ideas greatly influenced the young Toscanini. As a composer he had a gentle, lyrical gift, somewhat inspired by the chromaticism of *Tristan*, yet his talent was not strong enough to win him an enduring place in the opera house, where soft melody alone does not suffice. He is half-remembered for two works, *Loreley* and *La Wally*, both of which Toscanini tried his best to set before the public. (He gave *La Wally* at the Metropolitan during his first season; it lasted only one season.)

Toscanini was engaged to conduct *Edmea*, at Catalani's wish. The performance on November 4, 1886, marks Toscanini's Italian debut as a conductor. Its success was less spectacular than the Rio debut, though a few critics noticed that he "conducted with the sureness and energy of an experienced

---

* Twelve, according to another source, eighteen according to still another. The season took place in June, July, and August, 1886 (Rio's winter season).

maestro" and all were astonished that he conducted from memory. Catalani wrote a letter to a friend of his in which he prophesied, "I believe he is going to have an extraordinary career."

Yet Toscanini was not quite ready to give up the safety of the cello—safe because he could earn steady money—for the whirligig of chance of the baton, chance because Italy was full of opera conductors, able, older, one and all as wary of encroachment on their precincts as a village sheriff. In December he played in two concerts conducted by Giovanni Bolzoni, who many years later told Toscanini that he remembered those concerts as his most unnerving and unhappy experiences. "Why?" asked Toscanini, astonished. "Because of you. You sat there and I noticed that when you were not playing you were not counting the bars till your next entrance. You looked around you with an abstracted look as if you were not part of the orchestra. I was sure you would miss the next cue, that you would spoil everything. Then when you did come in at the exact split second, I got twice as mad. I was furious that my worries had been for nothing." "I am sorry indeed," Toscanini told him, "but I knew the music by heart and did not need to count nor to refer to the notes in front of me."

The following season, when Verdi's *Otello* was being rehearsed for its premiere at La Scala, Toscanini asked for and obtained the job as second cellist in the orchestra. He had heard that, though the opera was to be conducted by Franco Faccio, of whom the composer thought highly, Verdi himself would take a hand in the rehearsals. It was an opportunity to watch his idol at work, to be near him, though separated by the barrier which enclosed the orchestra, and, best of all, to be taking part in the disclosure of new music by Italy's greatest composer. They were rehearsing the first act, and were at the point which leads, after the "barbarous brawl" that "frights the isle from her propriety," to the starlit duet between Otello and Desdemona, the brief love scene based on an even briefer scene in Shakespeare: "If it were now to die, T'were now to be most happy." The transition is expressed by a quartet of cellos, a miracle of a passage, marked *pp*. (Transitions are a touchstone of the dramatic genius.) Verdi walked to the orchestra pit and asked who the second cellist was. Toscanini stood up, his veins pulsing with excitement. What did Verdi have to say to him? Verdi said, "Play a little louder," turned, and walked away. Toscanini felt bitterly hurt. He thought he had played the passage as it was marked in the score and true to the mood of the music. Only later did he come to understand that Verdi was used to the orchestra always playing louder than he meant it to, that he had accepted the exaggerated underscoring by the opera orchestra with the resignation derived from a lifetime of experience; Verdi knew that the second cellist, by playing exactly what was written, would be swallowed by his companions.

As usual, time has colored the true merits of that first performance of *Otello*, with the famous Tamagno as Otello and Maurel as Iago and with the audience bursting into an ovation to the superb tragedy. That tribute represented, at least in part, homage offered to the old Verdi. If we may believe an intelligent observer, the premiere was in fact not the matchless performance that it has come to be known as in musical history. Blanche Roosevelt wrote a series of letters to her friend Wilkie Collins in which she acknowledges Maurel's superb acting but says that the voice of Pantaleone, who sang Desdemona, was "invariably loud. When Tamagno sang, with one exception I felt that the Coliseum entire was being hurled in my face. This artist proceeds in blissful ignorance of the fact that there are some people who do not care for so much voice at the expense of even a little art." It was this pushing and shoving, then so prevalent in operatic performances—and is it not today?—against which Toscanini strove all his life. When he came to conduct *Otello*, he used to relate to the orchestra the little incident with Verdi; he used the anecdote to explain the transition to the scene in which two mature people deeply in love are as yet unaware of the "motiveless malignity" which is to beset them, and he used to insist that the tranquility be expressed by an absolute equivalence of the four instruments.

Very soon after, Toscanini put his cello away and became a conductor in various opera houses, hardly ever needing to worry about his next engagement. Opera companies were operating in Italy's small and large towns, and though some had to be content with makeshift scenery, small choruses, and few stars, every one of them needed a conductor. The opportunity for employment and for gaining experience was there, and though the competition was keen, Toscanini had already acquired a certain reputation.

We could follow Toscanini in his peregrinations to the Italian opera houses of greater or lesser quality. Their number was large, ranging from such tiny centers as Casale Monferrato, Novara, Brescia, Senegallia, Treviso, Macerata, and Volterra to such more populous cities as Genoa, Turin, Pisa, Venice, Lucca, Verona, Rome, and again Turin. But there is little point in chronicling the early career specifically. In sum it represents a crowded road along which he made few false steps and which led him, both by smooth and rutted stretches, to the acquisition of the vast practical experience on which he drew in later years. Not only did he conduct a cluster of operas then famous, only a few of which remained in his repertoire, not only did he study and bring to the stage Meyerbeer's *L'Africaine* or Ponchielli's *La Gioconda* or Donizetti's *Lucrezia Borgia* or Thomas's *Mignon* and *Hamlet* and Gounod's *Faust*, but in addition he interpreted works which were to become lifelong companions, such as *Manon Lescaut* and *The Barber of Seville* and *Rigoletto* and *Aida* and *La Traviata* and *Simone Boccanegra* and soon *Otello* and later *Falstaff*, the special object of his love. We do not know how willingly he gave his time and eyesight to the new efforts of Italian composers. Yet he did it because it was part of the task: if one calculates how much work a conductor has to expend to grasp an opera well enough to lead it—and surely "well enough" would never content him—one must marvel at the labor wasted, at the sheer repetition of effort which, like Sisyphus, had to roll the stone uphill only to have it fall down again. Each season Italian composers, effete or bombastic cousins of Rossini, Bellini, and Verdi, produced new concoctions which clamored for production. Most of these now lie in the graveyards of the encyclopedias, the commemorative tablet a mere mention of the title in tiny type. Who now knows Ponchielli's *I Promessi Sposi* or Cagnoni's *Francesca da Rimini* or Gnaga's *William Swarten* or Mascagni's *I Rantzau* or Franchetti's *Cristoforo Colombo* or Canti's *Savitri* or Lozzi's *Emma Liona* or Buzzi-Peccia's

Forza d'Amore? These are but some of the operas Toscanini brought to a transient existence. Was this work all waste, useless expenditure? Perhaps not. It helped to deepen his critical judgment and to separate the strong from the merely new. The organism of art needs the bad as well as the good; in no period was it possible to have good art without having bad art.

Did he *have* to conduct the rag, tag, and bobtail of Italian operas? In the very beginning, yes, but soon his reputation afforded him the luxury of choice. It was curiosity which drove him on, the inquisitive search by the artist, that curiosity of which Samuel Johnson said that it "is, in great and generous minds, the first passion and the last," sharply focused on whatever may be useful to the artist in the exercise of his art. If you tell him of Jacob's ladder, he wants to know how many rungs it had. Toscanini's curiosity was more encompassing than that of any artist I have known. It worked two ways: in his youth he rummaged through a whole house of music, including the dustbin in the attic. In later years he kept exploring the music he loved, digging tirelessly in its structure, holding it up to the light, again and again referring to the scores which he knew by heart, examining each phrase and dynamic sign afresh, always in the hope that the exploration would uncover a new discovery, reveal fresh meaning of the whole, disclose new understanding of detail. Edwin Bachman, the leader of the second violins in the NBC orchestra, of whom Toscanini was fond, remembers that when Toscanini was eighty-three he visited him at the Isolino in Lago Maggiore. Bachman was rowed over from Pallanza—it was the only way to reach the island—and Toscanini was waiting for him at the foot of the steps. "Come quickly," he said, "quickly! I have to show you something." They ran upstairs, Bachman doing his best to keep up with him, and there lay the score of Brahms's Second Symphony opened to a page in the second movement. Toscanini pointed to a small diminuendo sign in one bar of one instrument which he said he had previously overlooked. "I've conducted this symphony for sixty-one years," he told Bachman, "and I still don't know it." Such is the loving attitude, forever speculative.

35

Of course he had to make compromises in the beginning, conducting with inadequate orchestras, insufficient rehearsals, and brainless singers. But it didn't take long before he developed a bonze's obstinacy. He was going to take the girl from the market place, and wash her clean. He insisted that singers sing what the composer had set down and that they acquire an understanding of the meaning and plot of the entire opera, not only of their role. How necessary that was was demonstrated to me one day at a performance of *Aida* in which Kurt Baum sang Rhadames. In the second act it is a deep dark secret that among the captured Ethiopians their king, Amonasro, is hiding. Rhadames, pleading for mercy to be shown to the captives, has the line: "Amonasro is dead. . . . No hope is left for the vanquished." Baum, having apparently only the vaguest idea of *Aida*'s plot, sang, "Amonasro is dead," and with outstretched arm pointed to *him*, Amonasro, huddled among the chorus. And this happened at the Metropolitan Opera!

A new period of educating singers began. In opera productions of today we have become cognizant of the stage director's role. The knowledgeable devotees of the girl from the market place recognize the importance of his function; his name appears on the program—Ponnelle, Capobianco, Dexter, Felsenstein—his success or his failure is discussed in reviews of performances. He has become a luminary of his own. One or two of the current maestros—Karajan, Maazel—fancy themselves as regisseurs and assume a double task. In Toscanini's early operatic days the stage manager functioned as little more than a traffic policeman, seeing that the baritone did not bump into the soprano and that the road to center stage was cleared for the tenor. Each stellar singer acted—if that is the word—in his or her own style, that style being of course devised to display and buttress the voice. Toscanini wanted the performance to shed the motley garment of the carnival, with everybody displaying his own wares. Others before him had recognized that an opera is, or ought to be, an integrated work of art, its musical and dramatic components inseparable, its presentation demanding a total concept. But he had the tenacity, and the patience and the passion, to act on his belief and to fuse all the elements of the performance, from the flute in front of the curtain to the fortress painted on the backdrop.

He had to convince singers that the text, if it were less than deathless poetry, was vital to the music and the music vital to the text. Himself interested in poetry, he insisted that singers express the words, that—to put it simply—they not only sing but act through voice and speech. He met resistance. Much has been told of his peremptory and dictatorial treatment of singers, and there were a few singers, then and even later, who would not work with him. Not enough has been said about the sympathy which he showed, the respect for the work in hand which he instilled in the executants, the generosity he bestowed when he found the answering effort, the enthusiasm by which he gave his co-workers a new feeling of dignity, that enthusiasm bubbling as freshly at the hundredth rehearsal as on the first. He imparted a sense of discovery, as he himself seemed continuously to feel a sense of discovery. Those singers who were more than animalistic producers of sound acknowledged the value of what he taught them. The intelligent singers—more singers are intelligent than is usually assumed—understood that the man facing them was a force which, transgressing pedantry, could intensify all aspects of performance and thereby make *them* more effective. Mafalda Favero, who when she was very young sang Eva in the last *Meistersinger* he conducted at La Scala, said:

> I was not quite twenty years old. The whole thing was a dream. I remember that I sang and that I acted, but it wasn't I. It was the spirit of Toscanini which made me sing, with those two deep eyes always fixed on me, eyes which were so eloquent that one had to become excellent even if one was not. [Quoted from *Arte di Toscanini*]

Even on first contact he inspired them to do better than their best. Maria Caniglia, a fine soprano, who had never sung for him, was suddenly summoned to Salzburg to sing Alice in *Falstaff*. She remembers:

> In the sleeping car, leafing through the score of *Falstaff*, which I had already sung in January at La Scala with De

Sabata, I suddenly felt as if I did not remember one note; it seemed to me a score which I was opening for the first time. I was ready to die. At 9 A.M. we arrived in Salzburg. At the station we found Toscanini's car and Signora Carla [his wife] and several other people who had come to fetch me. They took me in the car directly to the theater, where the rehearsal had already begun. They had finished the first quartet of the men. I found myself on the stage without being able to take a breath, and for the first time in my life I saw Toscanini on the podium, in front of me. There wasn't a chair on the stage, not a piece of furniture against which I could lean, not even a prompter. What I did see in front of me was fire. It was the hand of Toscanini uplifted, signalling for attention. I made the sign of the cross and began to sing. When the first act was finished, I trembled all over with fear. Going to my dressing room, I met the Maestro, who said to me, "Not bad, Signora. It will go all right. Let us proceed."

We finished the opera and everything did go all right. I shall remember forever that hand uplifted, which seemed to say, "Take care that you do not make a mistake," that hand which guided me so securely. After the four performances, on the last night, I went to his dressing room to take leave and to thank him. "Maestro," I said to him, "this night my career could well finish, because I have achieved the greatest of my aspirations." He answered, "Signora, you did very well indeed and you can be satisfied. But I want to tell you one thing. It is possible that I am wrong but let us go and look it up in the score. Every night in the scene with the laundry basket you sang the word *cavoli* (cabbages) instead of *cavolo*." He took the score. We looked for the word, and we found that he was right. [Quoted from *Arte di Toscanini*]

But woe to the artist who committed an offense against the printed page! He wanted Toti dal Monte to sing the *"Caro nome"* in *Rigoletto* as it is written with the final trill in E-natural, not the E-flat above the staff. He wanted the aria sung *lyrically*, not as a staccato coloratura aria. He told her that

the pauses between the syllables of the first words indicated
Gilda's anxiety, the trembling of a girl in love for the first
time, a timid suspension, a silent sigh. She sang it that way
at the Scala—but then she went to nearby Bergamo and
there Guarnieri, the local conductor, who had quarreled with
Toscanini some time previously, said to her, "Here you can
sing your high note, which makes such an impression on the
audience." She admitted that she was vain enough to welcome
this and she sang the high E-flat.

When I came back to Milan, I had to present myself one
evening at eight o'clock for a rehearsal of *Lucia*. Suddenly
I got a telephone call from Scandiani [the manager of
La Scala]: "Dear Toti, I am forced to tell you that we
have run into a terrible squall. Toscanini, at the first rehearsal with the orchestra, took it into his head to ask in
what key Toti sang the '*Caro nome*' and somebody in the
orchestra answered, in E-flat." Toscanini said that he no
longer wanted to have anything to do with me, that he no
longer even would greet me. For him I was finished. Scandiani counselled me that the best thing to do was to have
patience and to wait. Perhaps the storm would pass. After
a long time, one morning I was bidden to the Scala, to
come to the red rehearsal room (it doesn't exist any
longer), that room which we used to call the room of the
heart attack, because every time we went there it was like
mounting the guillotine. At a certain moment Toscanini
entered. He looked at me, he sat down. Nervously he put
the score on the piano but he had hardly begun to play
when he interrupted himself and shouted, "Basta! I do not
want to see you any more. I do not want to hear you. You
are a circus artist. I put you among the elect and instead
even you have betrayed me." He closed the score, he
banged down the piano, and away he went.

I remained alone and I began to weep. After a little while
Scandiani came and told me to be quiet and to wait. Maestro had become calmer. Indeed it was so. Toscanini reappeared, and I began to sing. Perhaps feeling that I
understood Lucia, we continued the rehearsal without in-

terruption, and only in the duet with the tenor Toscanini
stopped. Then I saw that he had forgotten the incident
and that he was no longer angry with me. "Dear Toti,"
he said, "there is not enough breath here in your voice.
It is necessary that you bring forth all the warmth of
your soul in this passage, to express the drama of these
two who meet at night. You do not give it here. I do not
feel it. It is all too cold." When we finished the rehearsal,
we were friends again. He gave me a tap on the shoulder
and said, "Go ahead, go ahead! You have a beautiful
voice." [Quoted from *Arte di Toscanini*]

Mariano Stabile, the superb Falstaff highly valued by Toscanini, recalled that the first time he auditioned for Toscanini
was at the Scala, where both stage and auditorium stood
empty, the seats covered by sheets. Out of the corner of his
eye he could see across a "mystic gulf" a group of people
standing in the back of the theater, and he was asked to sing
something from the first act of *Falstaff*. Toscanini was one of
the group, and, while Stabile sang, Toscanini walked up and
down the aisle. Then he came close to the stage and said, "Sing
the monologue from the third act, '*Mondo ladro, mondo ru-
baldo.*' "

I began to sing, I finished singing, I left the stage, I went
up the aisle and past the little group of people. He
looked at me silently with that silence which kills people,
stroking his moustache. And finally he said, "You sing
too metronomically." "Maestro," I replied, "I did not
come here to let you hear how I sing Falstaff. I came here
to let you hear if I possess the quality that one day I
might be able to sing Falstaff, if you tell me what I
should do and how I should act." That made an impression. . . .

There was another eternal pause . . . and then he asked,
"Are you free of engagements now?" I said, "Yes, Maestro. I have nothing to do now." "You know where the Via
Durini is?" "Yes I do." "Come tomorrow at ten o'clock
to my house."

40

In those days I used to smoke like a Turk. I used to smoke thirty-five, forty cigarettes a day, with the result that in the morning I could not open my mouth. I was always hoarse. Therefore I got up at five o'clock and I started to walk like a crazy man through the streets of Milan. I was looking for a bar where I could get coffee and milk, hoping to overcome my hoarseness. I remember I finally wound up in the park, where there was a milk bar. I looked at the clock there. It was 6:30. I started to walk around the Via Durini in ever smaller circles and finally I arrived at No. 20 [Toscanini's house]. There was another problem—it is ridiculous now when I think of it, but in my state of mind it seemed an insoluble problem. Should I go up before ten o'clock, a few minutes before? Should I arrive exactly at ten? Finally it got to be two minutes to ten. I mounted the stairs to the apartment. There was the maid. She took me to the room where the piano was, and there was Maestro already seated at the piano waiting for me, with the score of *Falstaff* in front of him. At ten o'clock on the dot we began to rehearse the monologue of the third act, "*Mondo ladro*." From then on until 1:30 I repeated those few words because he wanted me to pull forth the regurgitation, that oh, ah of the fat man, of the drunkard, of the glutton, right from the belly. . . . It was not a question of the notes, not what was written down. The composer could not have written out those indications. It was Maestro who found what the author could not say by graphic means. In Falstaff's phrase, "*Ber del vin dolce è sbottonarsi al sole*" (To drink sweet wine is to unbutton oneself to the sun), he wanted the taste of wine to be heard. He said to me, "You are from Piedmont. You have good wine in Piedmont. Think of Nebbiolo wine, taste it in your mouth . . ." In the words "Unbutton oneself to the sun" the sun was never luminous enough for him. He said, "I want it luminous like our sun in the spring, I want a radiant sun in an azure sky. Try, use your imagination, and give me the sun I want." How often he made me repeat the phrase! For him there was always a little mist in my sun, but at last I succeeded in giving him what he wanted.

41

"Now it is luminous," he said, his eyes shining with satisfaction; "do it always like this!"

When we had finished, he said, "Goodbye, tomorrow at ten." Another night passed with wild visions. Well, after three days of this I became a little calmer. He addressed me in the familiar form. He began to tell me stories. He told me, for example, the scene that occurred between Verdi and Maurel when Maurel did not succeed in giving the "*Vado a farmi bello*" with the pianissimo which Verdi wanted. . . . The second or the third day it got to be two o'clock in the afternoon. Toscanini never got up from the piano. He didn't smoke. He didn't take a cocktail. He didn't eat. He wasn't hungry. At a certain moment Signora Carla entered and said, "But Arturo, don't you understand that Stabile has to eat something? It is two o'clock."

After seven days of that calvary he accompanied me to the door of the apartment and said, "Go to the Scala, go to Scandiani. I will telephone him to give you a contract." Can you imagine my elation? I think I broke the world's record in running down those stairs. I think I did the whole thing in two leaps. [Excerpted from a talk Stabile gave at a symposium to discuss Toscanini. The meeting was held in June, 1967, in Florence.]

In the contract it stipulated that Stabile was to be at the disposition of Toscanini every day from the first of November for a performance planned for December twenty-sixth.

Stabile's testimony shows that Toscanini was able to transmit his conviction so strongly that he rubbed the sticks into a fire. He was like a fire-god calling the frozen earth to life. But —to change the simile—powerfully though his will impressed itself, he was not the whipping-master of a row of galley slaves. He respected individual ideas. He said to an oboist playing the cadenza in the first movement of Beethoven's Fifth, "That is not the way I would have phrased it—but I like it. There is nothing absolute in music." An Italian critic, Eugenio Gara, wrote:

Nowadays one talks of the singers of the past with the inflection of saint-worship. One hears that record played over and over again until it becomes boring. Speaking of records, now we can listen to what the singers of the beginning of the century actually were like. What do we hear? Partly most beautiful voices, often marvelous virtuosity, but very often abominable offenses against the respect due to the original text. Toscanini was a restorer, especially in those wonderful five years at the Scala in the '20's. He made everybody respect his part, from the most famous tenor to the least important comprimario [singer of a small role]. . . . It is not true that singers felt themselves restricted or sacrificed. I deny this unequivocally. Even foreign singers have testified to that. One of the greatest interpreters of the happy years (one always calls the past "the happy years") was Lotte Lehmann, who sang *Fidelio* with Toscanini, and she asserted in her memoirs exactly the contrary to what is generally believed. Maestro's rages were caused solely by offenses which he believed to have been committed not against himself but against the exalted cause of music. Not only Lehmann told me that, so did Pertile, so did Stabile, and many others. Nobody could be gentler than Toscanini with singers who he felt really loved the music and demonstrated that love.

The courage he displayed all his life he showed before he became the famous Maestro. He fought the habit of audiences to demand repetitions of favorite arias. Scowling and with crossed arms he stood on the podium, outwaiting the cries of *bis*. Once, when he was only twenty, a fracas occurred at a performance of *La Gioconda*. He refused a repeat and a man in a military uniform shouted abuse at him. He lost his temper and shouted back, "You are a son of a bitch!" (the Italian equivalent of it). After the performance an emissary came to his dressing room to challenge him, on behalf of the military man, to a duel. The duel was never fought. In Palermo he ran across the command of the Mafia. Its local representatives, many of whom had girl friends on the stage, let the impresario know

43

that they wanted encores in *Cavalleria,* no fooling. The impresario pleaded with Toscanini. The answer was: no encores. At the first performance the audience showed its displeasure, at the second its fury. They paraded through the streets demanding Toscanini's abdication. He would not abdicate, but walked to his stand with seeming calm to begin the third performance. The audience was primed for an all-out free-for-all. Then the unexpected happened: the head of the Palermo Mafia decided that Toscanini was an antagonist whose nerve needed to be respected. Indeed, it would be advantageous to recruit him as a member. The word went out to the fellows that they were to *like* the performance. He was to be "protected." A few tardy noise-makers were peremptorily silenced and *Cavalleria* ended in loud clapping by horny hands. Toscanini did not join the Mafia.

When he was twenty-three he was engaged by the Politeama, the second opera house of Genoa. Arrived in Genoa, he went to the opera house and saw a man sweeping the floor. "I am looking for the impresario," said Toscanini; "could you please tell me where to find him." The man said, "I am Chiarella, the impresario." "I am Toscanini. I am told you have only twenty-four choristers. I need forty-eight." "Twenty-four is all I have," Chiarella replied peaceably and resumed his sweeping. "I insist on forty-eight." "Thirty is my limit," Chiarella conceded after more sweeping. "Then I'll go back to Milan," said Toscanini and turned to go. As he reached the exit, Chiarella shouted after him, "All right, forty-eight," and continued sweeping with such strokes of the broom as to indicate that he would dearly have loved to sweep this conductor out with the dust. Genoa was rewarded with performances of *Mignon* and *Carmen* of which the local critic said, "Toscanini has finally avenged all the crimes which for a long time have been committed in the name of art."

As to *Mignon,* one critic doubted that Toscanini really knew "so complicated a score" [*Mignon,* complicated?] by heart and that "it might have been better to place the printed score before him." Toscanini, though he did not reply to the critic, told a friend, "Tell him I'm willing to have myself locked in a room and I'll write down the entire score from memory. When

I do, I may also mark the inkblots and smears, because that's how I remember each page." His memory was as keen visually as orally. His glance absorbed a page in its entirety. And he did not, indeed he could not, forget it.

He was fortunate when he was engaged by Carlo Piontelli, the intelligent and forthright impresario of Turin, of whom Gatti-Casazza wrote with great respect in his memoirs. They worked together in Turin, Pisa, and Genoa, with Piontelli recognizing Toscanini's ability and probity. "The old man was like a father to me," Toscanini recalled.

Even so, he could prove himself an obdurate son. In Pisa he was dissatisfied enough with the orchestra to retain only twenty-six musicians. Only twenty-six—the others were no good, they had to go. The twenty-six declared their solidarity with the dismissed members and the whole orchestra went on strike. Piontelli, not to be intimidated, announced that he would "import" the entire orchestra of Milan. The prefect of police intervened and a compromise was reached. Piontelli generously proposed to pay the dismissed musicians their salary— but his decision had to stand. Toscanini got the orchestra he wanted.

Later (1896) Piontelli made it possible for Toscanini to conduct a full concert, an ambition he had long expressed. It was to be given in Turin and Toscanini remembered, a half century later, exactly what the program was; it was one that made little concession to easy taste: Brahms, "Tragic" Overture; Tchaikovsky, Nutcracker Suite; Wagner, "Entrance of the Gods into Valhalla"; and the long Schubert C Major Symphony. Toscanini rehearsed the orchestra first in the pit of the opera house and then told Piontelli that he needed two more rehearsals on the stage. He had to adjust the sound from the pit to the stage. Piontelli promised the two sessions, but the logistics of removing the scenery from the stage proved awkward and it was not done till the morning of the concert, a Sunday. That afternoon the orchestra rehearsed on the stage. When he had finished, Toscanini told Piontelli that he needed the second rehearsal for which he had asked. "Impossible," said Piontelli. "Where would we find the time?"

"Postpone the concert to next Sunday."

45

"What! The house is sold out—the people are coming. How are we going to notify them?"

"I don't know—but I won't conduct without another rehearsal."

"I heard the entire rehearsal just now. It sounded magnificent."

"It sounded magnificent to you—not to me."

Piontelli seems not to have taken all this literally. He and Toscanini had something to eat together before the concert; having eaten and chatted, Toscanini said, "Now I go to bed."

Piontelli thought he was joking. The people assembled. The orchestra was on the stage. There was no Toscanini. They sent a messenger to the hotel: there he was in bed, reading. Piontelli had to announce that the Maestro had been suddenly taken ill. All who wished it could get their money back, but he hoped that Toscanini would be well enough to conduct the following Sunday. Piontelli was roundly booed. Toscanini got the rehearsal he wanted and the concert did take place a week later.

When Toscanini told the story one day late in life, he was asked whether he realized into how serious a predicament and possible financial loss he had plunged his friend and well-wisher. He ruminated about this for a moment and then with a gesture of helplessness he said, "What else could I do? What else could I do?"

4

"What else could I do?" The artist sees things not as they are but as he is.

He is as twin a creature as the double eagle used in heraldic symbols. Jules Renard, discussing Verlaine, wrote: "People always confuse the man and the artist because chance has united them in the same body."

Toscanini was nine-tenths artist, one-tenth man. His body—all of it, not just hands and arms—was used as a servant of the artistic will. In moments of success, the body felt as exuberant as a little boy after he has completed his first pony ride. In moments of failure it was not only his mind but his body he punished, and he did so with an almost suicidal plunge, a desire to scratch and wound himself, to inflict physical damage on himself, an instinct of self-laceration, as a man maddened by rage thrusts his fist through a glass pane.

When the concert had gone well, or when he was not in the midst of work, Toscanini could be gracious, considerate, chatty, and charming. He was a superb host and as a guest could be the answer to a hostess's prayer. When he entertained he found out what his guests liked to eat. The food was always festal: ancient Anna, who lived in New York for twenty years but never learned a word of English, made ravioli as delicate as a Rossini melody. Toscanini ate two or three—that was all. But he liked it when the guests ate a lot, and after dinner he would proffer, with all the gravity of a high-priced medical consultant, a bottle of special drops, imported from Italy, guaranteed to cure an overfed stomach. As to conversation, all you had to say was the word "Brahms" and you were assured of a magnificent evening. He never usurped the conversation; sitting in his favorite chair with a lamp shining on him, he was quite ready to listen. But who would not have rather listened to him, as he reminisced of experiences with musicians, singers, writers—and beautiful women? When he discussed music, it was always in musical terms. He detested turgid philosophizing, the German habit of connecting sounds with sesquipedalian meaning. He read Mann's *Dr. Faustus* but found it murky, much as he admired *The Magic Mountain*. Of the first movement of the *Eroica* he said: "To some it is Napoleon, to some it is Alexander the Great, to some it is philosophic struggle, to me it is *allegro con brio*." He conversed in an accented and archaic English, which was pushed aside by Italian phrases as he got excited. Yet with all the mispronunciations he found the telling word, and his knowledge of literary English was incredibly inclusive. He could understand Robert Browning's daedal poetry and he knew Elizabethan English so well that he translated Shakespeare's sonnets into Italian. (The translation has been preserved.)

Sometimes he would ask his son Walter to bring the test pressing of a recording which was to be issued and sometimes, though rarely, a finished record. Walter would put it on the phonograph and play it at full volume, as loud as possible, as he was used to hearing the music. When he was reasonably satisfied—he was never wholly satisfied—his head would sink down, he would listen as it were with every hair on his head, and he would conduct with restrained gestures. Once, playing a test pressing of Berlioz's *Romeo and Juliet*, in the section "Romeo alone," I saw him fingering an imaginary cello, playing the cello part on his vest buttons. When he didn't like what he heard, he would scream, "Take it off!" and then wrap himself in gloomy silence. Once he asked Walter to play his Brahms's First recording. As the record proceeded, he began to mutter, "Horrible! . . . German slop (*porcheria*) . . . I am no good, ignoramus, stooopid!" his voice rising in a crescendo of self-accusation. It turned out that Walter by mistake had put a record of a German conductor on the turntable.

He could turn from a study of *La Mer* or from reading Tolstoy to the most primitive amusement: television. He never played cards, and once in his home in the Via Durini in Milan when we were playing cards with his daughters, Wanda and Wally, he came by, watched for a minute, and then walked away shaking his head and clearly implying that he could not understand how grown-up people could so waste their time. (How did he account for Wagner's and Verdi's fondness for playing cards?) But he would watch the wrestling matches on TV with utter absorption, practically crawling into the screen, and shouting the Italian equivalent of "Kill the bum!" When he was told that the grunts and the heaves were a fake, he wouldn't believe it. He became interested in boxing as well, and when he watched it, he stood up and feinted, sparred, attacked; he read a book on the art of prizefighting, thereafter discussing the sport like an expert of the arena. He was capable of enjoying the most idiotic of television comedians, such as Milton Berle, and much to the boredom of his family used to point his finger at the screen, "Look, look." Then he turned and went back to Dante.

In conversation, enterprise, liveliness, he could outlast people half his age. He hated to go to sleep and he needed only four or five hours of sleep, though it was suspected that once in a while he took a secret forty winks, just as it was suspected that his spartan abstinence at mealtime was relieved once in a while by unseen nibbles of cheese and fruit. When he spent a weekend at the country house of his adoring friends, the Chotzinoffs, they took turns as on a ship's watch: one would go to sleep, while the other stayed up to be with him.

He was never overbearing or conceited. He was proud, but never arrogant. He was aware of the good and bad fortunes of his musicians and singers. If they had troubles, he helped. He had been well-to-do for many years and money, as money, didn't mean all that much to him, though he certainly did not despise wealth, and though he liked to be paid the highest possible fee, because such fees constituted a mark of his position. He was paid $40,000 a season for his original NBC contract, the figure raised subsequently. (Income tax was paid by the company.) In addition, his income from record royalties rose from $30,000 a year to about $150,000, his recording of the Ninth Symphony being in the early fifties the best-selling LP of serious music. He took his affluence for granted. His wealth, surprisingly enough, was not impressive. It is difficult to determine where the money went; he spent freely without knowing what he spent and let others, chiefly a dedicated lawyer, concern themselves with income and outgo. There was never a scandal over his income tax, and he never employed a trickster to compute it, as quite a few Italian artists did.

He loved to give gifts to his friends, but even more he loved to receive them. He accepted them with the excitement of a seven-year-old girl on a sunny birthday. I used to rack my brains to think up little gifts to give him: I found a bronze statuette of Verdi, a replica of the Milan monument, which he treasured, two silhouettes cut by Rossini, an early French edition of *La Dame aux camélias*, about which he cabled, "Only today I receive your beautiful gift which I like and I love very much. Stop. I am very grateful and I thank you dear Muriel and George with all my heart. Arturo Toscanini."

This man who possessed a most sensitive appreciation of poetry and literature had no eye for painting. He knew exactly when Raphael or Leonardo was born and died and what they accomplished. The paintings which hung in his homes, both in Riverdale and Milan, were mediocre (or worse), for the most part effusions of the nineteenth-century realistic Italian style. He had a great many paintings, perhaps as many as a hundred, by men now forgotten, some of whom had been his friends, men such as Crubici, Fontanesi, Spagnolini, Israel, Sernese, and—better—of Boldini, who painted Verdi's portrait. He looked at the paintings owned by his son-in-law. Horowitz, whose eye is as fine as his ear, had bought them early—a superb Picasso clown, a Manet portrait of his wife, a Degas scene of horses, a Matisse odalisque—but they were all too "indefinite" for Toscanini's understanding.

Toscanini was vain of his appearance, though not in the peacock manner which is characteristic of many Italian males. He was slight and short; only on the podium did he appear nine feet tall. Early in his youth he grew an assertive moustache to make himself look older. The eyes, framed by eyebrows which when he drew them together signaled the coming storm, were always beautiful. But when he was in his forties his hair receded and he lost some of his handsomeness, to regain it in greater measure when he was old. He was one of those men whom age enhances. When he was late in his seventies he had the complexion of a child, not a wrinkle in his face. There was a radiance in him which shone on and illumined those who were with him. He had only to enter a room for the whole room to light up. He dressed with care and conservatively, though his clothes seemed to be a composite, the hat of a pianist, the dark coat of a professor, the striped trousers of a banker, the shoes of a ballet dancer. He was most fastidious; he exuded cleanliness. He smelled good even after a concert when he had sweated like a tennis player and his shirt was as wet as if it had just been pulled from a tub. On the day of a concert he used to lie for an hour in his bath, partly to think of the music, partly to overcome his nervousness. It is nonsense to believe that he was not nervous: *every* artist is nervous and as a rule the better he is the more nervous he becomes before he gets out on that stage.

He had so much sex appeal that women went to ridiculous lengths to please him; part of the attraction which drew them to him was an attribute of fame, but part was personal magnetism. When he was eighty, there were frequent telephone calls to and fro with female friends, usually between midnight and 1:00 A.M. When he first came to the Metropolitan, he had a flaming affair with Geraldine Farrar, which did not prevent him from railing at her when she did not do what he wanted done on the stage. His affairs, which he tried unsuccessfully to hide from his growing children, were casual amusements, trifles light as air. His children used to wonder where he got the time to spend in various beds, because he was always either in the theater or at home. His philandering, a sensual need which as he reached his fifties and sixties increased rather than decreased, bore a similarity to that of many creative men, men as diverse in temperament as were Wagner and Puccini. Puccini wrote to his wife:

> All the artists cultivate these little gardens in order to delude themselves into thinking that they are not finished and old and torn by strife. You imagine immense affairs; in reality, it is nothing but a sport to which all men more or less dedicate a fleeting thought without, however, giving up that which is serious and sacred; that is the family . . .

A love affair—if you could have called it that—was one thing, home was another. He had married the daughter of a Milan banker at the age of thirty. Carla de Martini met him through her sister Ida, who was a soprano in the little town of Voghera, where he conducted. Carla must have been the least theatrical girl imaginable, outwardly shy and soft, always keeping in the background, yet snoopy about people, interested in everybody who came to the house, and interested as well in clothes and scarves and pocketbooks, yet by no means shallow or ignorant. Sometimes she showed a more realistic instinct for the capabilities of a singer than he did. In an early photograph she looks like one of those ravishing girls by Renoir, walking in the Bois—black hair, black eyes, and a round roof of a hat on the top of which a dry garden grows. She was conscious of her charm and conscious as well of being Signora Toscanini, with all her modesty.

He fell in love with her, no doubt about it, as letters such as this show:

Turin, February 1897, 1:00 A.M.

Dearest:

I'm back home this very moment after four and a quarter hours of rehearsal. I began this morning at half-past ten to teach the man who plays the English horn his little solo in the third act [the *"alte Weise"* in *Tristan*]. At half past eleven I swallowed two eggs in a hurry, at twelve I rehearsed the orchestra alone, then till six o'clock with the artists. All in all eleven hours of rehearsal for your poor Arturo. I dare say I am earning my bread by the sweat of my brow. Tonight however not only my brow but my whole head is tired. That blessed *Tristan* is very, but *very*, difficult. To make it enter the bloodstream of a bunch of idiots . . . the orchestra, the artists, etc., etc., to make them expend the necessary exceptional efforts—I guarantee you that it needs more patience than I have. I hope to God I can summon enough patience. This morning I got mad with the clarinetist and I ended by chasing him out of the orchestra. The result of the altercation is that my poor nerves are now registering a low temperature. Day after tomorrow rehearsal with the artists and chorus. In the evening rehearsal of the entire opera with everybody, Piontelli will close the theater that night specially for the stage rehearsal in the evening. Saturday free for the artists and perhaps for the orchestra. Sunday the premiere. Will it go well? Let's hope. If my little Carla were here I'd be sure of victory. But since I can't hope that I can only say *ma!* [One of his favorite expressions—a sigh of resignation.] My heart is confident. I can say that I have done all my intelligence was capable of. . . .

My darling treasure, why don't you write me these days a few pretty little words? I have such need of a sweet and affectionate message which would help me wipe away an indefinable sadness which has tormented my heart for days and days. Who better than my Carlottina would send me such a message? Yet for two days you've kept silent. Are you rehearsing a Tristan of your own?

I'm continuously thinking of your suggestion that we live

in your house. I cannot persuade myself that this is a good idea. . . .

Goodbye, dearest. I'm going to bed, I really have need of it. Be patient if I don't write often. Know that I love you very much, that you are my little treasure . . . my beautiful girl and that I can't forget you even for a moment. All my kisses for your adorable lips.

Always your Arturo.

For the first six years the marriage was an untroubled union. Then the affairs began and Carla knew about them. She thought of leaving him. Though deeply wounded, she could not bring herself to do so. It was not the children which kept her at his side, it was her love and admiration for him. She accepted the condition; perhaps she even understood that the extramarital excursions, inconsequential though they might be to the deep core and meaning of his life, were necessary to him. He was able to keep them up to an age at which most men shift into the lean and slipper'd pantaloon. Even after that and as long as he had his eyesight, a pretty woman caused his face to light up.

Though marriage was unique and home was home, Toscanini saw nothing wrong in inviting his lady-loves to his house and dinner-table. Whether in the Via Durini or in the Villa Pauline in Riverdale, one met this or that woman, young or old, silent or rompish, who looked at him with moonstruck eyes. These worshiping caryatids, these occidental geishas, knew one another and spun secret consultations. What was "his" mood? What would please him? Would he like company today? Should one stay away or go to the house? One questioned the other, not so much for information as for the spying out how one could gain an advantage over the other. Endless telephoning was required for this stop-and-go game. A Hapsburg court would hardly have contained more complex ploys. An amorous network enmeshed him.

A little frantic a little meek, a little schoolgirlish a little Jezebel-ish, a little possessive a little sacrificial—such was the infatuation Eleanora Mendelssohn felt for Toscanini. Whatever its facets, it was a total infatuation, possessing all of herself. She was a late member of that branched family for which the philosopher Moses Mendelssohn had earned renown in the eighteenth and the composer Felix in the nineteenth century. She was an actress of more temperament than skill, a cultured woman, flamboyant in dress, extravagant in gestures, whose love for music was perhaps the one true-fixed quality of a mind all too unstable. After falling in love with Toscanini's back, as it were, from the other side of the footlights, she told everybody who would listen that experienced though she was—she had known many men—*he* was going to be the one and only man in her life. Bearing the name of Mendelssohn, it was not difficult for her to obtain an introduction. They met probably in Salzburg, in the 1930s. She lived in a castle near Salzburg. She was supposed at once to have taken off the wall of her salon a Guardi and a Canaletto and offered the paintings to him as a "tribute to his greatness." That seems doubtful—but it is certain that thereafter where he was there she was, at his feet. She worshiped him—and he rather enjoyed the worship, though from time to time he found it excessive. Later he used to visit her in her house in New York, not often but occasionally, slipping away from Riverdale very late at night. She went to Riverdale at all hours, even when he couldn't or wouldn't see her. Sometimes she would drive up to the house at night, sneak silently into the garden, and stand there behind the tree near the bedroom window, just to hear him clear his throat. When he was away, she used to occupy herself making drawings of him, some of them quite erotic. In her house she had a fine antique desk with a secret drawer; in that drawer she kept one of Toscanini's hats and a white shawl Duse had worn. The strangest feature of the relationship was that Carla liked her and used to talk to her about her problems. Sometimes when Eleanora overstayed her welcome, Toscanini would ask Carla to tell her to go home. Eventually they drifted apart. Eleanora swung from one unhappy affair to another and finally, in 1951, she killed herself.

Through all this Carla remained faithful. As the years went on, she got fat and nearsighted, but she never lost her femininity nor her curiosity nor the quiet warmth of her being, which could occasionally calm his agonies. She knew by instinct how long he would rehearse each piece in Studio 8H at NBC. She would be there at the start, then disappear to shop at Saks across the street, and come back just in time for the finish. He never knew—or pretended not to know—that she had been absent. The first time she came to our home for supper, she picked up the service plate placed before her, held it upside down, and peered to see what mark it had. I had arranged for a private showing of Olivier's film of *Henry V*. He wanted to see it, but he couldn't go to the theater because the autograph-hunters bothered him. After the film he talked about the use of the Chorus in Elizabethan plays, discussing its different use in Greek tragedy, and its still different use in opera. I sat with my mouth open, too scared to say much.

At the last they drew together again and he treated Carla with tenderness, as the symbol of a home, the center of the inviolable unit which is the Italian family. She compensated him for an early family life he had not known. He had cut himself off completely from that childhood home. His parents had not been present at his wedding, nor had they ever come to hear him conduct. Now, the most famous personality in music, the world's worship poured heavily on him, he never-theless liked to have Carla and his children at every concert. With all the infidelities, she was his wife and, according to him, a man has only one wife. He would not talk to Heifetz for two years when Heifetz got a divorce from his first wife, Florence Vidor. Such things weren't done. When Carla was dying, she wanted to return to Milan. We visited her there. She lay on her bed with a coquettish blue ribbon in her hair. When she did die, in June, 1951, he missed her very much, but he didn't talk about it much.

5

Becoming involved in the discussion of Toscanini's personality, I have neglected the tale of his career. I must turn the clock back.

We may date the beginning of the spread of a reputation larger than provincial from the year 1896. He was thirty—a young age for a conductor, especially in those days. He was called to Turin, the courteous and splendid city with the extravagant avenues, and to its *first*, not second, opera house, the proud Teatro Regio. The prize which its impresario, G. Depanis, had offered was the production of *Götterdämmerung*. Toscanini had experienced the "true, great, sublime revelation of Wagner's genius" (his own words) and had conducted *The Flying Dutchman* and *Tannhäuser*. But the giant structure of *Götterdämmerung*, as high as the Milan Cathedral, a work then unknown and strange in musical idiom to Italian audiences, that was something else again.* Depanis prepared the Torinese by publishing a booklet which explained the story of the *Ring*. Toscanini worked for months with the singers— the work was sung in Italian—but needed only ten days to rehearse the orchestra. Musicians, critics, music-lovers came from all over Italy to hear the first performance (December 22, 1895). A witness from the United States, S. Dalma, wrote in the magazine *Song Journal*, published in Detroit:

> Greatest of all was the superb manner in which Toscanini conducts. How sure, how calm he is: the best leader in Italy. And the only one in Italy capable of conducting Wagner's music in such a grand manner. . . . I hope that one day America will have this conductor.

From Wagner he turned to a new work by a composer who three years previously had delighted the youth of Italy by a vernal opera as prodigal in melody as an apple tree in blossom, *Manon Lescaut*. Puccini, now thirty-seven, had finally finished *La Bohème*. He was in Turin now, working with Toscanini. The composer wrote to his wife Elvira:

> We are working like dogs. I assure you that the orchestration is really prodigious. It is as fine as a miniature. I foresee a great and sensational success if—the artists will do their part. I had to transpose almost the entire part of the tenor. Now I hope it will go all right. Wilmant [the baritone] is still a dog, but Illica hopes to succeed in

* It was not, as is usually stated, the first performance of *Götterdämmerung* in Italy. Angelo Neumann's troupe had presented the work in German in Venice in 1883, about two months after Wagner's death. Toscanini's was the first performance in Italian by a resident company.

teaching him at least to behave less awkwardly. All the others are very good. And the orchestra! Toscanini! Extraordinary! Tonight I am listening to the chorus. We rehearsed today from eleven to four-thirty. Tonight we rehearse from eight-thirty to midnight. I have a bunch of letters to answer, including the thousand bores who want tickets for the premiere, and women who want to make an appointment with me. Ah! I seem to hear you! But be easy in your mind. I won't answer . . . [Elvira was a jealous woman.]

La Bohème proved to be, the night of February 1, 1896, but a mild success with the public, less so with the critics.* Like Cyrano about his nose they said a good many things, their opinions ranging from equivocal ("In truth music made for immediate enjoyment, intuitive music. In this judgment lie both praise and censure.") to damning ("It will not leave much of a mark on the history of our lyric theater."). It turned out to be a work so obvious in its appeal that it can be roughed up and knocked about and yet manage to draw breath. It is, on the other hand, an opera which needs a most sensitive adjustment between orchestra and voices, a most careful gradation of all the elements, if its porcelain colors are to be enjoyed to the fullest. I have heard Beecham and Karajan and Serafin and Schippers conduct it, not to mention a handful of operatic maids-of-all-work, and never have I felt such complete absorption in the fortunes of four really quite weekday characters, never have I perceived all that is in the score, as I did when I heard the Toscanini performance at NBC. That performance, he said, was no different from the first *Bohème*.

More Wagner came the following two seasons: *Tristan* and *Die Walküre*. For *Tristan und Isolde* Toscanini wanted the lights in the auditorium turned off. How could the dark apostrophe, how could the pleas of the lovers that night create forgetfulness of life, that eternal night unite them eternally,

* The best seat for that performance cost 60 lire, equivalent approximately to $25 in today's purchasing power, an astonishingly high price. Is it possible that the Turin audience resented this stiff price? It is also possible that after *Götterdämmerung* the Turin audience expected something "weightier." Toscanini thought that this might have been a partial reason for the lukewarm reception.

be summoned in a house full of light? The custom of keeping
the lights on during the performance was an old Italian custom on which Stendhal commented in his *Journal d'Italie*. Its
purpose was to enable people to follow the libretto, or to ogle
the women, or to see what celebrities were present. The audience
set up such an infuriated protest that Toscanini had to stop
conducting. He smashed the lamp on the conductor's stand and
left the podium. A compromise was hurriedly agreed on: the
lights were to be dimmed, but not turned off. This satisfied
nobody.

Turin was making ready for a World Exhibition in 1898.
Shrewdly estimating Toscanini's growing drawing power, the
committee offered him a series of concerts, the choice of programs to be entirely his. He gave forty-three concerts, ranging
over the music of different times and different nations, from
sixteenth-century Italian to contemporary Czech. He remembered that at no period of his life did he work more intensely
than in those five months, in which he brought forth four of the
Beethoven symphonies, two by Brahms, the Schubert "Unfinished," the first Italian performance of the Tchaikovsky
Pathétique, and music as dissimilar in style as that of Berlioz
and Smetana, in all 133 compositions by fifty-four composers.
Before the series was over, he received a call which represented
the summit of an Italian conductor's ambition: he was called
to La Scala.

La Scala—"The Staircase"—so-called because it was built
on the site of a church with steps, Santa Maria alla Scala—
could trace its existence back to Maria Theresa, the great Austrian queen. Rich Milanese, as well as the queen, had contributed to the cost of the land and the building, in return for
which their families became the owners of the four tiers of
loges. The owners used to decorate these boxes with their own
silks and furniture, turning a part of the theater into a kind
of private club, more or less aristocratic, a comfortable cubby-
hole in which to hear both music and gossip. In the early days
most of the cost of running the opera was derived from the
gambling tables which were set up in the lounges and foyers.
Emperor Franz, Napoleon's adversary, frowned on the prac-

tice and banned the gaming. Without the income from gambling La Scala got into financial trouble and had to close for two years. After that, the Emperor was persuaded that it was politically wise to reopen the opera house, and he subsidized it with a royal sum, 200,000 lire annually. He could afford to do so, Napoleon and his wars no longer draining the Austrian finances. When during the Risorgimento the Austrians were driven from Lombardy, in 1859, the municipality of Milan took over, though at first with paltry sums. By 1898 the municipal subvention had risen to 240,000 lire. Then the Milan Council took a turn to the left. The old question rose once again—why support an opera house "for the rich" when we need schools and hospitals and help for the unemployed? It looked once more as if La Scala would have to close—indeed it did close for a while—until a society of shareholders was formed under the presidency of the public spirited Guido Visconti di Modrone, an idealistic and patriotic music-lover. With the active participation of Boito, the hat was passed around among the public, the boxholders were asked to contribute, and the Council was persuaded to vote some kind of subsidy. La Scala was saved. To act as the Intendant of the reconstituted enterprise, Modrone called a young man two years younger than Toscanini—by the name of Giulio Gatti-Casazza, whose work at Ferrara had been favorably noticed by Mascagni, Puccini, and Boito. What Gatti found—in his own words— was a

> theater almost abandoned; finances and subsidy far below essential demands; no scenery, chorus, ballet, ballet school, orchestra, stage crew; everything gone and everything to be reorganized; publishers in bad humor; the press anything but friendly; no ledgers showing expenses or receipts or salaries during previous seasons, the impresarios having left not a scrap of written information behind them; and only a short time ahead of us to prepare for the coming season.

There was but one man in all Italy capable of assuming the musical regeneration of the theater—said Gatti—and that was Toscanini. Accompanied by Boito, Gatti went to Turin to talk things over with Toscanini. He welcomed the chance, but he carefully stipulated several conditions, the most important of which were unlimited rehearsals, freedom in the choice of repertoire, complete authority over the orchestra, and final approval of the singers to be hired.

He came and plunged into the work, without making concessions, to himself or the audience. The very first work to be presented was to be *Die Meistersinger*—unfamiliar to the artists, unfamiliar to the Milanese. It was true that some nine years previously Franco Faccio had conducted the first Italian performances of Wagner's comedy—with tragic results. Faccio, who had officiated at the premieres of *Aida* and *Otello* and had withstood that strain, could not cope with the complexities of *Die Meistersinger;* he went mad and was taken to an insane asylum, where he died after a year. Surely *Die Meistersinger* was a bad-luck opera.

Now it turned out to be the opposite. For more than a month Toscanini put every man and woman, orchestra, singer, chorus at the Scala through such tooth-and-nail rehearsals that the music haunted them in their sleep. Antonio Scotti was the Hans Sachs. He first looked at the score while he was appearing in Chile. He looked and said, "I am finished, I am dead. My career is over." But he was too intelligent an artist not to recognize the greatness of the role, and in the twenty-eight days of the sea voyage home he studied it with the help of Campanini, the conductor of the Chilean troupe. Toscanini had never heard a performance of *Die Meistersinger:* working from the printed page as exactly as he could divine Wagner's intentions, he breathed life into it. To prepare himself he had read extensively in Wagner's prose writing; a half century later he could still quote from Wagner's essay on conducting. The performance (December 26, 1898) was, according to Giulio Ricordi, "of the first rank, such as was not to be heard in Vienna, Berlin, Paris or even in Wagner's Bayreuth temple." The audience sat through the first act, which lasted one hour and five minutes, with complete attention, and burst into a great ovation after the fugue of the second act.

We meet here another characteristic of the artist's behavior, the   ish to challenge. He is a buccaneer boarding a forbidding frigate. He is a tightrope walker performing without a protective net. He cannot endure living in a safe castle but must break out to brave the challenge of the mighty line. Part of his daring springs from his egotism and self-assertiveness, the desire to impress his will on those who have come to hear him, his hubris, his wish to astonish. Part of it springs from the teacher's instinct, the missionary's alacrity. This makes him as willing to offend favor as to court it. He will play the *Hammerklavier* Sonata when his audience wants to hear a Chopin sonata. He will conduct *Die Meistersinger* with Italian singers to an unphilosophic Italian audience which wants to hear *Rigoletto*.

Let us remember that Toscanini's performance took place only a little more than a decade after John Ruskin, not a man given to spluttering, wrote to Mrs. Edward Burne-Jones:

> Of all the bête, clumsy, blundering, boggling, baboon-blooded stuff I ever saw on a human stage, that thing last night (*Meistersinger*) beat—as far as the story and acting went; and of all the affected, sapless, soulless, beginning-less, endless, topless, bottomless, topsy-turviest, tongs-and-boniest doggerel of sounds I ever endured the deadliness of, that eternity of nothing was the deadliest—as far as the sound went. [Letter of June 30, 1882]

After World War II Horowitz went to London, where he had not appeared for many years. He was a stranger now—how would he be received? The closer the ship came to Southampton, the more he worried about it. The last night on the ship he didn't sleep at all. The next morning Steinway sent over to the stage of Royal Festival Hall sixteen pianos. There they stood, sixteen silent pianos, while he went from one to the other, playing for hours, to make sure of finding the instrument which would suit him. The only auditors to this strange performance were his wife, his friends Benno and Anita Moiseiwitch, and myself. After trying all sixteen, he found none satisfactory. He then went to Steinway's depot and began all over again, tried more pianos, finally choosing one. As to the program he played—he was not content with the bravura pieces for which he was famous and with which he was sure to capture

61

the public, nor was he content to play Chopin, but included Scriabin, a composer then largely unfamiliar to the British audience, and one hardly "effective."

The challenging spirit serves the artist as the antidote to the fear he feels, as courage is often the fear of running away. Bruno Walter, in *Theme and Variations*, speaks of "the shyness I had to overcome before every rehearsal":

> I clearly recall how, when I had to wait several hours at Brussels on my first journey to England, I felt so great a dread of the impending orchestra rehearsal at Queen's Hall that I was tempted to telegraph a cancellation of the London concert. I was comforted by Toscanini's assurance, when many years later I casually told him of my Brussels attack, that he himself had had the same inclination and had been in a similar condition before his first orchestra rehearsal at the Metropolitan Opera in New York.

From his *Die Meistersinger* performance at La Scala, Toscanini proceeded to Mascagni's *Iris*, Meyerbeer's *Les Huguenots*, Massenet's *Le Roi de Lahore*, Rossini's *William Tell*, and Verdi's *Falstaff*. After the performance of *Falstaff* with Scotti, Verdi, always sparse in praise, sent Toscanini a three-word telegram: "Thanks. Thanks. Thanks." Verdi had not been at the performance—the old man now avoided being seen in public because he was "so very ancient"—but Boito had given him a full report.

Toscanini planned to give *Norma* that first season. To him the opera represented a masterpiece of a combination of the *bel canto* and the dramatic style, stern strength wrapped in a cloak of velvet. He cast *Norma*, he began to rehearse it, he tried, he failed, and he canceled the performance. Tullio Serafin, who was then a young assistant conductor at the Scala, wrote:

> After three full rehearsals Toscanini was dissatisfied. First he changed the soprano, De Frate, who sang well but would not succeed in giving the character of Norma as he saw it in acting, vocal, and miming concepts. Then

he changed the tenor twice. After all that he felt that the execution was inadequate: it wasn't Bellini, it lacked tragic force and urge. After three rehearsals he canceled the whole thing, declaring it wasn't good enough for the Scala. I believe he never found a soprano who could adequately realize the protagonist he had in mind. . . . [True, he never performed *Norma*, just a few excerpts.] [Quoted in *Arte di Toscanini*]

What about postponing the performance? Gatti asked. Toscanini said No. What about giving it to another conductor? Toscanini said No—he was artistically responsible and he would not permit a second-rate performance of such a work at what was supposed to be a first-rate institution.

The labor of regeneration proceeded with the second season: the Italian premiere of *Siegfried*, followed the next night by *Otello*, later the same season the Italian premiere of *Eugen Onegin*, then *Tosca* and *Lohengrin*. The first performance of *Lohengrin* caused the fashionable audience to protest with unfashionable vigor. They wanted the Prelude repeated; it was of course not repeated. Between the first and the second scenes of the third act they wanted an interval for rest and more probably for refreshment, but Toscanini had the curtain lowered only for the twenty-seven bars which Wagner stipulated. More anger! (Well, *Lohengrin does* make a long evening.)

During his first tenure at La Scala, which lasted, with interruptions, from the beginning of 1899 through the spring of 1908, Toscanini ranged over a most diverse repertoire, strong works and limp works, from *A* to *Z*, from *Aida* to *Zazà*. He introduced new creations and scraped the rust off old metals, such as *Trovatore*, a statue so weatherbeaten that after half a century it seemed like a caricature of everything that makes opera ridiculous. He had no "specialties" and would turn from Siegfried's threnody to the hop-skip-and-jump of *L'Elisir d'Amore*. When he wanted to revive Donizetti's little masterpiece, he could not find a bass who would express the ironic lightness of that adroit charlatan, Dulcamara. They remembered an old-timer, Franco Carbonetti, a singer long past his prime who was making something of a living in provincial theaters. Carbonetti was sent for, he came on a bitter cold day without an overcoat and with a battered canvas bag held together by a piece of string. He had no need of an overcoat—he was young and hardy still, he said, he still had wonderful top notes in his voice. Would Toscanini let him sing those notes, just a few of them, even though they were not written in the score? Toscanini would not, and Carbonetti sensibly submitted himself to Toscanini's direction. When the news of Carbonetti's engagement became known, some of the subscribers protested. What was the Scala—a home for has-beens? An asylum for hand-me-down casts? Carbonetti with great courage went on, using every inflection and gesture Toscanini had shown him. He gave a superb performance and the audience took him to their hearts. It was a triumph of age over youth. But the tenor in that performance was a very *young* man who sang *"Una furtiva lagrima"* with such beauty of tone and phrasing that the people couldn't believe their ears. His name was Enrico Caruso.

The ladies in the audience were requested to remove their hats, high-plumed as they were, to enable those sitting behind them to get a view of the stage. Not to be able to show off that new hat from Paris—it was presumptuous! The audience was to arrive on time, or else wait in the corridor. Whoever heard of arriving any place on time?—it was ridiculous! Artists were chosen without chauvinism, so that when Toscanini gave Boito's *Mefistofele* his selection for the titular part was Feodor Chaliapin; he was little-known then and this was his first appearance outside Russia. "How can a Russian sing an Italian opera? Aren't there plenty of good basses in Italy? Do they have to go to Moscow to fish up a barbarian?"—much discussion in the *Galleria,* the glass-roofed gallery where the opera-lovers argued about musical matters while they strolled to and fro Leonardo's statue and the Duomo. In their third season Gatti and Toscanini eliminated the tradition of following an opera with a ballet. The custom, dating back to the eighteenth century, had become absurd in a period when *Siegfried* was performed. Evenings lasted till 1:00 A.M., everybody's attention wandered, but all the same some of the subscribers felt they were not getting their money's worth. Similarly Toscanini kept fighting the custom of granting encores, the *bis* affliction, sometimes winning the fight, sometimes not. The ban became official as late as the season of 1906–1907; even then, when Toscanini returned to conduct *Carmen*, according to *Illustrazione Italiana,* "the audience settled into the glacial severity of judges."

With all the triumphs he experienced, with all the appreciation penned by the critics in phrases fulsome, with all the fervid love of fervid audiences, he had no paucity of enemies. Enmity, often a component of love, stalks the footsteps of an unusual artist. Giulio Ricordi, the powerful publisher and panjandrum of Italy's musical life, declared in 1901 that he would not permit the Scala to perform *Trovatore* if Toscanini was the conductor.* Ricordi hated Toscanini, partly for personal reasons, because Toscanini had refused to perform in Turin an orchestral piece by one J. Burgmein, alias Ricordi. In the magazine he published, the *Gazzetta Musicale,* Ricordi would attack Toscanini for his rigid tempos and "mathematical accuracy," and he once compared a Toscanini performance of *Falstaff* to a "mastodontic mechanical piano." (Later Ricordi changed his mind.) To what billingsgate journalists of those early days could descend may be exemplified by excerpts from an article which appeared in the Milan newspaper *Il Corno,* shortly after the cancellation of the *Norma* performance:

> There is no particular merit in boasting when one's predictions fulfill themselves to the letter. Anyway, who could *not* have predicted that the Scala would become the laughing stock of art under the sceptre of that Dwarf King who responds to the name of Maestro Toscanini? . . . Here is a man who has erected his fame on the basis of absolute disregard of good manners and on an exercise of unconscionable stubbornness, made possible by his being

* But he did conduct *Trovatore* (February 9, 1902) in a performance of which one critic wrote, "There never was a performance so complete, so just in every detail, as the one Toscanini has given us by his true artistic devotion" (Gianbattista Nappi in *Perseveranza,* February 10). Another critic, Carlo D'Ormeville, observed that to present *Trovatore* in such a manner "needed greater talent and greater authority than to conduct *Tristan* or *Walküre*" (*Gazzetta dei Teatri,* February 20).

freed from artistic responsibility. This was done by a management which childishly trembles before him and submits to him.

We have said it repeatedly: if we really wish to save the Scala, we must not give plenipotentiary powers to that monster of Mephistophelian arrogance who has been incautiously chosen to manage its artistic fate. Like any other director, Toscanini ought to be considered an employe, and as such subject to dismissal by the firm, if he ruins the enterprise by his eccentricities and exigencies.

The facts confirm our prophecies all too fully. . . . Our words seem harsh but they are inspired by the great love we feel for the first theater of our paramount artistic city, a city which serves as the hearth of our Italian art.

Let us review the facts which have led us to a judgment which we believe just even if severe.

As the first ukase of his Czarism, Toscanini objected to seven—yes seven—comprimari. He has already dismissed a quarter of them. Result: considerable financial damage and artistic malice. Seven artists, who have had to fight for their living, ruined. A slap in the face of the group of theatrical agents who evidently are not capable of finding even one satisfactory one. . . . De Marchi, the well known tenor, was another target of the intolerance of this new Bluebeard.

Then he chose the celebrated tenor Brogi. . . . The carriage—that famous carriage of the institution—was late in fetching Brogi for a rehearsal. Everybody understood that Brogi would arrive late: however, this drew a reprimand from the Bluebeard and an irrefutable answer from the tenor. Do you know, my friends, what this blown-up frog of a Toscanini had the imprudence to reply? These were his actual words: "I do not believe you, I believe the call-boy." Brogi reasserted his statement, giving his word of honor, and Toscanini answered, "I do not believe you." Brogi replied, "*You* are the one who is lying," and threw the score at the head of his adversary. He should not have done that . . . because he should have thrown something more solid. Toscanini started to hurl himself against his enemy, but in doing so he fell, without however doing himself any harm. The injustice of heaven! Brogi, after such an act of lèse-majesté, was of course no longer called and the tenor Cosentino was substituted. He is a creature of Bluebeard's. . . .

Rehearsals, rehearsals, and after two general rehearsals, *Norma* is cancelled. Nice going! Malibran, Fricci, Galletti can no longer show themselves in the role, to their loss and ours. Now De Frate, who made a success in Trieste and Barcelona, is not given a chance to submit her interpretation to the judgment of the public. Since none of the artists made a formal protest, it is necessary to pay everybody, but the opera is not given. . . . In addition to art and the public, the ones who suffer are the shareholders. . . . Toscanini, that ferocious Bluebeard, only knows how to conduct works which are unknown, such as the *Meistersinger*, with which he intends to prove his own superiority, and he consigns to oblivion the standard repertoire, such as *Norma*, in order not to uncover his own incapacity . . .

Pompeo Ferrari, January 17, 1899

Did Toscanini read this dulcet diatribe? Did he read any of the thousand reviews in which critics, sickly from having to drink too deeply the fizzed-out liquid of mediocrity, chased excited pens over paper and wrote in exhilaration that what happened last night was a unique event, that music once more was brought to them sparkling clean? Toscanini did read some of his reviews and he thought some of the critics "intelligent," such as Olin Downes of the *New York Times*, Samuel Chotzinoff when he wrote for the *World*, or B. H. Haggin, who wrote for *The Nation*. Toscanini liked to discuss music with Haggin and hardly anybody could understand the reason for the relationship, Haggin being an acidulous man, his temperament the opposite of Toscanini's. But reviews did not influence Toscanini one way or the other. He was not like Thomas Mann, whom I once saw fretting because some unimportant scrivener in a newspaper in Bern, Switzerland, did not like *Dr. Faustus.* I do not believe that there is an artist who does *not* read his reviews. Erich Leinsdorf says he never reads them. Well, perhaps a friend reads them to him. Nor do I believe what Charles Lamb wrote: "For critics I care the five hundred thousandth part of the tythe of a half-farthing"—I'm sure Lamb still preferred getting good reviews to bad ones.

The stronger the artist, the more is he exposed to the Everest of praise as to the Grand Canyon of condemnation. I believe that critics are inclined to overpraise rather than to derogate; I know of no artist who has undeservedly been killed by the critics. Not one. And for one self-important, rancorous critic I give you two who extol where they can. As Pope observed in *An Essay on Criticism*:

> *The generous critic fann'd the poet's fire*
> *And taught the world with reason to admire.*

As to Toscanini's art, they did not have to teach much to the world.

Still, and perhaps because in later years his idolators burned too much incense around his podium, a few protests were heard, some legitimate, others prompted by the desire to disagree with general opinion and thereby to show how sagacious their iconoclastic judgment was. Long after Toscanini died, David Wooldridge, perhaps a conductor manqué, wrote in his book *Conductor's World*:

> . . . For the Italian temperament worships nothing so adoringly as the *prima donna,* of whose arts Toscanini was the exceptional and preeminent exponent. He combined the jealousy of Furtwängler and the vanity of Koussevitzky with the musical sensitivity of neither, and over a period of twenty-seven years successfully turned the musical life of New York over to the tender mercies of commercial exploitation, and created of her musicians arrogant and swashbuckling caricatures of themselves. His musical legacy is sparse, for the much-vaunted Toscanini recordings are largely shallow and of no enduring worth, and the few memorable performances which he gave—for

68

his instincts were too professional to be ignorant of the art of rising to the occasion—too high a price to pay for a man who seemed bent on the very destruction of music in his insistence that it serve his will, and be compelled to sing instead of being allowed to sing.

This sort of twaddle is inevitable, one supposes. There must have been some men in Troy who did not find Helen all that beautiful. When there is a lion in the lobby, there is a frog in the house, croaking away. Most artists, however confident they may appear, listen to the frog.

6

On New Year's Day, 1901, Verdi and Toscanini sent greetings to each other. Ever after Toscanini carried in his wallet a card, smudged by age, on which the composer had written friendly wishes in an old man's handwriting. In early January of that year Toscanini called on Verdi and Verdi, still interested in the new music Italy was producing, wanted to know why Mascagni's opera, *Le Maschere*, had failed. Verdi was now almost eighty-eight years old, his mind still active, but his body becoming weary, his strength at ebb tide. A few days later Toscanini called again; this time the decline was evident, the conversation proceeded haltingly, Verdi sometimes losing the thread of it, and Toscanini stayed for only a little while. He left sadly, knowing that his idol was nearing the end.

On the morning of January 21, 1901, Verdi was dressing himself. His collar button fell to the floor. He bent to retrieve it and suffered a brain hemorrhage. For nearly a week he lay unconscious, while Milan, and indeed all of musical Italy, seemed to walk with a soft step, waiting for the inevitable. The city put straw on the streets surrounding Verdi's hotel so that he would not be disturbed by the noise of horses' hoofs. On January 24 Verdi's doctor put his gold watch to Verdi's ear; it chimed the hours with a little musical phrase. Verdi listened, opened his eyes, smiled, and fell back into unconscious-

ness. On January 27, at 2:50 A.M., he died. Some time later
Boito described his death in a letter to Camille Bellaigue:

> Today is Easter Day, day of forgiveness; you must for-
> give me then. I used to spend this day with him at Genoa,
> every year; I arrived on Good Friday (he kept in his
> heart the great Christian festivals, Christmas and Eas-
> ter) ; I stayed until Monday. The tranquil charm of that
> annual visit comes back to my mind, with the Maestro's
> conversation, the patriarchal table with the customary
> dishes, strictly according to ritual, the piercing sweetness
> of the air and of that great Palazzo Doria, of which he
> was the Doge. . . .

> Verdi is dead; he has carried away with him an enormous
> measure of light and vital warmth. We had all basked in
> the sunshine of that Olympian old age.

> He died magnificently, like a fighter, formidable and mute.
> The silence of death had fallen over him a week before he
> died.

> . . . With head bowed on his breast and knitted brows he
> looked downwards and seemed to weigh with his glance
> an unknown and formidable adversary and to calculate
> mentally the forces needed to oppose him.

> His resistance was heroic. The breathing of his great chest
> sustained him for four days and three nights. On the
> fourth night the sound of his breathing still filled the
> room, but the fatigue . . .

> My dear friend, in the course of my life I have lost those
> I have idolized, and grief has outlasted resignation. But
> never have I experienced such a feeling of hatred against
> death, of contempt for that mysterious, blind, stupid, tri-
> umphant and craven power. It needed the death of this
> octogenarian to arouse those feelings in me.

> He too hated it, for he was the most powerful expression
> of life that it is possible to imagine. He hated it as he
> hated laziness, enigmas and doubt.

Now all is over. He sleeps like a King of Spain in his Escurial, under a bronze slab that completely covers.

Boito himself was to die seventeen years later, exhausted by his futile struggle to finish his opera *Nerone*. When they told him on his deathbed that Toscanini would conduct the first performance of the incomplete *Nerone*, Boito wept. He had a clear and modest view of his destiny: "To the faithful ser vant of Verdi, and of that other, born on the Avon I ask no more."

Italy mourned and offered Verdi obsequies he would have thought excessive. He had stipulated in his will that his funeral was to be "as modest as possible" and that it was to take place either at dawn or "during the evening *Ave Maria*, without chanting or music." This wish was not respected. Verdi wanted to be buried with his wife in the chapel of the Casa di Riposo, the home for aged and indigent musicians, which he had founded and endowed with his fortune. But the chapel was not quite ready and Verdi's body was buried in a temporary grave. On February 1, Toscanini conducted at the Scala—which had closed its doors as soon as Verdi had fallen mortally ill—a commemorative concert. Giuseppe Giacosa, the playwright who served Puccini as librettist, spoke. Toscanini chose eight excerpts from Verdi's works. Caruso, Tamagno, and others sang. Then on February 27 the coffin was transported through the streets of Milan lined with a thousand men and women, the procession followed by an honor guard of dignitaries and soldiers accoutered with theatrical glitter—sabers, feathered helmets, gold braid, and all. They halted in the open square before the Casa di Riposo, and there Toscanini, clad in solemn black, conducted a chorus of 830 voices in the chorus from *Nabucco*, "*Va, pensiero*" "Fly thought on golden wings."

To Toscanini Verdi remained a god, no greater a god to be sure than Beethoven or Wagner, but a more personal one, a god with whom he had held converse. In Toscanini's old years, he expressed the hope that he could live as long as Verdi and, probably unconsciously, he adopted Verdi's stiff-legged way of walking. When he was rehearsing *La Traviata* with the NBC he said to the orchestra, "You play this as if it were Wagner.

It is not Wagner, it is Verdi. Wagner was right, Verdi was right. They were *both* right." In that sentence, "They were *both* right" is to be found one of the keys to Toscanini's art . . . He gave me as a gift a large reproduction of Boldini's portrait of Verdi. When I asked him to autograph it, he said, "I cannot sign my name next to Verdi's."

This identification of the executant artist with the creative artist is not exceptional. Wanda Landowska, not a phantasmagorial woman—she liked dirty jokes, the dirtier the better —said quite casually, "I spoke with Bach during the night. He showed me a better way of fingering a passage in the fourteenth Goldberg variation." Ordinarily one would find this unbearably pretentious and arch. She was so matter-of-fact about it, she said it in so offhand a way, that one began to believe Bach *did* speak to her.

7

In the Scala season of 1902–1903, Toscanini committed an act for which his biographers find it hard to offer an apology. It happened at the final night of the season, during a performance of *The Masked Ball*. The tenor in that performance was Giovanni Zenatello, a popular star who was later to sing the first Pinkerton at Covent Garden. In the second act the audience shouted for Zenatello to sing an encore. Toscanini stood immobile, waiting for the tumult to die down. It would not die down; indeed, the howls increased in volume, the cries of *bis* became harsher, and it became clear that the demonstration was aimed not only for Zenatello but against Toscanini. In a sudden rage Toscanini turned, flung his baton into the auditorium, and stomped out. When he arrived home, Carla, who that night happened not to go to the opera, looked up: "Is the opera over already?" "No," he said, stalked into his room, and said nothing further. During the interval, they sent a lawyer over posthaste to tell Toscanini that he had to conduct. Toscanini blazed. "You conduct!" he shouted, slammed the door, and locked himself in. An assistant conductor finished the performance. That was the end of Toscanini at La Scala for three seasons.

Walking out in the middle of a performance is a breach of obligation so severe that it has almost never occurred. His fury must have been engendered by a cause deeper than the rowdy demand for an encore. After all, he had previously yielded to such pressure, if not with good grace. His nerves must have been rent raw after a season which included not only the study of new works, the staging of Berlioz's *Damnation of Faust*, the third act of *Parsifal* (first Italian performance), but also three performances of the Ninth Symphony. Verdi's *Luisa Miller* had bored the audience, an opera by Ponchielli, *I Lituani*, was judged deficient, and the one act of *Parsifal* was not understood; in short, Toscanini had experienced disapproval. He was angry not only at the public but at the management of La Scala, which had made facile compromises on bargain nights, not keeping up the standard. He was angry at certain singers whose vanity chafed under the discipline imposed by him. He was angry at the claque which haunted the house like a phantom of the opera. Perhaps most of all he was angry at himself: he had failed to draw the public—or a large part of it—up to the level where music meant more to them than sociable entertainment. Mahler had a similar experience at the Vienna Opera. He said that he knew he was butting his head against a stone wall, but all the same he proposed making a hole in the wall. The pride which lay in Toscanini and which expressed itself more than once in throwing the baton at somebody's head was a pride in the glorification of music, not in his own glorification. It was a trait which served him to accomplish what he did accomplish, feeding the task not the ego, however wounding and intransigent it could appear to those around him. It was a pride that flowed "as hugely as the sea," certainly not a pride which rustled "in unpaid-for silk," to use both of Shakespeare's definitions, and it merged with humility toward the work itself. And yet—sometimes it overflowed the measure and became an unmanageable tantrum.

The famous incident has been embroidered by adding that he packed his bag that very night, took a train to Genoa, and boarded a ship to South America. So incensed was he that he did not return to Italy for years. The facts are that his bags were already packed, as he was scheduled to leave the next day anyway for a season in Buenos Aires that summer. Toscanini did return to Italy, working in 1904 in Rome, Bologna, and later in Turin.

Upon his return from South America, Toscanini turned toward concert-conducting, and he toured northern Italy with the Turin Orchestra, presenting such novelties as Debussy's *Nuages* and *L'Après-midi d'un Faune*, Borodin's *In the Steppes of Central Asia*, Strauss's *Don Juan* and *Till Eulenspiegel*. However, when the Scala asked him to return, he accepted because he did love the Scala. He found the expected: singers had slid back into their old habits, the orchestra was careless and indifferent. The orchestra was busy organizing a musicians' union. Toscanini, in a rehearsal, suddenly asked who was to be the head of the union. The first trombonist stood up. "Tell me," Toscanini asked, "are you writing the by-laws?" "Yes, Maestro." "Do you mind if I make a suggestion?" "Of course not, Maestro." "Rule Number One: an orchestra should play in tune." "Yes, Maestro." "Because you are playing shamefully out-of-tune today."

In his first season back (1905–1906) he put Strauss's new opera *Salome* on the program. He had written Strauss (July 27, 1905) that he had studied the original French text by Oscar Wilde, that he intended to translate it into Italian, and that he found the subject "beautiful and very musical." Strauss wrote his publisher Fürstner five days later, "As far as Toscanini is concerned I do *not* share your view. He is the greatest living Italian conductor, a supreme artist and a man of complete authority. If a performance in Italy is to be possible at all, then only under his guidance. Conclude an agreement with him and send him the material as soon as it is ready." This from a man who was himself a great conductor. Gatti obtained a promise from Strauss for the Italian premiere of an opera which, hardly a year old, was sure to prove a *succès de scandale*, if nothing else. However, probably unbeknownst to Strauss, Fürstner had already signed a contract with Turin, for a high fee which included the condition that Strauss himself was to go to Turin and conduct the premiere. When Toscanini heard of it he at once took the train to Berlin, accompanied by Carla and his brother-in-law Enrico Polo, who was to act as the interpreter. Two meetings with Strauss and Fürstner took place. Yes, they said, the contract had been signed and an advance had been deposited. However . . . However, if La Scala were prepared to offer a substantially higher fee than Turin, perhaps something could be done, or rather undone. When Toscanini heard this, he paled visibly—Polo testified later—exploded in fury, turned, and took the next train back to Milan.

Gatti felt that Strauss had broken his word. He devised what in effect was revenge: the Turin performance was scheduled for the very day of the originally scheduled Scala premiere (December 22, 1906). Gatti turned the dress rehearsal at the Scala (December 21) into what was virtually a performance, with a full audience, inviting celebrities, critics, and subscribers, and claiming the credit for pride of place. Though Gatti's and Toscanini's anger is understandable, it was a trick which now seems unnecessarily un-neighborly.* Gatti was able to pull it off because the performance was ready.

Toscanini had rehearsed each element so punctiliously that at the penultimate rehearsal he went through the opera without stopping once. How could he do it? "There were no mistakes," he said. Strauss went to Turin and because he himself needed justification for his action, he managed to justify it. He wrote to his wife:

> . . . You tell me: "I didn't chase you to Turin." Yes, yes. But that it was necessary that I come here to straighten things out, that was proved by the Milan performance. Toscanini and a mercilessly furious orchestra absolutely murdered the singers and the drama (à la Mottl). It's a miracle that the work had success in spite of it. If I had not arrived here in good time and demonstrated to the public what the work was really like, *Salome* might have been lost to Italy for years to come. . . .

> Turin, December 26, 1906

Nothing could have been further from the truth, the truth being that *both* performances were equal successes.

---

* The "official" Scala premiere took place on December 26.

Many years later, Strauss sent him the first page of the score of *Salome* copied by his own hand. He wrote that he hoped that Toscanini "would not think it presumptuous to include this in the collection of autographs which I admired in your office at the Scala" (September 26, 1928). Toscanini thanked him with a long telegram in which he said that for him the beginning of *Salome* was "one of the most picturesque and inspired pages of your art." When Toscanini met Strauss later, he said, "For Strauss the composer I take my hat off," and proceeded to do so; "for Strauss the man I put it on again," and proceeded to clamp his hat back on his head.* At that, there were quite a few men in Europe who put their hats on for Strauss the man, long before he turned to be a Nazi play-along.

In the following season, 1907–1908, Toscanini conducted *Götterdämmerung, Tosca, Mefistofele, The Force of Destiny,* and brought forth two French operas, Charpentier's *Louise* and Debussy's *Pelléas et Mélisande*. When Toscanini reminisced of that first *Pelléas* performance, he said that the work had presented him with his severest challenge, that it was more difficult to conduct than *Götterdämmerung,* and that he was "stupid" to give it in Italian, words and music being so finely smelted that translation is impossible. Even today *Pelléas* usually empties the opera house; few can gaze long at its nubilous beauty without fatigue. It is like a Monet waterlily painting of the last period. Most conductors mistake its absence of detonation for delicacy and conduct *Pelléas* as if it were a fabric embroidered by a feminine hand, though its passion is as real as that of *Tristan*. To be sure, that passion is expressed in different language, in a pellucid whisper. And unlike *Tristan, Pelléas* holds a sense of hope, a sense of dawn. "It is you who will open for us the door of the new era I foresee," Arkel sings to Mélisande. He sings it quietly. How must this work have struck the audience at La Scala, used to the firmly drawn line of Italian melody?

Toscanini, wrote Gatti-Casazza, "transfused his entire being" to each of the participants. Yet he was not sure he had

* The truth of the episode is not quite certain.

succeeded and was relieved to learn that Debussy, who was supposed to come to the performance, could not come. Before he went out to conduct he told the company that whatever happened they were to go on, following his beat. The first scenes passed off quietly, the audience probably being too stunned to protest. Then the murmurs of protest began, rising in the scene of the subterranean vault to an un-Debussian fortissimo. What kind of mad opera was this, without a single tune? Toscanini recalled that the shouts became so loud that he could not hear the orchestra. Nevertheless he kept on. Somebody behind him was exclaiming, "*Some* beautiful music!" He turned and bellowed, "Yes, yes, for *me* it is beautiful music." Yet, after a while the audience began to listen, almost in spite of themselves. The scene between Golaud and little Yniold under Mélisande's window moved some of them and then more became caught up in the story and music. At the end a few responded to the beauty of the work, while most of the audience rushed to the cloakroom and went home. Toscanini, contrary to his usual custom, appeared before the curtain and applauded those who had stayed, saying, "*Molto intelligente, molto intelligente.*" Debussy sent Toscanini his photograph, on which he inscribed a few bars from the Golaud-Yniold scene and wrote underneath, "Here is where the tide turned." Later, when Toscanini heard a wretched performance of the work in Paris, he said, "Perhaps ours was not so bad."

With all the dissensions and vanities indigenous to the opera house—a kindergarten for nervous children supervised by nervous teachers—those were glorious years for La Scala. The period ended when Gatti received an offer to head the Metropolitan, which was then considered, with some justice, the foremost lyric theater in the world and was the one which paid the highest fees. Gatti made it a condition that Toscanini was to be engaged with him. Toscanini accepted. An overt cause contributed to his decision, or furnished an excuse for it: he had been asked by the "Council of the Scala" (the board of directors) to conduct, at one of three concerts scheduled for the end of the season, some music by Gaetano Coronaro, who for years had been professor of composition at the Milan Conservatory and who had recently died. Toscanini, though he had admired Coronaro as scholar and teacher, thought him a feeble composer and refused to play his music. The Scala officials then turned the last concert over to Panizza. Toscanini felt that this constituted a breach of contract, since it was he and he alone who had the right to determine what music the orchestra was to play. He turned the matter over to his lawyer, who went to court over "an illegal imposition." The court found against Toscanini, holding that the board had the right to exercise some control over programs and that Coronaro's music was not of such low quality as to injure a conductor's reputation. It was all a tempest in a kettledrum, and one would guess that it represented merely the outward sign of Toscanini's disappointment and restlessness. There was a bit of Joshua in Toscanini. He set out to conquer a new world and arrived in New York in the autumn of 1908. The Metropolitan engagement was to be a cancellable arrangement, a trial. As it turned out, he, an Italian artist, would make New York the center of his work and America his home.

8

Toscanini came to the concert hall by way of the opera house. Though in his early years he conducted a number of concerts, his main activity lay in a realm fronted by Donizetti and Verdi. His career differed, then, from that of Mengelberg, early occupied with symphonic music, who built and directed the Amsterdam Concertgebouw; or that of Furtwängler, who began as an assistant to Mottl and in 1922 succeeded Nikisch as the head of the Berlin Philharmonic; or that of Thomas Beecham, wealthy enough to begin by forming an orchestra of his own and who only later became enamored of opera; or that of Koussevitzky, who did not conduct opera at all. (Bruno Walter, on the other hand, began as an operatic coach.)

The early experience in the lyric theater shaped the formation of the Toscanini style. He bestowed on symphonic music the warmth and expressiveness of which the human voice is capable. He was concerned with bringing to the surface the

melodic content of a score, which, of course, is not to say that
he conducted Brahms as if he were Bellini, nor that he spread
honey on a bitter passage. He knew that the voice can speak
in both austere and in dulcet accents and he did not soften
it when it cried out in mordant tones. Yet his continuous admonition to the orchestra—"sing!"—so frequently repeated
that it is the Leitmotiv of his work, indicates that he sought
the sense of music in melody. Once he had the line and phrasing
of the melody ordered to his satisfaction, he felt that half the
work was done.

The other half was work to fix the mood, particularly the
drama of music. Of all interpreters Toscanini, I believe, possessed the keenest sense of drama. Perhaps here too his early
training may have influenced him, as did his lifelong interest
in all forms of dramatic expression, "tragedy, comedy, history,
pastoral, pastoral-comical" . . . Seneca was not too heavy nor
Plautus too light for him. In the noblest sense Toscanini made
music into a dramatic experience. One may cite as an example
his conducting of the *Leonore No. 3* Overture, which was melod-
ically so beautiful as to make your eyes brim over, and dramatically so exciting that listening to it should have been forbidden to a man with a heart condition.

It goes without saying that the two parts of his labor were
not performed separately, but as a whole. And two halves do
not make a whole: much remained, propelled by a sense of duty
for "playing what was written" down to the tiniest dynamic
mark, and a marvelous instinct for what the composer meant
by what was written. With the statement that I have previously
quoted—"It is easy to be a conductor. All you have to do is to
play the notes"—he was fooling himself. To play the notes
is of course the first requirement, but it is no more than reading aloud the text of Hamlet's speeches exactly as they are
written. That does not make Hamlet come alive. The same text
can serve astonishingly different interpretations.

Beecham was quite right in his witty remark when he took
over the New York Philharmonic after a spell with Toscanini:
"We've had so much fidelity to the score around here, let's
have a little interpretation."

Of course Toscanini interpreted. Textual fidelity—"it is

written here"—was only the beginning. To it he added his ideas of how what was written was to sound. He began with the premise that the composer knew what he was doing when he wrote down his score. Elementary as that supposition seems, it is not always acted upon by the interpreters with flowing locks. Respect for the text needs to be expressed through decisions on such matters as dryness or wetness of tone, comparative loudness or softness, balance of orchestral choirs, relative importance of inner voices, judgment of the right tempo and variations of tempo, and a dozen other musical problems. The solution of these problems represents interpretation. Toscanini's solutions were encompassing, though it would be an exaggeration to say that they included all music. His understanding did not include Bach, for example. His repertoire was wide enough and, at his best, set forth with what seemed to us an indisputable rightness. When he played Smetana's *Moldau* you thought he must have been born in Prague. When he played the *Enigma Variations* you wondered how often he had strolled down Pall Mall.* He once said to me, "When I look at a score, I see the profile of the composer on the page."

Olin Downes, reviewing a performance of Beethoven's First in 1936, wrote, "It is extremely hard, it demands supreme mastery, to give a performance of that simplicity" (*New York Times*, February 21, 1936). Toscanini's preoccupation with melody and drama tended to make music clear. Indeed, it tended to make music simple. And communicative. Here we have one reason why audiences loved him. Renato Simoni, one of Italy's most perceptive critics, commented in *Ritratti*:

> Our pleasure is no longer a self-centered pleasure but a communal one: it becomes stronger by being nourished by the pleasure of those around us. . . . It becomes something more than an intellectual treat. . . . It is not limited to the knowledgeable, or to the musician or the connoisseur, but turns into a popular festival, for which the hall is never large enough. . . . Those present are impatient to share their enthusiasm with others, in the way that people grab

* I chose these two examples because some critics felt that he did *not* conduct these compositions in the correct style.

hold of good news and spread it through the city. In that sense Toscanini is a formidable propagandist.

If Toscanini brought melodic and dramatic drive to symphonic music, he applied as well symphonic thought to operatic music. He was not content even in the older operas to let the orchestra merely strum an accompaniment to the girl from the market place. Bellini's orchestra contained more than a gentle oom-pah movement. To quote the excellent Olin Downes once more, this is what he reported from Milan on May 8, 1929:

It has been an exceedingly great pleasure to this reviewer to encounter a certain aspect of the genius of Arturo Toscanini with which Americans of this day and generation can scarcely hope to become familiar on the other side of the water. This aspect is not that of the conductor of symphonies nor yet that of the interpreter of *Tristan und Isolde*, or *Götterdämmerung*, or *Ariane et Barbe-bleue*, or any of half a dozen other masterpieces of music drama which Toscanini re-created for Metropolitan audiences in bygone years. Those achievements are written large in the operatic and symphony records of the golden metropolis.

But have the music-lovers of that favored metropolis, by any chance, heard Toscanini conduct an old outmoded opera long since consigned to the ministrations of linnet-headed coloratura sopranos to their audiences, and disgustedly relegated by musicians and reviewers who profess to know anything to the ash heap of hoary antiquities? It is an opera composed by one Donizetti. Its name is *Lucia di Lammermoor*. . . .

. . . One visitor at La Scala sat absorbed through three hours of this opera, engrossed by its aristocratic style, by the curve of Donizetti's phrases, his surprisingly dramatic touches of orchestral commentary, and the actual poignancy of much of his music.

Well, there was Toscanini near by and in perfect profile, his eyes blazing, his lips moving with deep shadows in the lines of his face cast up by the light of the conductor's desk. He was singing with the orchestra, as he always does when he leads, directing the players less with his hand than with his piercing eyes, fashioning every note and phrase, as completely "on fire" as if he were conducting *Tristan* or *Otello*. The emergence of certain orchestral phrases—as, for instance, at the moment of Lucia's fatal signing of the marriage contract—and the intensity of the orchestral utterance were as unexpected as they were thrilling to hear.

Again and again the orchestra assumed such significance that one acquired a new idea of Donizetti. . . .

It was immediately evident that every singer was held as in a vise to Toscanini's ideas. . . . With Madama dal Monte—who, if she has not a voice of unequaled beauty and brilliance, interpreted her music with the most admirable intelligence and style and with equally admirable clearness and finish of her coloratura—Toscanini fairly breathed. The smallest punctuation of her phrases, the slightest occasional pause or retard which gave a true emotional inflection to a passage commonly considered one of mere ornament, was reflected instantaneously as in a mirror by the orchestra. . . .

As one listens to the fourth act of *Rigoletto* (that is all of *Rigoletto* one can hear, an off-the-air recording of a Red Cross benefit concert he conducted at Madison Square Garden on May 25, 1944), one seems to be face to face with Greek tragedy. The curse seems as large as that which hovered over the house of Atreus. Milanov of the beautiful voice becomes not the simpering coloratura which Gilda usually is but a pawn of fate, while Warren, though he had previously sung many fine Rigolettos, is lifted to new power, never again to be equaled. The orchestra becomes "symphonic."

His concern with opera as a totality—which encompassed the orchestra's role in the predominately "vocal" works of Bellini, Rossini, or early Verdi—his watchfulness over line and phrase, whether the phrase belonged to a peak of an aria or to a casual recitative, his conviction that everything the composer set down came from his heart and soul and therefore made a legitimate claim on the interpreter's heart and soul—it was these qualities which suffused his music-making. They confirmed the impression that one was hearing the familiar piece for the first time. One felt as if one saw the first spring and walked in a pristine meadow. One felt that when, like Downes, one heard Beethoven's First Symphony, and one felt that, perhaps even more intensely, when one was lucky enough to be present at one of his opera performances.

The girl from the market place has often been treated with careless condescension. Toscanini took the girl from the market place and turned her into an actress of patrician style.

CHAPTER THREE

THE MAN

F AUST's sigh—"Two souls reside, alas! within my breast, one striving to part from the other" *—has been cited often enough to become a commonplace of psychology: the duality of man, the sundering of two elements, the contrariety of traits, is more sharply marked in talented beings than it is in men and women whose mediocrity holds them in equilibrium. As I have suggested, the higher the scale of talent the more pronounced the contradiction. Nor, of course, does an easily discernible connection exist between artistic excellence and excellence of character. Similarly, the dependence of artistic endowment on intellect, though it does exist, has not been satisfactorily assayed. "I am as bad as the worst," wrote Walt Whitman, "but thank God I am as good as the best." One observes that "bad as the worst . . . good as the best" in biography after biography. One observed it in Toscanini.

One of his biographers, J. Cuthbert Hadden, wrote of Chopin:

> You could as little get hold of him, said Louis Enault, as of the scaly back of a mermaid. Kind, generous and forbearing, he could yet rate his friends as "pigs" and

* *Zwei Seelen wohnen, ach! in meiner Brust*
Die eine will sich von der andern trennen.
—*Faust*, Part 1, Scene 2

"Jews" when they failed him in any of the least of the menial services he so often demanded of them. Punctual and precise in his habits, he was halting and irresolute to the point of imbecility—an "undecided being," as he called himself. . . . Simple and open as a child, fond too of children, he nevertheless showed himself somewhat of a *poseur*, as when he grew a little whisker on one side of his face, the side he turned towards his audiences. A man of education and culture, he was yet influenced by the most absurd superstitions. George Sand said of him in Majorca that he lived under a nightmare of legends.

Brahms could be as modest and considerate as a village priest, deprecate his own achievement, praise that of others, help young composers—but the next moment be as jealous as a Siamese cat and as feigning as a Borgia. How did the *Siegfried Idyll* spring from the mind of a man as malign as Wagner was? Why did he need to clothe himself in satin and perfume himself with attar of roses to create the fire which guards Brünnhilde's mountaintop?

Rossini pretended that composing was child's play to him. He let it be known that he finished *The Barber of Seville* in thirteen days and that as he lay in bed composing a duet a gust of wind blew the sheet to the floor; rather than bend and pick it up he composed another duet. Is this true? I do not believe it. The lightheartedness and the carelessness were poses, designed to hide a dichotomy. Herbert Weinstock in his biography of Rossini speaks of his "moods of black despair, at times so unreasoning as to resemble incipient madness." His supposed ease of working habits is contradicted by the testimony of the painter Gugliemo De Sanctis:

Rossini takes the very greatest pains when copying out his writings, never wearying of perfecting them, often going back to read them over and alter notes, which he is in the habit of erasing with a scraper with truly singular patience.

Possibly the most inexplicable of inexplicable geniuses was Mozart. Our loving imagination wants him to have been as he appears in certain idealized portraits: we expect that angelic smile, the tender, balanced head, the luxuriant silky hair (of which we know he was vain), the clouded eyes which seem to gaze into posterity, the immaculate grooming with the peruke and the jabot made of the finest material. It is a fact that he was particular about his clothes and "wore a good deal of embroidery and jewelry." Clementi, meeting him for the first time, took him for one of the Court chamberlains. He was the famous child prodigy grown up, a man used to walking on the polished parquet of the salons of counts and bishops, who as a boy had been kissed by an Empress and who had been called— and not by his father alone—a "miracle of nature." This aristocratic man who poured out music—he wrote music as other people write letters, said his wife Constanze—and who could sit down at the piano and lose himself in such inspired improvisation that Haydn averred with tears in his eyes that he would never forget Mozart's playing as long as he lived— "it went to the heart"—this apparition who seemed to be an immigrant from the Elysian Fields—*of course* he was too good for this world. That is our hero-worshiping view of him, which is only strengthened when we learn how gay he could be, how *ausgelassen*, how he loved to dance, how he played billiards expertly, and how he enjoyed convivial evenings, drinking a quantity of punch. He was so modest that he was highly flattered when he observed that in the dance halls of Prague the tunes from *Figaro* were being used for people to dance to and chat over. "I looked on," he wrote to a friend in Vienna, "with the greatest pleasure while all those people flew about in sheer delight to the music of my Figaro, arranged for quadrilles and waltzes."

We think of him as sublimely innocent. (We could never think this of Haydn or Beethoven.) That innocence endears him all the more to us. We are not altogether mistaken. Part of Mozart's nature was childlike and remained so all his short life. He delighted in spinning nonsense, in writing clownish, clumsy doggerel, in shaking silly puns from his sleeve, and in inventing crazy names for everybody. He called his wife Schabla Pumfa, his dog Schomanntzky, while Notschibikitschibi, Runzifunzi, Roska Pumpa, and Gaulimauli were his names for some of his friends.

If we read his letters—they fill three volumes in the English edition edited by Emily Anderson, a work of superb scholarship—we are struck by his charm and good nature, but we wonder as well over the quantity of prattle he gives forth: local gossip, advice to Constanze on how to behave properly, excuses made to his father, reports of court intrigues, how he was entertained by this or that celebrity, how so-and-so was jealous of him—these occupy much more space than his feelings and his thoughts on music. We know that he read copiously—particularly writings which could furnish material for librettos—but not once, I believe, does he discuss a book. He lived at the time of the American Revolution and the French Revolution (it occurred in the year *Così fan tutte* was performed), but he never mentions these world events. It was as if somebody writing today were unaware of Vietnam. Perhaps we begin to wonder how Mozart could have written Mozart's music.

There is another Mozart. The man who wrote those eighteen bars at the beginning of *Don Giovanni*, which accompany the duel between the Don and the Commendatore, a trio of dark voices in which we seem to "see" the shadow of death passing over the scene—not only the death of one man but all death, mortality itself—that man peered into the well of tragedy. How could this scene, or the *Don Giovanni* churchyard scene, or the brooding restlessness of the slow movement of the Symphony No. 40, or the whole of the D Minor Piano Concerto (K. 466), be created by a man who saw only the beauty of the world and not its pain, one who was merely an extraordinarily endowed innocent?

No, he was a creature of Lucifer as well. The demonic element in him was strong, and though he seems on the surface to have been what we today would call a "nice man," though in point of fact he *was* a nice man, he was no stranger to the seamy side of character, nor was he untouched by bitterness. The modesty which we, who know how the plot ends, now find excessive, must not mislead us: when the demonic in him came to the fore he could be sharp, overbearing, arrogant even.

When his father warned him that he was making himself detested in Vienna by his overbearing manners, Mozart replied:

> The whole world declares that through my boasting and criticizing I have made the professors of music and also other people into enemies! What world? I presume the world of Salzburg . . .

W. J. Turner, one of his biographers, comments:

> Here is another instance of Mozart's inevitable blindness. In his hatred of Salzburg he finds an easy explanation for the criticism his father retails. But what his father told him was true. The professors of music and many others hated the superiority of this man who always spoke on musical matters as if he were a god, "as one having authority."

We are moved by pity when we contemplate the poverty of the last year of his life. He died at the moment when his final opera, *Die Zauberflöte*, gave signs of making him into a truly popular success—what irony lies in this fate! But that does not change the fact that *Figaro* and *Don Giovanni* were appreciated by many, and that he did have quite a number of powerful and perceptive friends among the members of the Viennese aristocracy. His poverty sprang, not from a lack of fame, but from his financial imprudence, from his wife's bad management, from illness, from some unfortunate money speculations, and from a social condition in which no laws existed adequately to protect a composer's income.

Neither his suffering nor his profundity could be documented by his letters. Those letters—they are, well, just plain silly and filthy. They show a coarseness irreconcilable with our image of the composer of the G Minor String Quintet (K. 516). Granted, we must understand the letters in terms of the eighteenth century, a century uninhibited in its language, scatological expressions being as prevalent then as they are in the talk of today. Mozart's interest in the natural functions and in the parts of the lower body is apparent in the famous letters to his cousin, Maria Anna Thekla (the *"Bäsle"*), which may have been love letters. Even to his mother he writes, "I kiss my sister's backside." He often wrote to Maria Anna in rhyme, and the Emily Anderson translation gives us some of the flavor:

> . . . now I have the honour to inquire how you are and whether you perspire! Whether your stomach is still in good order? Whether indeed you have no disorder? Whether you can still like me at all? Whether with chalk you often scrawl? Whether now and then you have me in mind? Whether to hang yourself you sometimes feel inclined? Whether you have been wild? With this poor foolish child? Whether to make peace with me you'll be so kind? If not, I swear I'll let off one behind! Ah, you're laughing! Victoria! Our arses shall be the symbol of our peacemaking! I knew that you wouldn't be able to resist me much longer. Why, of course, I'm sure of success, even if today I should make a mess, though to Paris I go in a fortnight or less.

> Forgive my wretched writing, but the pen is already worn to a shred, and I've been shitting, so 'tis said, nigh twenty-two years through the same old hole, which is not yet frayed one whit, though I've used it daily to shit.

Like Raphael and Goethe, Mozart was sexually oriented. He was probably not a Don Juan, everything and anything in skirts exciting him, as Leporello says of his patron, yet sex played a considerable role in his life and he must have been attracted to a number of women. His eroticism was muscular. He writes to his sister before she gets married:

> Wedlock will show you many things
> Which still a mystery remain;
> Experience soon will teach to you
> What Eve herself once had to do
> Before she could give birth to Cain.
> But all these duties are so light
> You will perform them with delight.

When he went on a journey with Prince Lichnowsky, he wrote to Constanze:

Arrange your dear sweet nest very daintily, for my little
fellow deserves it indeed, he has really behaved himself
very well and is only longing to possess your sweetest . . .*
Just picture to yourself that rascal; as I write he crawls
on to the table and looks at me questioningly. I, however,
box his ears properly—but the rogue is simply . . .* and
now the knave burns only more fiercely and can hardly be
restrained.

This is not the letter of a newlywed; they had been married
seven years.

Foul language and fair melody, plump persiflage and win-
some wit, fine grains and rough granules—they show the two
sides of the artist, this artist, and they alert us to the obser-
vation of a diversity which is generic to most artists.

2

Gentle and harsh, loving and indifferent, disciplined and un-
bridled, helpful and merciless, reasonable and raging, tolerant
and prejudiced, now lamb now lion, such was the man Toscanini.

He was a failure as a father. When the children were young
he could summon neither the time nor the patience to be with
them, to play with them, to laugh with them, or to understand
their needs. When they were little sometimes he fondled them,
sometimes he scolded them, in either case to dismiss them
quickly. Toscanini was totally devoted to his task, Carla was
totally devoted to him, and the children were entrusted to a
nurse, Nena, who acted as the real mother. The children had the
advantages of a well-to-do house and good schooling—but they
were cool advantages, hemmed in by the hush required for
the father who was studying, always studying. On Sundays
Nena, who had a relative buried in the Milan cemetery, used to
take them there, and there was their playground, jumping
leapfrog over the graves. The children admired their father,
but loved Nena. Wally was the first born, then Walter, then

* Word made illegible in the autograph.

Wanda. Because of his early friendship with Catalani (*La Wally*), he named his children with names beginning with the letter *W*, though that letter is not used in the Italian alphabet. A fourth child, Giorgio, was taken with his parents on one of Toscanini's South American tours. In Buenos Aires the child, four years old, contracted diphtheria, a disease which was then one of the chief infant-killers. Carla fought desperately to save the boy. In vain—one evening—it was very late and cold, and Carla and a nurse were alone in the hotel room—the little Giorgio died (September 10, 1906). Toscanini at that moment was with Rosina Storchio, the pretty soprano whom he admired as an artist and with whom he had an affair. Carla sent for him. They wept. Carla wanted to leave him, he begged her not to. She stayed. One of Toscanini's biographers, Filippo Sacchi, who knew him well, wrote that Rosina Storchio had a son by Toscanini. He was supposed to have been a beautiful boy with large black eyes and his father's unmistakable brow, but the child was retarded, palsied, and unable to talk, and died at an early age. (I am not certain that the story is true.)

As Wally, Walter, and Wanda grew up, they all showed talents, though none strong enough to develop without encouragement. Wanda, a superb mimic, might have become an actress. Walter was almost as studious as his father, loved books, and for a time became a dealer in rare books. He was a fountain of diverse bits of information, and his sisters nicknamed him "Monsieur Je-sais-tout." He married a dancer, Cia Fornarola, and made the cardinal mistake of living with his wife in the parental home. Like his father, Walter had a number of affairs. He was handsome, a voluble raconteur, a generous friend. Again like his father, he had no idea where the money went. RCA employed him, more as a courtesy than as a necessity, though he was helpful in getting Toscanini to approve recordings, it being always a struggle for Toscanini to say Yes to any recording—he was never happy with the several tries at *La Mer* or the Berlioz "Queen Mab"—though there were instances when he did approve something he knew to be faulty, because he felt a spirit in the performance he was not likely to recapture. He held up the opera transcriptions from the broadcasts for years. He would not approve *La*

Traviata because in one spot Merrill had made a trifling mistake in the text. Joe Gimma, Licia Albanese's husband, kept telling him of the lively black market that had developed for his *Traviata* broadcast. He finally said all right, and thereafter it became easier.

When Toscanini moved to Riverdale, Walter became, in effect, his father's servant. For the seventeen years Toscanini conducted the NBC Symphony, Walter was backstage at every concert wiping the perspiration off Toscanini's brow. He led no independent life of his own, accepting the fate that as long as his father was working the son was to be at his beck and call, the man with the towel. Patiently he endured his father's black moods, his rages at inadequate performances; patiently he tried to shoo off the bores; and always he lived in awe if not in fear of his father. To make himself useful, Walter appointed himself as the guardian of the treasure, the keeper of the keys. In the basement of the Riverdale house he had installed elaborate electronic transfer equipment, turntables, equalizers, etc., a veritable cabinet of Dr. Caligari. Walter loved the wired hocus-pocus and employed an engineer full time, and a secretary. He transferred the earlier material to tape—but when Walter himself died the whole accumulation was left in so disorganized a state that it will take a long time to straighten it out. (The tapes and some of the correspondence and documents now repose in the New York Public Library, Lincoln Center.)

When his father died, Walter was free at last. He was still youthful and capable of zest. Yet, a curious psychological twist pulled him awry: the cage had been opened but the bird could no longer fly. Instead of freedom he subconsciously sought bondage. He began to re-create in himself—as a subconscious act and not as a conscious pose—the image of his father. He wore shoes similar to his father's, he would stand and walk like his father, he would speak like his father, pausing before the first word and lowering his eyelids like his father. He would say "*Ma!*" in the same sighing tone that his father used. Even posthumously his father's power squeezed the marrow out of him. He was destroyed; no freedom was possible for him.

Wally saved herself. She came nearer to normality because she got away early and stayed away. When she went to her father and announced that she intended to marry a Count Castelbarco, he said, "What nonsense! He is blond and an aristocrat. Who ever heard of marrying a blond man? Whoever heard of an aristocrat being worth anything?" That his prediction eventually proved true, though for the wrong reasons, merely firmed his belief that no count, baron, or duke could be trusted. Wally made her home in Milan, while her father was in New York. She took an active part in Italy's musical life, befriended musicians famous or obscure, and was forever helping an unlucky family or an acquaintance short of funds. "She is the Countess with the golden heart," the Milanese said of her. Today (1975) she is in her seventies, still beautiful, looking like early fifties, and still rushing around Milan. Both she and Wanda inherited their father's physical energy. They wanted, indeed they needed, bodily peasant exertion; they liked to push furniture around like moving-men. When Toscanini's birthplace in Parma was being turned into a museum, and the day before the opening, at which the President of Italy was to officiate, nothing was ready, Wanda and Wally worked all night to set it in order and finally got down on their knees to scrub the floors. At the appointed hour they appeared as *grandes dames* and loved every moment and every word of the publicity shining on them.

On the comparatively rare occasions when the whole family was gathered around the dining table, they could quarrel in voices as heated as those of rug merchants in a Syrian bazaar. It sometimes sounded like an orchestral fugue, fortissimo, some of the musicians having lost their place. At other times, one or another member would be punished by being ostracized: Toscanini would not speak to him or her and messages would be relayed by him to Carla and by Carla to Wanda and by Wanda to Walter. Dark balls of silence floated through the room. Away from home each could say nasty things about the other, "my beloved brother" or "my fine sister" one heard pronounced with heavy sarcasm—but let any outsider utter the mildest word of disapproval about *any* of the Toscanini clan and he was banished on the instant.

93

Toscanini thought he loved his family. He did love them in his way, giving them whatever love he could spare from his love of Beethoven. His grandchildren were toys to him, to be caressed, dangled, and petted. Sonia, Wanda and Vladimir Horowitz's daughter, inherited the double curse of talent, a child all too brilliant. Grandpa asked Edwin Bachman to give her violin lessons. Then he would accompany her on the piano, smilingly enduring her mistakes. Yet when the child did something childish, when she committed some harmless bit of mischief, he wouldn't speak to her for days. With the children of his friends he could be adorable and he could establish complete communication with them. He would play with them, knowing instinctively what would delight them. A grandchild of Wilfred Pelletier, four-year-old Margo, was brought to him at his request. She had a little woolen doll in her hand and they played a game. She would mischievously drop the doll and Toscanini would bend and retrieve it, time and time again, indefatigably. After she tired of that game, he sat her down on top of the piano and played little songs for her.

Though his love for his own stood in the second row, though it lacked understanding, it was there and never so much as when he was separated from Wanda or Wally. When they were apart it flowed at spring tide, when together at neap tide. The letters he wrote Wally, when during World War II she remained in Italy, are redolent of concern:

Monday, May 17, 1943

My adored Wally:

Some weeks ago I finished my concerts and I am now resting in Riverdale, that exquisite spot which reminds me so much of our dear Isolino, though in a diminished tone.

I will soon take up my work again and conduct a few concerts, but only for charity purposes (June 20, July 18 and 25, September 19); the real season begins on October 31.

As you see, my activity has not lessened, in spite of my 76 years, a sign that God (or somebody representing him) is protecting me and maintains my good health. I live in

the hope, ever more fervid, that we shall see each other
again sooner than we thought. Dear Wally, how often my
thoughts—*our* thoughts, for mama, Walter, and Wanda
love you no less than I—fly to you, longing to know how
your life is getting on. You can imagine the anxiety you
cause us. But, I repeat, I hope that we will meet again
much sooner than we thought. Everything must crash
down—it has already begun. Let us endure still for a while
the immense misfortune which has wounded the world. The
fifth act of the tremendous tragedy is about to unfold. The
curtain will finally fall. Let us hold our hearts high!

And our dear Emanuela [Wally's daughter]? How we all
would like to see her! Sonia and Walfredo [Walter's son]
are darlings, handsome, vivacious and good.

I am very happy about the "Colony" [Wally had offered
a group of friends and relatives asylum on a Toscanini
property in the country near Crema, removing them from
Milan] you established. You are marvelously good and
wise. I am happy not only for you but for the relatives and
friends. I embrace and kiss you with much, much tenderness, as I embrace and kiss relatives and friends, all of
them . . .

Papa

Wally then fled to Switzerland. He wrote her at Lugano:

September 26, 1944

Wally, my adored one:

Only the thought that you will receive in a few days these
few lines which I am tracing on this sheet of paper with an
agitated hand and a suffering heart—only that thought
lets me breathe a little more freely. I am beside myself. It
seems a thousand years since I saw you. The complete lack
of news from you makes me unreasonable. That you were
unable to write I can understand. . . . But that none of our
friends could substitute for you—that seems improbable
to me. But I don't want to sadden you with my lamenta-
tions. If God is good, it seems that the beginning of the

95

end of this huge tragedy is in sight. Let us hope for a rapid solution and that you'll soon be able to return home. My health is good. In a few weeks I'll begin my concerts. I'll conduct 16 this year—four more than last season. You see, your old father goes once more onto the breach and does what he can. Last winter I made a propaganda-film [the film for the O.W.I. with Verdi's *Hymn of the Nations*], very successful, according to everybody. . . . I know a print was sent to Switzerland. Find out. I would so much like you to see it. [Wally obtained a print and showed it for the benefit of Italian refugees] . . .

Dear Wally, now that I've been able to talk to you, I am a bit calmer than before.

In both letters he mentions God. God was to him the one who created Mozart and Wagner and to whom one needed to speak sharply in the matter of inept clarinet-players. Of organized religion he would have no part, though he carried in his pocket a tiny crucifix on a silver chain which was obviously and atavistically a good-luck piece. He never went to church and his dislike of priests was only a little softer than his dislike of aristocrats. Like most artists, he was superstitious. Most artists observe a complicated ritual before emerging from the dressing room. Lotte Lehmann carried with her a heap of trinkets—medallions, amulets, pressed flowers—without which she did not dare to appear. She kissed them all, and at the last moment before her entrance she made the sign of the cross. Scotti could not sing unless a certain rag doll was on his dressing table. Like most Viennese of her time, Selma Kurz, the coloratura, believed that passing a chimneysweep would bring her luck. Her manager used to hire one to saunter "accidentally" past the stage door. On one occasion she called the sooted fellow to her, fumbled in her purse, and wanted to give him a tip, whereupon the honest man said, "Not necessary, madame, I have been paid already." Tettrazzini carried a lucky dagger with her: it was one which, one night when she was singing Lucia exceptionally well, had fallen from her hand and stuck upright in the floor. Thereafter the dagger served as a barometer: she would drop it before going onstage. If it stood upright—success, if it fell flat—failure. She cheated a bit, of course.

Toscanini turned his dressing room into a photographic gallery as personal as a mother's sewing table on which she displays her offspring. There were photographs of his family, several of Verdi, one of Brahms, one of Wagner, and a miniature of Beethoven. Wherever he conducted, these pictures were set up. He believed that certain men possessed the *malocchio*, the "evil eye." Chotzinoff told the story (in *An Intimate Portrait*) of Gatti-Casazza calling on Toscanini in Milan. The two elderly men sat and discussed in great seriousness one Giovanni, who had years before ruined the first performance of Weber's *Euryanthe*. Giovanni had the evil eye, he was a *iettatore*. He had greeted Toscanini as he entered La Scala. Full of foreboding—"my blood froze"—Toscanini had let himself be persuaded against his better judgment to proceed with the performance. What happened? The orchestra played the overture so magnificently that the audience clamored for a repeat. They yelled while Toscanini stood. They wouldn't let him begin the opera. He waited patiently—"I am really a patient man"— but then he couldn't stand it any longer. He broke his baton and went home. Disaster! Then he understood: obviously it was all the fault of Giovanni's evil eye. He had put the hex on the proceedings. *Euryanthe* was postponed a week and they took great care that Giovanni not be around. The two men shook their heads, reminiscing over the evil fate; can such things be? They could, indeed . . . In later years there was a photographer hovering about Carnegie Hall and NBC who worshiped Toscanini and took superb camera studies of his work. But Toscanini suspected him of *malocchio* and the poor fellow had to be hidden away with his camera.

To the end of his life he believed that little Giorgio died because he and Carla had not named him with a name beginning with *W*.

Toscanini read Webster's *The Duchess of Malfi* and he must have come across these lines:

> How superstitiously we mind our evils:
> The throwing down of salt, or crossing of a hare,

Or singing of a cricket, are of power
To daunt whole man in us.

But he still believed in the evil eye.

3

He was utterly unselfconscious, as simple and direct in movement as the rain—and as driven by his task as the rain is by
the wind. On an off-the-air transcript of a Verdi *Requiem* performance, one can hear him shouting at the brass during the
Dies Irae: he had forgotten that he was in a concert hall, forgotten that an audience was present, and remembered only
Verdi.

He was of course cognizant of his fame—how could he not
be?—and once in a while he could get himself to admit that
as an executant he had been "not so bad." More often he would
say, "I was stupid." He never postured, not on the podium,
not off the podium. He was the only conductor I have known
whose gestures were more pronounced in rehearsal than in performance. His singing, his shouting *"Piano!"* in a voice that
would go right through to your spine, urging, begging with
two hands folded, his whiplash downward movement of the
baton, the raising of the left hand in the caressing of a lyric
phrase which resembled a lover's caress, the circular motion
which seemed to stir some unseen brew and which served to keep
the rhythm flowing, the precise patterns he drew with the tip
of the stick—all these were strictly means to a musical end,
and all of them were toned down in performance. Certainly
there are more ways than one for a conductor to achieve the
results he wants. Grace is not a *sine qua non.* Furtwängler was
and Solti is awkward, but awkwardness does not detract from
the worth of a performance. I am unwilling to stigmatize
Leonard Bernstein's behavior as out-and-out charlatanism.
Those falling-locks swoons, that rhythmic pirouetting, the
high jumps off the podium, the feline crouching, those Death-
and-Transfiguration grimaces, all the mannerisms which prove
disturbing to part of the audience and are loved by the old

ladies, are they altogether acting? It is more probable that they are necessary to him, that they are an ineluctable part of his music-making, that they are his means to a musical end, honestly used. He behaves the same way in recording sessions when nobody but a few hard-headed engineers are around. Of the simulations of many another conductor, gazing like Narcissus at his image, I am more suspicious. I doubt the musician who lets you know by outward show how much he loves music.

Toscanini abhorred excesses. To see him was to receive a visually gratifying experience, a proportioned pleasure, a study in restrained and aristocratic grace, the better part of which the audience could hardly witness—his face. Nor was the simplicity with which he left the podium false modesty. Otto Erich Deutsch, the Viennese scholar to whose work on Schubert we are indebted, once wrote that Toscanini "ends like a victor but exits like a plain soldier, bows with a questioning mien—'Was it good?' or yet 'Did you really understand me?'—no more often than is absolutely necessary, and swerves the applause to the orchestra, convincingly, not rhetorically" (*Basel National Zeitung*, September 11, 1934).

However, it would be erroneous to assume that he repulsed the approbation tendered to him. As I have suggested, he liked the honest detonation of applause by a public moved and thrilled, and he acknowledged the tribute with the most gracious and least coquettish of smiles. What he loathed was greenroom gushing. What he appreciated was the natural response. There was an Italian waiter at Voisin's who loved music; he managed to buy a ticket for one of the New York Philharmonic concerts, and what's more he managed to make his way to Toscanini's dressing room after the concert. "Maestro," he said to him simply, "tonight I was back in Italy." Toscanini understood and valued the compliment.

All but the most self-worshiping artists learn to detect the difference between the fashionable hosanna and the stammer of truth. One summer, after we had recorded *Tosca* in Rome, Leonard Warren invited us and a few friends for dinner at an outdoor restaurant. During dinner there appeared, inevitably, the little band of strolling musicians. The head of this group of four, who doubled as singer and fiddler, wore a red fez. They came to our table and performed the usual Neapolitan songs and Roman ditties. Suddenly Warren, who knew the songs and who had had enough wine to drink, began to sing with them, at full voice. The street singer at once stopped singing, listened, and without saying a word took his fez off his head and placed it on Warren's head. Warren said, "That was better than an ovation."

Toscanini remained unpretentious even in his last years, when his name had become so famous in America as to be almost synonymous with music. He could have asked for a special police escort to transport him from Riverdale to Carnegie Hall; it would never have occurred to him to make such a request. Once he asked me, "*May* I record the Kabalevsky Overture?" and when I answered, "You can record anything you like," he laughed.

He was usually unaware of the sensation his appearance created. Once in Paris he saw in the morning paper that Furtwängler was conducting a gala performance of *Die Meistersinger* at the Opéra. "Tonight we go," he announced to Carla. He, Carla, Wanda, and Horowitz, all dressed *à quatre épingles*, appeared at the theater, whereupon a murmur of excitement flickered through the entire audience and all opera glasses were trained on the four figures. Toscanini did not notice it. The Overture began, it was ill-rehearsed and inexact, he started to curse to himself; the curtain rose, the chorus was singing the chorale in French and a quarter tone off-key. At this moment Toscanini rose and announced, "We go." The four of them groped their way out of the theater. Wanda, recalling the incident, said it was the shortest performance of *Die Meistersinger* she had ever heard. The next morning Furtwängler phoned and said that he had come from Berlin and had not had sufficient time to prepare the performance.

Toscanini could be cruel. Beginning a rehearsal of Verdi's *Requiem* in Vienna, he stopped after a few bars and, out loud and in front of everybody, called for "Another soprano." I doubt the story that to another soprano who was endowed with an ample bosom he said, "Oh, Madame—if only those were brains," but I have heard him lacerate a blundering female singer in such language as to make the luckless creature dissolve in sobs. In an early performance of the Ninth I saw him pull Matzenauer by the hand to acknowledge the applause of the audience, while he more or less ignored the other three singers. Matzenauer had sung her part by heart, and magnificently. He himself had chosen Friedrich Schorr, the poetic interpreter of Hans Sachs, for the Salzburg performance of *Die Meistersinger*. He began rehearsals with the singers alone, Erich Leinsdorf accompanying on a piano, and for two weeks took this cast of experienced and devoted artists through every nuance of the score, he himself beating the rhythm with his hands. It appeared that Schorr could not or would not accommodate himself to Toscanini's ideas; he was not malleable. He had to go, declared Toscanini. In vain did friends appeal to him that such a dismissal would greatly harm the singer's fame, that Schorr had come to Salzburg relinquishing other engagements, rented a house, brought his family. It didn't matter: "He must go." He was excused because of "ill health" and another baritone, Hans Hermann Nissen, substituted. Nissen, in my opinion, was not half the artist Schorr was, but he was able to fit into the mold. Schorr, deeply hurt, left Salzburg at once. The sad incident was obliterated by a dress rehearsal in which Toscanini worked up orchestra, chorus, and singers to such a pitch of emotion that when the curtain fell and was raised again for the usual final comments, not one of the hundred people on the stage, not one member of the Vienna Philharmonic in the pit, not one stagehand behind the scene, moved. The cast stood, silent, overcome, almost like statues except that tears trickled from many eyes. Even Toscanini remained motionless at the podium and covered his eyes with his right hand.

Frances Alda, the Australian soprano, came to Milan to sing Charpentier's Louise for him. She was young, enthusiastic, eager. He let her sing without interrupting her once. When she had finished, she looked expectantly at him. He said, "Tell me, my dear, in what language were you singing?"

At a party in Riverdale a man approached him to say, "Maestro, I am sure you do not remember me, but twenty-five years ago you were the judge in a prize competition and I submitted a composition. I never heard anything about it." Toscanini replied, "Oh yes, I remember you very well. The reason you didn't hear from me was that I did not think your composition was any good." With that he went to the piano and began to play the composition, the score of which he had read a quarter of a century ago, shaking his head and ruminating continuously, "No, no good, no good."

His lashing of musicians followed an upward line, fitting his judgment of the magnitude of the crime, but in the early years with the New York Philharmonic, when he thought he ought to speak in English, depending as well on his facility in the language. In the first year—red in the face and choking—all he could manage to say to an offending trombonist was "You bad, *bad* man." The lexicon of opprobrium soon became enlarged: "Asses" . . . "Imbeciles" . . . "Don't be stupid" . . . "Shame, shame, shame" . . . "Are you sleeping?" . . . "You have no blood. Put blood" . . . "Impotent old men" . . . "You are not musicians, you are lackeys and sloppy ones" . . . "You understand nothing, not Beethoven, not Mozart, not Debussy, nothing, nothing" . . . "You eat the notes" . . . "You play a dirty mess" . . . "You grunt like pigs" . . . "You scratch your bellies" . . . "You are supposed to be an orchestra? Go play in a village band." All this in English and Italian intermixed. Strung together like a laundry list these invectives seem offensive, wounding, and insupportable by anybody with an ounce of self-respect. But they must be understood in the context not only of the long working hours, during which 90 percent of patience and 10 percent of impatience formed a sum of 100 percent inspiration, but in an ambience of love, trust, respect, and understanding which he had created with his men, not one of whom would have tolerated one similar outburst from another conductor, and all of whom understood—understood both with heart and brain—that the malediction was only the obverse side of the benediction. Each man felt like a volunteer for a skilled knife-thrower at the Fair; the knives flew and landed close to his skin, they made fear surge but caused no lethal wound.

In a way it was more difficult when he waxed sarcastic, though that did not happen often. "I believe," he would begin with ill-simulated calm, "that there is an accent on this G-sharp." Pause. "But," he would continue, looking at the transgressor menacingly, "I am probably mistaken. I am only Toscanini. Let us look at the score." He would take the score, flip its pages quickly, arrive at the bar, and holding the page so near to his face that he could kiss it, would exclaim in feigned amazement, "Well—can you believe it? I am right. Beethoven has written an accent here." Then in a voice that had the force of a cannon shot he would let loose: "But"—pause—"but that means nothing to you. *Ignoranti! Da capo!*" He often addressed a man not by his name but by the instrument he was playing; he called Karl Glassman "Tympano," but if he didn't like what Glassman played, he called him "*Signor* Tympano," with a heavy stress on the "*signor.*"

To an offending flutist he said in one of the last rehearsals of the season, "I am going soon on my holiday to Italy. If you ever come to Italy be sure to let me know: I will leave the country." To a group of brass players who had been guilty of a wrong entrance at the end of *La Bohème*—it was by but a fraction of a second and none but the offending players and he would have noticed it—he spoke more in sorrow than in anger: "You will go home and sleep with your wives as if nothing had happened. But for me—for me life is over. How can I face anybody after this? I am finished." He meant it at that moment.

Samuel Antek, the violinist, who played in the NBC Orchestra, wrote:

> One of Toscanini's most enigmatic qualities was the almost unbelievable combination of saint and demon, poet and peasant, that was such an essential and paradoxical part of his temperament. As he stood on the podium at rehearsals in his severe black alpaca jacket with a thin white piping made by a handkerchief tucked in underneath the high collar, sharply creased striped trousers, and finely shaped ankle-high slippers, he looked the personification of a priestly leader or a venerable saint. His face was transfigured with a spiritual light as he worked on a passage of surpassing beauty. He seemed lost in the mood. And suddenly, like a thunderbolt out of the blue, the saint

103

would flee and the demon lash out at the orchestra in language that would blanch the face of a longshoreman. I sometimes had to have some of these phrases translated before I could understand their full earthy tang and barnyard flavor. If a minister, in the midst of a sermon on the serenity of heaven, would suddenly interrupt himself to curse out roundly a parishioner who came in late, the effect could not be more startling. Toscanini had one favorite curse in Italian of purest gutter flavor that he indulged in with not too much provocation. He would hurl it with particular relish at a fellow Italian, saying, "Good! You are Italian. I don't have to explain. You know what I'm talking about!"

The insult to which Antek was referring was the Italian word for "Prick!"

It was not only *what* Toscanini bellowed that gave it its special flavor, but the way he said it. It was among the most horrifying sounds I have ever heard and seemed to come from his entrails. He would first almost double up, his mouth open wide, his face red, as if on the verge of an apoplectic fit. Then a raucous blast of unbelievable volume would blare forth. The only sound that comes to mind to equal it is the horrible shrieking of stuck bulls in a slaughterhouse I once visited as a boy in Chicago.

He would suddenly seize on one word like "No!" or "Short!" or "Longer!" and keep repeating it, slowly drawing out the vowel sound with a rising, wailing inflection until it filled the hall and all but shook the walls.

These bursts of anger were the safety valves of a brain strained to the utmost capacity. They were the manifestations of a mind so hotly functioning that when it was exposed to a cold temperature it began to foam, as do two inimical chemicals thrown into the same retort. It is certain that the bursts were unpremeditated, spontaneous, not planned for a purpose, even a teaching purpose. He did not indulge in vituperation because he wanted to spur his men on and achieve results. Not consciously, at least. He did it as instinctively as one shields one's eyes when somebody pokes a finger at them. He was often sorry. He said to Wally, in a sad small voice, shaking his head: "I should have told them gently." And then, in the next rehearsal, he hurled the lances like a young Olympic athlete. Who knows in what dark childhood experience these turmoils, so like "Nature's elemental din," had their origin?

His outbursts were most cruel when they were directed against himself. If he failed to reach the standard he had set for himself, his reaction was sheer violence, a hurling and breaking and kicking and tearing of music stands, scores, furniture, clothes, anything that was near to be hurled or broken, kicked or torn. In the fullest sense he was his own severest critic. On one occasion he stormed into the green room, where the artists were assembled, and pointing a finger in turn at each, exclaimed, "Shame on you, shame on you, shame on YOU!" He then closed the door, disappeared, opened it again, stuck his head in, said, "And *shame* on Toscanini," and slammed the door shut. The most frightening incident I personally witnessed occurred in a rehearsal of the Ninth Symphony. The first movement was going along superbly, or so it seemed to me, in the taut tempo—*allegro ma non troppo, un poco maestoso*—he had worked out long ago, the strings were bending into the phrases mining from them all their wealth, on the podium he was swaying with the music, his face contracted, his eyes obscured by sweat—when suddenly he stopped and shook himself as if he had been hit by a flying object. What had happened? What was wrong? The cellos! The cellos they were careless, they were not giving their all, they had smeared a phrase, they were taking it easy. How *dared* they? They were not working as hard as he, the old man, they were not respecting the music, they were not respecting the Ninth, they were insulting Beethoven! He screamed, he broke the baton, he hit the score, he tore pages from it, he tore at his rehearsal coat, he ripped open the collar in search of air and in doing so his hand caught the watch he was carrying in his breast pocket. Still not knowing what he was doing, he took the watch and heaved it at the orchestra. It fell to the ground and smashed into a hundred pieces. It was the end! It was beyond him! How could he conduct Beethoven with such a bunch of slothful, apathetic idiots? Cursing and shouting and banging his fists against whatever was in the way, he left the stage. The orchestra sat without moving, many of the men as pale as if they had just heard a judgment of guilt pronounced on them. The few of us in the hall did not stir. We waited.

He did not come back. It appeared later that he had dug his nails into his chest so hard that the wound bled and needed to be bandaged. He could not continue rehearsing that day. The orchestra was dismissed. The next day he began all over again with unabated zeal and utter patience.

It is natural to blink at the flashes of lightning. But emphasis on the storms would present a false picture of the prevailing climate. The weather was sunny for long stretches. His punctiliousness knew tolerance, provided that he felt that the player was trying his best, that he was playing with "blood" and understanding. He could say after the fourth attempt, "Is no good. Come—we try again, *together*." No rehearsal was calm—but many rehearsals passed in good-humored cooperation, orchestra and conductor working together like fellow-laborers in the vineyard. Often he understood and made allowances for the troubles of others. Often he was as generous in praise of singers as he was sparing of praise for himself. He admired Peerce, but he wanted Bjoerling for *Un Ballo in Maschera*. Then Bjoerling suffered one of his alcohol attacks and canceled. Peerce was asked to substitute. His pride wounded, he refused at first. Alice, Peerce's sensible wife, said, "If you don't do it I will leave you." So he consented, though he had not sung the part for six or seven years. He prepared himself carefully for the first rehearsal, he approached with fear, but Toscanini put him at his ease:

I'd seen Toscanini upstairs [at Carnegie Hall] for a minute; and he'd said to me: "Just sing. I follow." "I'll follow *you*, Maestro." "No, no, you just sing." We went through the first act without a mistake; and he called an intermission; but before that he jumped off the podium and threw his arms around me and kissed me. This was the side of Toscanini that seldom came out; and I felt just like a kid. And upstairs he said to me: "You afraid? You afraid? I told you: you just sing." I said, "But Maestro, I was worried about not satisfying you." He said: "Don't worry. Just sing." [B. H. Haggin, *The Toscanini Musicians Knew*]

In the *Nocturne* of Mendelssohn's *Midsummer Night's Dream,* the first horn has a long sustained note at the end. At one performance Toscanini perceived that the first horn player of the Philharmonic, Bruno Jaenicke, who was one of the world's best masters of that difficult instrument, was not feeling well. Toscanini cut the note short, a musical error he committed on purpose to save Jaenicke from embarrassment.

But shortly after, when the orchestra did not satisfy him, he announced, "After I die I shall return to earth as the proprietor of a bordello—and I won't permit one of you to enter. No—not one!"

He never lied, disdaining even the white lies of social conventions, though his sense of the dramatic sometimes would make him touch up a reminiscence to form it into a better story. At such time Carla would quickly say, "Tosca"—and that sufficed to lead him back to exactness. At other times he would turn to her for corroboration: "*È vero?*"—"Is it the truth?"

When he liked somebody that person could do no wrong. His house was open to his friends—except of course when a wrong note had been played at the concert. He was no snob, not a grain of it. He liked and admired David Sarnoff, but he liked quite as much a minor employee of NBC, Al Walker, a little man-of-all-work who saw to it that the automobile arrived on time and that there were iced melon-balls in his dressing room. He behaved toward his servants, the cook, the chauffeur, with completely unforced friendliness. It would not have entered his head to behave any other way. Yet if he thought, rightly or wrongly, that somebody had acted disloyally or even just equivocally, that person was banished, without explanation and sometimes without reprieve. He did not, he could not, moderate his moods. Lizette Sarnoff, David's wife, asked him to give a benefit concert for her favorite charity, the New York Infirmary. He agreed at once and

107

chose the Verdi *Requiem*. The soprano, Herva Nelli, sang off-key in the last few bars. Sarnoff was giving a party for him after the performance. He came, sat in the corner, would not eat or drink, never took part in the conversation, which, any-way, had been embarrassingly dampened; and when people went up to him he uttered but one word, "*Ma—*" and turned his head away.

If he suspected somebody of having tolerated Mussolini or Hitler—that was the end. He could not forgive "compromis-ing with the devil." He helped many who fled from Europe, Friedelind Wagner, Winifred and Siegfried's daughter, among them. He paid for her voyage to South America, then to New York, and supported her in New York for a long time. His acts of kindness were performed without fuss or fanfare and usually anonymously.

Yet he was not impervious to the intrigues that spun around him, and he could be misled into unjust judgments. It wasn't he who indulged in miching mallecho, it was his entourage. Every artist, however unimportant, has an entourage turning in his orbit. These leeches do not necessarily expect to gain financially by the proximity; they do not "exploit" the artist in the raw sense; all they gain is a feeling of importance, a vicarious, backstage, in-the-know excitement. It is enough. They are willing to pay for this excitement by gifts and elab-orate dinner invitations. (I have often marveled how many boring dinner invitations an artist is willing to accept.) Tos-canini's Italian acquaintances, the men at NBC, and as pre-viously mentioned, the various lady friends, were constantly jockeying for position, even as in a king's court. He paid little attention, yet once in a while the gossip got to him.

He was a man baked of solid peasant dough who in looks and manner and—once removed from the task of pulling eighty or ninety men to the heights—in courtliness was every inch the patrician. He was the tyrant with the soft heart. He is "a good soul," Bachmann said to me, after Toscanini broke a baton, of which Bachmann retrieved the pieces and kept as a cherished memento. He was a complicated and learned intellec-tual—with very simple reactions. That he sometimes overawed the men and women near him was not his fault. Vincent Shee-han in *First and Last Love* wrote:

> I was presented to both Lehmann and Toscanini and could not utter a word to either. As a matter of fact I have never been able to originate any remark to Toscanini, though I met him fairly often for the next twenty years; the most I could ever manage was the mumbled conventionality of hail and farewell. Once in New York we were left alone in the same room together for well over half an hour (perhaps deliberately) but I did not dare to speak, and he finally took up a book and read it while I looked at some photographs. This is the limit of imbecility, of course—there are innumerable things I have long wanted to ask him—but the effect of Schwärmerei upon me is something akin to paralysis. I do not have it with the ordinary great of the earth. As a journalist I talked often and freely to presidents, prime ministers and the like; neither Mr. Roosevelt nor Mr. Churchill nor Mr. Nehru ever had such an effect upon me in public or in private, and I had quite long conversations with all of them at different times. . . .

But once you conquered your own shyness, he was not in the least formidable.

He had the ability, rare in famous men, to laugh at himself. At a party given at the Sarnoffs—one more successful than the one mentioned above—Wanda, in a white wig and wearing his clothes, impersonated him. They gave a little skit representing a meeting of the board of directors of RCA. The men sat at a huge table while they discussed projects involving millions and millions of dollars. Then "Toscanini" sitting there—the real Toscanini had once been invited to such a meeting by Sarnoff—sitting there quietly, asked in a small voice for twenty-six dollars cash for some new harp strings. This was voted on and vetoed. "He" got up, and as he turned to go he noticed the sexy stenographer who was taking notes. He stopped, stroked her knee, whispered "cara"—and left. No one relished the spoof more than the real Toscanini.

He was exceptionally free of the jealousy which one artist

displays toward another. There was nothing of Sir Benjamin Backbite in him. He thought in all honesty that his own achievement was flooded by too much praise, but he also knew that he stood high. Yet, being an artist, he had to see his art his way. He showed scant appreciation of other conductors' interpretations if they differed from his. He did respect Bruno Walter, though he often disagreed with Walter's milk-and-honey approach. He thought well of De Sabata, until De Sabata became one of Mussolini's adherents. In his last years he admired Solti. But for other men of the baton he didn't have much use. He particularly loathed Stokowski and would not acknowledge Stokowski's enormous contribution to orchestral development, nor his ability to make music sound with a smooth and luscious, a sheerly beautiful sound. When Stokowski pulled a phrase like taffy—which he sometimes did —it went against Toscanini's whole creed of propriety. Nor had he the least tolerance for Stokowski's affectations and vagaries, the spotlight shining on his hands. Usually when Toscanini listened at home to a radio performance he disliked, he would vent his anger by shouting, kicking the radio, and by cries of *"Vergogna."* One day he listened to an especially eccentric Stokowski performance of a Brahms symphony, but this time Toscanini said not a word; quietly and patiently he listened to the end. Then he disappeared into his room. Walter knew that no good would come of it. That night Walter saw in the outgoing mail-basket a letter addressed to Stokowski. He abstracted it and showed it to me. The letter read, "Dear Maestro Stokowski: I have known two assassins in my life. One was Hitler, the other was Mussolini. You are the third." The letter was, of course, never sent.

As to his own interpretations, Toscanini was quite amenable to discuss them with men who knew what they were talking about. Yet he was human enough occasionally to be piqued at disagreement. Milton Katims, the first violist of the NBC Symphony, was often invited to Riverdale, partly, he suspected, because he had a beautiful wife, who in addition to being decorative was an excellent cellist. Somebody had given Pablo Casals a movie camera. Casals said he would love to have a film of Toscanini at home and he asked if Katims would do him the favor the next time he went to visit Toscanini. Katims took Casals's camera with him. When they arrived at the Villa Pauline, Toscanini greeted them both most warmly and at once plunged into a discussion of obscure cello literature with Virginia Katims. On and on they chatted, but when the two stopped a moment for breath, Katims brought forward Casals's request. Toscanini did not answer. Katims repeated the request. Could he take those pictures for Casals? Again no answer. Katims dropped the matter. At the end of a long evening, as Toscanini accompanied his two guests to their car—he always treated guests with great courtliness—he suddenly turned to Katims and said softly, "Casals thinks my Brahms too fast. No pictures."

4

"Poetry," wrote Congreve, "the eldest sister of all art, and parent of most." Toscanini loved that eldest sister, his interest encompassing the literature of several languages. He felt the music of those languages when he read them, though he could not speak them easily. He read, in addition to his native poets, German, English, and French writers. He knew much of Shakespeare by heart, some of it in Italian and some in Victor Hugo's French translation, as well as in English. Once when an actress quoted some passages from *A Midsummer Night's Dream* in German, he continued the recital, quoting the next lines both in English and Italian. He read Walt Whitman, Washington Irving—for some reason he read every word Irving wrote—Goethe and Heine, Keats and Shelley. He loved Poe—"such music in his words!"—and berated himself that he forgot to visit Poe's birthplace when he gave a concert in Richmond, Virginia. One evening in Riverdale somebody mentioned Rainer Maria Rilke; it appeared that Toscanini knew Rilke's poetry and had read the *Duino Elegies*, not an easy work for a foreigner to understand. He phoned Bachmann one night at 1:00 A.M. to ask what the word "unwillkürlich" meant: he liked its sound. Dorle Jarmel, who as a young girl handled publicity for the New York Philharmonic, sent him a book at the end of his tenure and wrote on the flyleaf, "Farewell, thou

111

art too dear for my possessing." He recognized at once this quotation from a Shakespeare sonnet and replied, "Farewell, thou art too young for my possessing."

It was to be expected that he knew Dante. But how he knew him! He could take you, through Hell (which "endures eternally," and he spoke in his croaking voice with infinite sadness, "All hope abandon, ye who enter here"), through Purgatory to Heaven. To hear him quote Dante was an unforgettable experience.

He himself tried his hand at writing poetry, as in his youth he had attempted to compose music. He soon relinquished composition, judging himself to be insufficiently talented. Likewise, he destroyed most of his poems. Two, however (written in English), have survived. They were written in his old age and are poems of longing, longing for youth. Even he knew he had to die. One is a variation on Goethe's *Mignon*. I give the poems here exactly as he wrote them, including the grammatical errors, which seem to me to make the verses all the more touching:

Autumn

The leaves already are falling from the trees
And my unhappy love likewise is waning,
It smiles to the agonizing olden world
But it will never see another May.

Unhappy love of my past youthful years!
Your torbid destiny pursue relentless—
In sorrowfulness always you have grown
In sorrow you expire for your life's last day.

Mignon

Did you ever see that beautiful dear country
Which the sun enfold up with dazzling splendour?
That charming country where May is eternal
And eternal the smiles of stars and flowers?

There every whisper of waters or wind
Resemble an harmony of celeste harpes.
There every single sound of human idiom
Resemble a song a tender sigh of love.

Of that dear and sweet native country of mine
I have a vague remembrance in my heart,
I see it in my dream—there must I go,
And there I want to love, to weep—to die.

Perhaps it was after writing "Autumn" that he called an
extra rehearsal for Strauss's *Death and Transfiguration*. It
was on a Sunday morning and the musicians groused at having their day of rest disturbed. They crept most unwillingly
to school. At first he addressed himself to the problem, often
previously rehearsed and always difficult, of the beginning of
the piece, which is not only technically tricky but emotionally
precarious, with the violins and violas suggesting the troubled
sleep of the dying man, his irregular heartbeat, his suppressed
fear, life's assertion dragging thin and weary. It is a study of
dying.

Toscanini stood there, almost immobile, creating with the
sparsest of means, with slow, small indications of his hands, the
still scene, the stale air of the sickroom. The light in the hall
seemed suddenly to dim and each musician in the orchestra felt
the presence of death, each was conscious of pain he had suffered, each felt the tremor of mortality. This was no longer
a performance of a famous tone poem; it was a contact, pal-
pable and physical, with a body about to fail. Then, as the
struggle began and the Transfiguration theme was heard for
the first time, he built and built the theme to a climax of such
titanic force, of such superhuman annunciation, that the
brasses seemed to have gone mad with the challenge and the
hall seemed to split asunder. Toscanini rehearsed the tone poem
for three hours; after it was over the men sat, drenched, exhausted, pale with the thrill that they themselves had just experienced, looking at one another and not believing it. To this
day the musicians with whom I have spoken remember that rehearsal as a high-point of their lives. The performance, marvelous though it was, fell short of what happened on Sunday
morning.

After the rehearsal, his chauffeur Emilio drove him home
at top speed. The older he got, the more did he enjoy driving

fast. Did he wish to husband time or did he wish to repudiate an old man's tempo?

He hated growing old and would not admit to any of the infirmities which age heaps on one. He had all his teeth even in his seventies, but once a tooth had to be pulled, and he made a great mystery of his visit to the dentist, allowing no one to accompany him. In his seventies he was—after canceling two appointments—finally persuaded to have his eyes checked: for years he had worn the same pair of glasses which some doctor in Italy had prescribed for him. The New York eye-doctor, a famous one, found his eyes sound but changed the prescription to one twice as strong. Toscanini was delighted. "Now I can see the girls better," he said.

CHAPTER FOUR

THE METROPOLITAN

T HE seven seasons Toscanini worked at the Metropolitan Opera were seven fat years. Or at least six and a half fat years.

The Metropolitan was, and is, a maddening place. It is an artistically capricious institution. Its audiences—there is more than one audience—are capricious as well, ranging from the ignorant to the bewildered to the finically knowledgeable. However they are constituted and whatever the transgressions perpetrated on stage and in the pit, the Metropolitan manages to maintain a special love-hate relationship with its public, the audiences returning to their opera house again and again, after staying away again and again. The relationship smacks of caprice, proving that Oscar Wilde was right: "The only difference between a caprice and a life-long passion is that the caprice lasts a little longer." The Metropolitan has lasted a little longer.

On certain nights the Metropolitan has been capable of presenting performances greatly sung, magnificently conducted, and not too badly staged. The next night the performance would fall below the level of that of a third-rate *Stagione* playing in Brescia during an off-season, with some "robustious periwig-pated fellow" strutting and bellowing and the orchestra sawing and scratching. The chance one takes when one innocently purchases a seat, the never-knowing-what-one-will-

115

get, is as true today as it was on the day Gatti and Toscanini took over.

It is not true that in the Toscanini years the audience consisted solely or even largely of dowagers and socialites, incapable of distinguishing bravura singing from music or responding to an integrated performance. The Metropolitan was not merely a hothouse where the tiaras grew. New York, with its large Italian and German population, with a long tradition of first-class music-making behind it (the New York Philharmonic began in the same year as the Vienna Philharmonic, 1842), was not musically naïve. Gustav Mahler wrote to Bruno Walter (in December, 1909), "The public here is very nice and behaves relatively more decently than in Vienna. They listen attentively and with good will." Yet Metropolitan audiences, then as now, have had a curious way of behaving. They have responded to faulty, loud-mouthed performances with enthusiasm, only to be left as indifferent by a fine presentation of Gluck's *Armide* (with Toscanini) as Thackeray was by *The Sorrows of Werther:*

> Charlotte, having seen his body
> Borne before her on a shutter,
> Like a well-conducted person,
> Went on cutting bread and butter.

Swings in quality are inevitable in a theater performing repertoire night after night: the performance cannot always take place on the mountaintop. Yet the unevenness of the Metropolitan standard was (and is) greater than reasonable divergence. And that unevenness was usually due to the absence of leadership, strong, artistic, free-acting leadership. The inspiring authority was missing. No muscular hand kept the performance from sliding.

In former years the Metropolitan rightly claimed that it employed the world's finest singers. All too often it let these singers splash at will in operatic waters. If nothing quite so ludicrous happened as on the pre–David Garrick British stage, when the actors took over and gave *King Lear* a happy ending, or made comic characters of Macbeth's witches, the stars

116

often managed to pollute the flow of a work of art. They held on to the high C's while they performed the standard attitude of the outstretched arm, the palm upward, in a gesture about which Toscanini used to ask, "Is it raining?"

When, intermittently, an excellent conductor entered the house, he was hardly ever given sufficient time or authority to perform his task. Mahler arrived at the Metropolitan when he was already ill, and soon became discouraged. Bodanzky, who led the German repertoire for many years, often settled for routine. Others, such as George Szell, could not get along under restrictive conditions. When a good stage director was employed—which happened frequently in the early Bing years—he left his staging, after the initial presentations, in the hands of a timid assistant, and presently the singers ruined it. Zeffirelli's fine staging of *Falstaff* was in a season or two perverted into a vulgar farce, Bardolph and Pistol hogging the stage, and everybody acting in the belief that the seat of humor is the humor of the seat.

A new era began with Toscanini. At once he let everybody know who was in charge. At once he put all talent at the service of him who must be served, the composer. In an early rehearsal Geraldine Farrar, singing Butterfly, said of him, "Maestro, you must conduct in the tempo I sing. I am a star." He replied, "Geraldine, the stars are in heaven. Here we are all artists, good artists and bad artists. You are a bad artist."

In his very first performance—*Aida*, November 16, 1908 "there was every evidence that there were new forces at work," wrote Richard Aldrich, the critic of the *New York Times*. Henry Krehbiel of the New York *Tribune* welcomed him:

> Of the new conductor it must be said that he is a boon to Italian opera as great and as welcome as anything that has come out of Italy since Verdi laid down his pen.

With the orchestra he began to rehearse *Götterdämmerung* before he rehearsed *Aida*. Obviously, the Wagner work presented the new conductor with a more complex problem, though the score was fresh in the musicians' memory, *Götter-*

dämmerung having been given as the last performance of the previous season under Alfred Hertz.*

Toscanini did not draw back from a comparison of his handling of Wagner, against Hertz's traditionally German Wagner. At a certain point during the first rehearsal, Toscanini said to the cellos, "That is B-flat, not A." They showed him their parts: they all had an A, they had played an A for years. It was wrong, said Toscanini. It was right, said the men. He called for the full score. It was brought—the correct note was B-flat. At the next rehearsal, which went badly, Toscanini tore into the orchestra, using his armament of Italian invectives. A delegation of the orchestra marched to Gatti's office. He listened to their complaints—"never have we been called such dreadful names"—shrugged his shoulders, and said, "You should hear what he calls me." Nevertheless the orchestra went on strike. The matter was arbitrated and soon the men got used to their leader's language.

His mind filled every phase of all his performances, supervising diction, miming, gestures, grouping of the chorus, lighting. No ensemble was too large, no detail of costuming too small for his care. He did have extraordinary singers at his disposal: Alda, Destinn, Eames, Farrar, Fremstad, Gadski, Gay, Gluck, Homer, Nordica, Sembrich, later Matzenauer, Ober, and still later Bori. Among the men, Amato, Bonci, Burrian, Didur, Feinhals, Goritz, Pini-Corsi, Rothier, Schmedes, Scotti, Slezak, Urlus. And Caruso!

Caruso had a mind as well as the incomparable voice. He was a serious artist. Perhaps that is not saying much, for most artists are serious in the exercise of their profession, few play hopscotch with their gift. But many artists, having arrived at a certain level, are unwilling to change or unable to learn. Curiosity deserts them. Caruso, though his endowment placed him *hors de combat*, though he knew he was unique, was willing to take instruction and search for help. Left to his own devices he would do some tasteless things; guided by somebody he re-

---

* That season (1907–1908) saw and heard as well Chaliapin in *Mefistofele, Lohengrin, Tannhäuser, Die Meistersinger,* in addition to the usual *Fausts, Pagliaccis, Bohèmes,* etc. Mahler made his debut, conducting *Die Walküre, Siegfried, Don Giovanni, Tristan,* and *Fidelio.* The repertoire shows that the Metropolitan was much more than a Caruso-dominated "Faustspielhaus."

spected the giant and pliant voice became a giant and pliant artist. He and Toscanini worked together and Toscanini loved him. Perhaps their natures shared certain traits: "Caruso was not a happy man," wrote the Italian critic Leporello; "he paid for his triumphs with torment and anguish. Every time he went before the public he did so with the anxiousness of a first trial. His clamorous successes did not give him joy; he was perturbed and bitterly discontent." This may be exaggerated, but does contain some truth. At any rate—there was the Caruso-Toscanini combination which illumined the house in *Aida*, *Butterfly* (with Farrar, three days after the *Aida* debut), *Carmen*, *Cavalleria*, *La Gioconda*, *Germania*, *Armide*, *La Fanciulla del West*, *Manon*, *Un Ballo in Maschera*, *Tosca*. Geraldine Farrar was Toscanini's favorite soprano, notwithstanding the early spat. "She was very, very beautiful," he remembered smilingly, beautiful as Mimi and Manon and Cio-Cio-San and Tosca. They were lovers, as I have said, and when many years later Toscanini visited her she served caviar before dinner. "I slept with that woman for seven years"—he confided to a friend—"wouldn't you think she'd remember that I hate fish?" But to her, now grown old, he was still gallant and he swallowed the caviar.

In the seven fecund seasons Toscanini conducted twenty-nine operas, including every opening night except that of 1912. His capacity for work was that of a demon, but a young demon in excellent health. Only once did he have to cancel an appearance; he had injured his hand. Could many artists accomplish the physical labor, let alone the mental effort, required for his schedule at the beginning of the 1914–1915 season, November 16, *Masked Ball*, November 19, *Carmen*, November 21, *Aida*, November 27, *Carmen*, November 28 (matinee of the day following), *Boris*, November 30, *Butterfly*, December 3, *Tristan*, December 4, *Tosca?* Seven operas in two weeks—he had the strength of Antaeus when he touched music.

Of the great works he presented to the New York public, perhaps the most glorious performances were those of *Falstaff* (with Scotti and Destinn) the first season; *Otello* (with Slezak, Scotti, and Alda); *Tristan* (with Gadski and later Fremstad and Nordica, three different Isoldes, and Burrian as Tristan);

Orfeo (with Homer and Gluck) the second season, with two performances of *Die Meistersinger* at the end of that season. Among the American premieres were *Le Villi*, Puccini's first tentative opera, Catalani's *La Wally*, Franchetti's *Germania*, Dukas's *Ariane et Barbe-Bleu*, Wolf-Ferrari's *Le Donne Curiose*, and *L'Amore Medico*, Montemezzi's *L'Amore dei Tre Re*, and Gluck's *Armide*, already mentioned, with decorations by Puvis de Chavannes. These were failures, with the possible exception of *L'Amore dei Tre Re*, which was revived several times in later years, partly because its sensuous music is reminiscent of *Tristan*, partly because it contains three stellar roles. Toscanini prepared two world premieres: Puccini's *La Fanciulla del West* and Giordano's *Madame Sans-Gêne*.

This record can give us lovers of the opera no idea of the beauty which suffused the performances, nor of the sense of fulfillment one carried home. All we can do is to read what the critics wrote and be envious. For example, Richard Aldrich in the *New York Times* (March 27, 1910) on *Die Meistersinger:*

> That Wagner's comedy did not reach a performance at the Metropolitan Opera House till the last days of the season has been a matter for surprise and disappointment. But this season it was transferred to the care of Mr. Toscanini; and the delay in the production has been due to his exigencies in the matter of rehearsals. Although many of the principal singers are the same and the scenic arrangements have not been changed, the work was necessarily entirely restudied under Mr. Toscanini. And how thoroughly this was done yesterday's performance bore eloquent testimony. It was, indeed, worth waiting for. It was in almost every respect a profoundly beautiful and poetical performance. Upon the musical side especially it reached a pitch of perfection, of ravishing, intoxicating loveliness, of pure beauty of sound, of instrumental color, that was perhaps unique in its kind. New York has heard representations of "Die Meistersinger" in the last quarter of a century that have been memorable in many ways; but yesterday's was one of the most remarkable of them

all, and in its way had qualities rarely equalled. Nothing Mr. Toscanini has done, not even his reading of "Tristan," has equalled his performance of "Die Meistersinger."

2

Trouble arose over *Tristan.*

The matter has been variously reported, depending on the narrator's being a Mahler or a Toscanini adherent. Mahler's wife Alma told the story thus in *Gustav Mahler, Memories and Letters:*

> Toscanini had gone so far as to make it a condition that the first production at which he was to conduct should be *Tristan,* an opera Mahler had already studied with the company. Weary of conflict he gave *Tristan* up. Toscanini immediately took it in hand and rehearsed it all over again in a manner entirely different. Mahler bitterly resented this and took no further pleasure in opera in New York. We had all read the cables between the Metropolitan and Gatti-Casazza. The Metropolitan wanted Toscanini, and he made *Tristan* his supreme object and an indispensable condition. So Mahler relinquished it to him. Instead of thanking him, Toscanini from the first moment contemptuously ignored him. He even went so far as to hold him up to scorn during rehearsals. He was always telling the orchestra that Mahler "could not do that" and that he had no understanding of *Tristan.* We went to the first night of this production of Toscanini's. The nuances in his Wagner were distressing. His style has been simplified since those days.

That is not the truth, but we are quite used to the dazzling Alma playing hide-and-seek with the truth. It is not true that Toscanini made *Tristan* "a condition" of his accepting the Metropolitan post, nor that it should be his "first production" nor that he "immediately took it in hand." Nor does it seem to be true that Mahler "bitterly resented" Toscanini's *Tristan.*

It is true that Toscanini had originally asked to conduct

Tristan in his first season. Andreas Dippel, who was still co-manager of the Metropolitan before Gatti-Casazza took over exclusively, wrote to Mahler about this request and received a reasonable reply:

> [Undated, but probably early August, 1908]
> If recently I was willing to give a free hand to the new manager and to consider the wishes of my colleague, I must insist on an exception for *Tristan*. Last season *Tristan* cost me much labor and I believe I am right in saying that the form in which it is now given in New York is my spiritual property. If Toscanini, for whom I have the greatest respect and whom I am honored to salute as a colleague, though I do not know him personally—if he is to present *Tristan* previous to my return, the interpretation would necessarily assume a different character. It would be painful to me to have to re-study it in the middle of the season; I must insist therefore that the opera be reserved for me until December 17.

A moderate enough request!

Mahler's wish was respected: he conducted *Tristan* during the 1908–1909 season, Toscanini not till the following season. For a time, then, two supreme musicians worked in the house and the standard of performance reached a height never equaled since. Whatever Alma's recollection, it is improbable that Mahler found Toscanini's performance "distressing"; he told Bruno Walter that "he [Toscanini] conducts it in a manner entirely different from ours, but magnificently in his way." On the other hand, Toscanini thought Mahler's interpretation lacking in passion: "But the poor man was tired and ill." Nor did Toscanini care much for Mahler the composer. He examined all his major works but found them too enigmatic and too diffuse. In effect, the two men remained strangers.

Mahler's words "my spiritual property" point to a characteristic of some interpretative artists who stake out claims to artistic territories. "Don't tread on my grass," they post. Bruno Walter has not a word to say in his autobiography of Beecham's conducting of Mozart, while Beecham in *his* autobiography (*A Mingled Chime*) mentions Bruno Walter just once in passing, keeping mum about Mozart. Each considered himself the one and only Mozart Mohammed. Clemen Krauss saw himself as the official representative of Richard Strauss, while Mengelberg admitted only one "authentic" performance of *Ein Heldenleben*, the tone poem Strauss had dedicated to him. (Both Krauss and Mengelberg, however, allowed that Strauss's conducting of his own works had some merit.) Wanda Landowska said to another harpsichordist, "You play Bach your way, I play him his way." Koussevitzky, a generous and warm-hearted artist, said to me at the time that Toscanini was conducting the NBC Symphony, "He is a superb *opera* conductor."

3

The socially diamantine event of the Toscanini years, perhaps the most glittering evening in the Metropolitan's history, was the first performance of Puccini's *The Girl of the Golden West* on December 10, 1910. To obtain the world premiere of a work by the most beloved living opera composer—that represented no small coup for an opera house. Gatti had gone to Italy to negotiate the matter. He had been able not only to offer a handsome sum but to point out that an opera with an American locale should first be heard and seen in America and that he could put at the disposal of the baptismal feast a uniquely stellar cast, headed—and this was most important to Puccini— by Toscanini as conductor and by David Belasco, author of the play and brilliant regisseur, as stage manager. The agreement was concluded and Puccini consented to be present at the premiere.

Excitement over the event was slowly heated by planned publicity, bits of which were dropped into the public prints as early as May, 1910, and which continued with increasing frequency to bob up right to the day of the premiere. The New York public was told, for example, that "Puccini is the most successful of all modern composers from a box-office point of view. His income averages $15,000 a week during the season, for not less than one hundred performances of his operas are given throughout the world at a royalty of $150 each."

Caruso stated that the new opera was Puccini's best. . . . Puccini was going to conduct the opera himself. No, he was not, said another story, he was going to stage it. In the meantime, Toscanini had brought Puccini and Mascagni together and the two estranged composers had kissed and made up "and should now collaborate on an ode to macaroni" (New York *World*). Puccini's operas had earned so much that he owned "three automobiles, three motorboats, and a well-stocked game preserve." Mme. Nordica said, "Mme. Emmy Destinn, who will sing the title role, is a wonderful artist. . . . I cannot but regret, however, that the artist selected is not an American."

Puccini arrived on November 17 accompanied by his son Tonio and by Tito Ricordi. Having given his usual brilliant shipboard interview (what he said was precisely this: "Thank you, thank you! Much pleased! Long live Italy!"), he went that very night to hear Toscanini conduct *Aida*, sung by Caruso, Destinn, and Amato, the three who were to assume the principal roles of *The Girl*. In later interviews he spoke more fluently. He declared that "the music cannot really be called American, for music has no nationality—it is either music or nothing." Contradicting himself, he then said, "For this drama I have composed music that, I feel sure, reflects the spirit of the American people and particularly the strong, vigorous nature of the West. I have never been West, but I have read so much about it that I know it thoroughly." Asked about his next opera, he said that he wanted a good, lusty comedy, that he was tired of tragic subjects. "Like Wagner's *Meistersinger?*" someone asked. Mr. Puccini assumed a reverential air. "No," he said, "there is only one *Meistersinger*" (New York *Herald*).

Puccini wrote home, "The opera emerges splendidly, the first act a little long, but the second act magnificent and the third grandiose. Belasco has attended all the rehearsals with great love and interest. Caruso is magnificent in his part, Destinn not bad but she needs more energy. Toscanini, the *zenith!*— *kind, good, adorable*—in short, I am content with my work and I hope for the best. But how tremendously difficult it is, this music and the staging!"

The demand for tickets was frantic. Subscribers to the

Metropolitan had first choice of seats, at doubled prices. In order to buy a seat, one had to sign the ticket stub; before entering the theater, one had to countersign the ticket. The two signatures were then compared by the doormen at the entrance. If they tallied, you were allowed to enter. This measure was to prevent ticket speculators from getting hold of the tickets. It was only partially successful; nothing invented by man can stump a ticket speculator. They asked—and received—incredible sums for tickets (as high as thirty times the box-office price) and a brisk business was done in forged signatures. The delay necessitated by countersigning the tickets clogged the lobby of the Metropolitan and in turn created such a traffic jam that all traffic in the vicinity of the opera house came to a standstill. Special police were called out to push back the mob of curious sightseers. The opera could not start on time, though the first automobiles and carriages had drawn up to the opera house an hour before curtain time.

The performance, led by Toscanini, was resplendent and fiery. He brought to the surface every last flake of gold—that wasn't there. The staging was splendid as well, thanks to Belasco's master touches. No trouble had been spared: eight horses galloped onstage during the last act. The elegant audience forgot to be elegant and shouted its pleasure. When Puccini appeared for the first time before the curtain, a silver crown was placed on his brow by Gatti-Casazza. Bouquets of flowers were hurled onto the stage. There were fifty-two curtain calls in all, twenty of them after the end of the opera.

When the curtain was lowered for the last time, everyone congratulated everyone else, and Puccini was kissed by one and all. He said to Toscanini and the singers, "My heart is beating like the double basses in the card scene. I am tremendously pleased with this reception. I couldn't have had better interpreters for my work." He believed, as did everyone else connected with the production, that the new opera was destined for a long life.

A six-thousand-word review by W. J. Henderson in the New York *Sun* and only slightly shorter essays in the *Times* and *Tribune* gave perspicacious estimates of the new work, which boiled down to the statement that it "shows considerably less fecundity of melodic inspirations" (Aldrich). They all agreed that the conducting was "one of Mr. Toscanini's masterpieces."

The Girl is a remarkably poor opera. Its first weakness lies in the libretto. We can understand how Puccini may have been led astray by the fascination of Belasco's production of the play, which he had seen in New York on a previous visit. William Winter, in *The Life of David Belasco*, writes, "Nothing of the kind which I have ever seen in the Theater has fully equaled in verisimilitude the blizzard on Cloudy Mountain as depicted by Belasco in the Second Act of this fine melodrama—such a bitter and cruel storm of wind-driven snow and ice as he had often suffered under in the strolling days of his nomadic youth." In order to produce this snowstorm and the accompanying moaning of the gale, Belasco employed no fewer than thirty-two assistants, a symphonic band of stagehands, so to speak, who were directed by a centrally located "conductor" and who operated wind and snow machines with the precision of an orchestra, underscoring the lines. In addition, Belasco used a moving panorama which first disclosed to the audience a view of Cloudy Mountain in all its majesty, then seemed to wander down a winding path until it stopped at a settlement where Minnie's saloon, the *Polka*, was found. The lights were then dimmed for an instant and the scene changed to the interior of the saloon. The action was accompanied by the music of minstrel instruments playing Western and Stephen Foster melodies. No doubt extraordinarily effective! Yet the story of Minnie, who lives among brawling miners but who remains as pure as one of Louisa May Alcott's girls, only to fall in love with a mysterious bandit who is also pure in heart, indeed, a fine fellow who at once resolves to give up his old life—this story is sufficiently mucid to stick to the palate of even the opera lover who is willing to swallow the plot of *La Gioconda*.

To American audiences, the opera is an impossibility. Puccini, needless to say, is totally unsuccessful in suggesting an American atmosphere. Italian audiences might pardon the libretto's absurdity were they to be rewarded with such music as can be reasonably expected from Puccini. Here and there, in a turn of melody, a phrase voiced by Minnie, we do hear the Puccini of *Butterfly* or *Bohème*. But only here and there.

Nine-tenths of the opera sounds as if it had been written by somebody who was imitating Puccini and was not doing it very well.

The enthusiasm Toscanini expended on this opera (which, in spite of attempted revivals, once with Jeritza, then with Leontyne Price, then with Tebaldi, refused to stay alive) he was to devote later to music by Italian second-rate composers, such as Martucci, Respighi, Sammartini, and Sonzogno. Again one may observe that neither the creative nor the recreative artist is necessarily a good judge.

Puccini was grateful for all his friend had done for the opera. The composer, though wealthy, was by no means free-handed with his money: all the same, he bought the Toscaninis a silver candelabra at Tiffany's which cost three hundred dollars, then a considerable sum. He duly reported this to his wife, Elvira. But from then on the friendship took a curious "go-away" and "come back" course, one which we may as well relate here, though it disturbs chronology. It leads once again to the eyrie which people of talent inhabit and to which only yea-sayers are usually welcomed.

Puccini's next opera was a slight affair, *La Rondine*, which he had composed on commission for Vienna. It was completed during World War I and the composer had been imprudent enough to let it be known that he did not hate Italy's German or Austrian enemies, and indeed he was willing to serve the enemy. Were not his operas beloved in Germany and a mainstay of the Vienna Opera? Did the public there not appreciate him better than the French did?

La Rondine out of the way, Puccini turned to the *Triptych*, the three one-act operas of which one, *Gianni Schicchi*, is a masterpiece; one, *Suor Angelica*, a bore; and the third, *Il Tabarro*, a fascinating work of tone-painting influenced by Debussy. Toscanini heard the *Trittico* in Rome, declared that he did not like any of it and that he would not conduct it, though he had no objection to the Scala scheduling it for the season of 1921–1922. He thought *Il Tabarro* was bad *Grand Guignol*. Was this a purely musical judgment? Perhaps not. During the war Toscanini had been an ardent patriot and Puccini's unpatriotic attitude had offended him. Now Puccini was deeply hurt: he thought that Toscanini's refusal would cause him "not only material but moral damage." He lashed about him. To Sybil Seligman, his adoring English friend, he complained:

> Torre del Lago, 16 March 1919
>
> I protested to Ricordi's because I don't want that *pig* [in English] of a Toscanini; he has said all sorts of nasty things about my operas and has tried to inspire certain journalists to run them down. He didn't succeed in every case, but one of his friends (of the *Secolo*) wrote a beastly article under his inspiration—and I won't have this *God*.

To his intimate friend Riccardo Schnabl-Rossi, a man of the world who must have smiled when he received the letter, Puccini wrote:

> (Torre del Lago. Undated but probably July 1921)
>
> The *Trittico* will be given at the Scala, but Panizza will conduct. Toscanini conducts only *Falstaff* and operas he knows already. That's what he tells me and I believe he does so because he doesn't want to conduct my works. He really is an awful man, perfidious, heartless. I deny that he has the soul of an artist, because anybody who truly has it cannot possess such meanness and I think envy, too! I really don't give a damn. I only worry on account of the Milanese. That public, more or less intelligent, thinks there is something derogatory if one of my operas is conducted by another conductor.

To Renato Simoni, with whom he was working on *Turandot*, he wrote, "I have a thorn in my side—Toscanini. He persists in being my enemy. Why?"

Yet less than two years later Puccini informed Schnabl: "Toscanini is now really the best man in the world; as conductor he has everything, soul, poetry, *souplesse*, organization, dash, dramatic subtlety—in a word, a miracle."

What caused this turnabout?

Toscanini had decided to rethink and restudy *Manon Lescaut*, Puccini's fragrant youthful opera; he was going to conduct it at the Scala in the season of 1922–1923. Both men discussed the score as if it were yesterday's product—*Manon* was then twenty-nine years old—Puccini did a little editing of the orchestration, and Toscanini brought forth all the charm, the melodic fullness, the free-breathing ardor of this treasurable work. Two middle-aged men held the mirror up to youth. The performance on December 26, 1922, proved a sensation, *Manon* washed in morning light.

Puccini wrote to Senator Luigi Albertini, then the editor of the influential *Corriere della Sera* and later the author of a definitive study, *The Origins of the War of 1914:*

[Milan] December 27, 1922

Your music critic states that I have retouched the instrumentation of *Manon:*—"There are quite a few changes in the second and fourth acts and even in the first act alterations are evident."

The fact is that aside from some unimportant modifications in orchestral coloring, my score as it was published by Ricordi would show that I did *not* change the instrumentation. My *Manon* is exactly as it was thirty years ago. Only—it has been conducted by Arturo Toscanini, which means that it has been conducted in a way that provides the composer with the great and rare pleasure to see his music illuminated by the same light which he envisaged and imagined at the moment of composition—and which then disappeared forever.

All too long have we in Italy fallen into the habit of giving the so-called repertory operas, those which resist time and sloppy performances, in an indecent way: one rehearsal for the orchestra, none for the stage, and away we go, carrying all the foul rubbish with which little by little the abuses and the bad habits of conductors and singers have encrusted the work.

Arturo Toscanini, with the faith and love which inflame him, grasps the chisel and chips away until the work is revealed to the public with the true intention of its author.

The old opera appears new to the public and the people say, "It is different." No, it is simply the work brought to life by the greatest recreator whom music possesses. . . .

Last night *Manon* seemed a new opera even to me, so much so that I felt myself thirty years younger. When I left the Scala I forgot I was leaving from a seat in the stalls and not from the topmost gallery, and I was just on the point of guiding my steps toward the Aida [a little restaurant where he ate when he was a student] to consume my alas! very, very modest repast, the cost of which would be inexorably added to the account which the good Signora Assunta kept.

Giacomo Puccini

But again, and soon, their relationship soured. Puccini no longer loved Toscanini in May as he did in December. Again he was angry: why did Toscanini "waste" his substance on Pizzetti's new opera, *Dèbora e Jaéle*, and why was he working so hard bringing Boito's *Nerone* to life, neglecting his, Puccini's, operas? Well, he wrote Schnabl from Vienna, *Bohème* had been newly given at La Scala, "God" (*il Divo*) did not conduct, but "it was a great success all the same."

Puccini's nerves were strung taut. Struggling with *Turandot*, he could not get the text shaped to his satisfaction, and he became discouraged with the music of what he intended to be his most ambitious work, "a new kind of opera," the theme of which he had first loved and now thought of abandoning altogether. The piano was closed, he said, and when he touched it his fingers got covered with dust. In February, 1924, he began to complain of a persistently raw throat. He was coughing and the cough disturbed his sleep. Then he got better, he took up the work with refreshed energy, hoping "soon to see the end of this blessed Princess." By September all that remained to be done was to finish the love duet and the finale of the last act, which he thought would take him but a few weeks. It was time now to play the music for a competent authority. To whom should he turn? Puccini called Toscanini. He came to Viareggio. Puccini played. The gulf between them was bridged—they were friends once more. Toscanini liked what he heard, except the love duet. The day after, Puccini wrote to one of his librettists, the poet Giuseppe Adami, "Toscanini has just left. We are in perfect agreement and I breathe at last. The incubus which has oppressed me since April has been lifted. . . ."

In October the two men met in one of the rehearsal rooms of the Scala. Renato Simoni, who had worked on the text of *Turandot* as well, was present. He recalled that Puccini played the music and sang in a hoarse, small voice. As the audition went on, dusk fell and the light faded, but Puccini did not notice. He was pale, his face was gray, he was utterly absorbed in his playing—his body hunched over the score. Toscanini sat next to him and turned the pages. He said little but every so often he patted Puccini on the back. When Puccini had finished, Toscanini expressed himself quietly but decisively. Turning to the exhausted composer with simple solicitude he said, "This is a fine work."

Puccini did not live to finish *Turandot*. Later in October the trouble in his throat changed to ominous pain. After trying to ignore the pain he finally went to see a doctor in Florence. The physician was noncommittal: he advised rest and told Puccini to stop smoking. Now frightened, he consulted a throat specialist, who called the condition a "papilloma." Puccini did not know what that meant. He asked his son, Tonio. Tonio guessed and went to see the doctor. To him the physician called the disease by its right name: cancer. Puccini was hurried off to Brussels to a radium clinic. On the train he suffered a hemorrhage. Always fastidious, he was ashamed and threw the soiled handkerchiefs out of the window. The radium treatments proved ineffective. He died during the night of November 28, 1924.

On December 3, Toscanini conducted a commemorative concert at the Scala. It took another year and a half before *Turandot* was made ready for its premiere. On April 25, 1926, Toscanini conducted the performance with Rosa Raisa as Turandot and Michele Fleta as Calaf. At the dress rehearsal the opera was given with the ending composed by Franco Alfano. At the performance Toscanini laid down his baton at the point at which Puccini had stopped, and turning to the audience, made his one and only public address: "At this point death forced Giacomo Puccini to break off his work." The audience left in silence.

The premiere of *Turandot* was almost canceled by a political incident. The Fascists were holding a celebration in Milan to which Mussolini had come especially from Rome. He was invited to the Scala. He let it be known that he would come to the premiere if Toscanini would precede the performance by the playing of the Fascist hymn, the *"Giovinezza."* Toscanini's answer was short: either *Turandot* was to be performed without the hymn or they could look for another conductor. Il Duce, wanting to avoid an open scandal, decided to stay away. The official news-bulletin stated that "the President did not wish to distract by his presence the attention of the public from the Puccini dedication."

Toscanini did not conduct *Turandot* after that season. The seesaw of his feeling toward Puccini continued long after the composer had become part of history. I once questioned him about Puccini: "He was a pretty good composer," he answered and turned the subject.

4

Though Toscanini entered the Metropolitan for what turned out to be his last season with greater energy than ever, his enthusiasm waned in the early months of 1915. Neither the war, with the certainty that several German singers could or would no longer cross the Atlantic, nor nostalgia for Italy, seems to have been the main cause. Gatti, he felt, was cutting artistic corners. His friend, become paunchy and self-important, took great pride in running the Metropolitan at a profit. Having bought out the dangerously competitive Hammerstein in 1910, the Metropolitan was favored by an era in which the demand for entertainment ran high, wide, and handsome. High, indeed, were the prices of the seats, not only those printed on the tickets, but those actually paid: the ticket agencies bought up large blocks and sold them adding whatever "service fees" the traffic would bear. For a Caruso performance it got to be well-nigh impossible to obtain a seat by standing in line at the box office. Toscanini performances were almost invariably sold out. Prosperity penetrated to the corners of standing-room space. Improbable though it seems today, the opera was making profits, and not just penny profits. Geraldine Farrar claimed that Gatti kept two sets of books: one he showed the artists when they asked for higher fees; the other, the true one, he showed his board of directors. Gatti proposed to maintain and if possible to augment this happy state. To do so he was willing to compromise, by skimping on rehearsals and employing inexpensive artists for unimportant roles. He was being cautious, particularly since the European war created an atmosphere of uncertainty, even though America was still standing neutral. As Irving Kolodin wrote in *The Metropolitan Opera:*

> The twin pillars of the structure he [Gatti] had created were Caruso and Toscanini. It was his good fortune that Caruso was satisfied with a top fee of $2500 a performance from 1914 on. No pittance, to be sure, but substantially less than a man of his popularity might have demanded. This not only assured Gatti of a satisfied star, but put him in an advantageous bargaining position with lesser artists. Toscanini's nature was otherwise. Neither adaptable nor inclined to compromise where artistic standards were at issue, he could not bear with restrictions on the free exercise of his talent when the money was available to assure that freedom. . . .
>
> Unlike most other conductors, even the most conscientious, Toscanini made his dislike operative not by fretting or "making do" but merely by giving up the thing he disliked. . . . Gatti's creed, often quoted, was Verdi's dictum: "The theater was not built to be empty." Toscanini's *idée fixe*, if never articulated in words, was that, empty or full, the theater, like the concert hall, is the place for maximum effort or nothing.

Toscanini resigned. The usual excuse, "ill health," was given as the reason, but he was seen around New York evidently in the best of health. Gatti then offered him "whatever fee he wanted." Toscanini replied that it was not money but artistry he needed. For many years after Toscanini's departure, he and Gatti were not on good terms. Occasionally they saw each other, accidentally and without pleasure. When Gatti was ill in 1939, his wife begged Toscanini to visit him. He went, somewhat reluctantly, and the two men were left alone. By and by, friends who were gathered in another room could hear their voices raised in a loud argument. Presumably they were still arguing about artistry versus box office. At any rate the reconciliation was a compromise which advancing years allow. Toscanini said, "I was willing to please the old man [Gatti, the reader may remember, was two years younger than Toscanini]; after all, we didn't have to put on any more opera performances."

No doubt Toscanini left the Metropolitan with a heavy heart. There were rumors in the newspapers that he left "because of personal problems," whatever that may have meant. (One rumor said he left because he was weary of his liaison with Farrar. That seems improbable.) He did not answer the rumors directly but he wrote to Max Smith, the music critic of the New York *Press*, an amiable man who was bilingual and whom Toscanini regarded as a friend:

[Undated, Spring, 1915]

. . . At the same time, I beg you, my dear friend, to furnish this, my explicit declaration of the reason for my spontaneous withdrawal from the Metropolitan. You may have this published wherever you think necessary. "I gave up my post in that theater because my artistic aspirations and ideas could not find the fulfillment of which I dreamed when I entered it in 1908. Routine is the ideal and the basis of that theater. That may serve *for the artisan not for the artist*" [these words in English]. To renew oneself or to die. Voilà tout. That is the only reason which removed me from the Metropolitan. All the others which the newspapers have circulated are false and unfounded. . . .

Toscanini's departure caused little regret among New York's critics. Not one of them got red in the face with anger. Kolodin, in *The Metropolitan Opera*, summed up the curious indifference:

> It shows a grievous unawareness of an axiom of opera production: while a bad conductor can do more to spoil a performance than a bad singer, a good conductor can do more to ennoble it than a good singer. And a great one can do more to set the tone of an opera house as high as it was at the Metropolitan in those several years than all the singers in the company combined. If New York's discriminating press did not more highly value what it had, it deserved no better than it eventually got.

CHAPTER FIVE

THE WORLD OF THE SYMPHONY

Not again would he undertake a task in which he could not exercise complete artistic authority. Not again would he submit to a manager, impresario, director, or a board of directors. Not again would he attempt to produce performances under routine conditions. More stubbornly than before he would pursue an all-or-nothing goal, recognizing only one necessity, that of bringing music to life as he heard it in his mind's ear. All other necessities, inseminated by finances, contractual obligations, promises tendered, weaknesses accepted, all those were the debris of music-making and were to be as resolutely swept away as wrong notes.

Now he wanted no part of New York, but longed to go back to Italy, far away from the Metropolitan and close to his own country which, he knew, could not remain untouched by the blaze that was burning up Europe. Toscanini had booked a cabin on the *Lusitania*, scheduled to sail in a week or so. Why wait? He had no further business where he was; he felt that "I had rather than forty pound I were at home." So he changed to a smaller and less luxurious steamer, and left at once. The *Lusitania* was sunk on that voyage.

Arrived at the Via Durini, he closed the door. But soon there was much knocking on that door: offers from opera houses poured in, from the Colón in Buenos Aires, from La Scala, renewed blandishments from the Metropolitan, etc. He would have none of them. He sat in his room, at times with the shades drawn, the lamps unlit, the door barred even to his family. When the war was going badly for Italy he would not talk or eat and he paced up and down half the night waiting for the morning newspaper. Walter had enlisted in the army: he was at the front.

At the beginning of World War I, Italian conservatives counseled neutrality, as did—paradoxically—Italian Socialists who adhered to the Marxian interpretation of war as a clash of imperialistic forces. Soon enough, however, the entire country was drawn toward the wish for combat, the desire for alarums and excursions, and that partly for idealistic reasons, but much more so for selfish reasons. The few idealists who clung to the tradition of Mazzini were deeply offended by Teutonic aggression and by the brutal invasion of Belgium. The many who were motivated by what the Foreign Minister Antonio Salandra called the *sacro egoismo*, the "sacred egotism," wanted to be at the side of the probable winner, hoping to be rewarded with the Italian Tyrol or bits of Dalmatia or other delicacies eventually to be served up at the conference table. Gabriele D'Annunzio, one-quarter genius, one-quarter charlatan, one-quarter hero, one-quarter tenor, inflamed the minds with patriotic poetry which needed only to be set to music to be thoroughly operatic, and rushed from town to town making torrefying speeches which never used a simple phrase when a grandisonant could be found. These are a few sentences typical of the apostrophes he devoted to Toscanini (though the speech from which they are taken belongs to a later patriotic occasion, the signing of the treaty of Rapallo in 1920):

> Brave captain [*condottiero*, a play on the word] whom our forebears would have called "the Overseer" like those men who in armed ships beat out the rhythm of the battle . . . look at him! He is of your race, emaciated like you, with bones like yours, nerves like yours. . . . Look at him! Look at the hand which holds the sceptre! His sceptre is a slender reed like the twig of an elder-tree. With it he lifts the great billows of the orchestra, releases the mighty

torrents of harmony, opens the cataracts of the vast flood, plumbs the forces of profundity and holds them on high, reigns in the tumult and reduces it to a whisper, creates light and darkness, serenity and tempest, sorrow and jubilation . . . [Quoted by Ferdinando Gerra: *L'Impresa di Fiume*]

D'Annunzio was joined by Mussolini, who as a young journalist had outspokenly opposed Italy's own imperialistic effort in Tripoli. Mussolini now clamored for intervention with equal loudness.

The war demanded real sacrifices from Italy's people. The army showed much bravery, operating high in the Alps under the most difficult of conditions. Walter, promoted to artillery captain, was often in danger.

Toscanini emerged from his seclusion to help in the only way he could: he conducted benefits, such as forty-two opera performances at the Dal Verme Theater in Milan (receipts 369,000 lire, equivalent to more than $100,000 in today's purchasing power), a monster concert to raise money for the Red Cross, several concerts in Rome. He organized a troupe to play band music at the front. A photograph exists showing him surrounded by officers, wearing puttees and a steel helmet, looking most unmilitary and Chaplinesque. This was taken just before the battle of Monte Santo, one of the war's bloodiest battles. There, "sheltered only by a huge rock, he conducted a concert which did not stop until word had been brought to him that the Italian soldiers had stormed and taken the trenches of the Austrians to the music of the band" (*New York Times*, September 3, 1917). This work he did without being paid one lira. He lived on his savings, still refusing any paid engagements, and when the money ran out he sold his house in the Via Durini. (Later he was able to repurchase it.) At the low point he unwrapped his cello, which he had not touched for years, and began to practice. He would rather make his living as an anonymous cellist than to return to the podium, except on his own conditions. His children and Carla begged him to relent. He would not. The sum of his work for almost five years—1915 to 1920—is slight. Used to the most intense kind of labor he must

138

have suffered profoundly by not doing what he loved. The anguish must have torn his mind. Yet—an intransigence which approaches the unreasonable is a characteristic of strong artists, though few indeed are those who will refuse money and fewer still those who will refuse fame.

In spite of his patriotic efforts, he did not escape an instance of the sort of bobbery to which he was by now used. In Rome he conducted a concert (November 19, 1916) at the Augusteo, the first part of which consisted of Italian music, a Corelli *concerto grosso*, the first Martucci symphony, a tone poem by Tommasini. The fourth number was the *Siegfried "Waldweben"* and the *Götterdämmerung* Funeral March. During the silence which follows one of the drum beats at the beginning of the March, a man in the balcony shouted, "That's for the dead of Padua." He referred to an aerial bombardment which had taken place in Padua a few days previously. The cry was taken up by others, the audience began to stamp and whistle, one affecting the other with the bellicose virus. Toscanini interrupted, played the "Royal March," then resumed the program and conducted the last number, Sibelius's *Finlandia*. A few days later an editorial in one of Rome's newspapers, headlined "Holy Whistles," approved the rowdyism:

> . . . Is it any wonder that in a time of a war bitterly fought against Germany (because even against Austria we are fighting principally against the German spirit) the people rebel at the imposition of German [artistic] examples?

> It could have been borne with patience had Toscanini at least selected works of Beethoven, who represents the lofty Germany of Goethe and Kant. But he had recourse to the most brutally German of modern composers, to Richard Wagner, who with his romantic mysticism and his orchestral rant anticipated and represents the barbaric reawakening of the imperialistic Germany, the Germany of Krupp, Tirpitz, and Zeppelin. For that reason the public was right when it whistled. . . .

Lest we feel too superior at such purblindness, let us remember that German operas were banned at the Metropolitan dur-

ing the season of 1917–1918 and that when *Parsifal* was revived in 1919–1920 it was sung in English. I still remember
Didur, a Pole, as Klingsor, singing, "Ha, he iss handsome,
der you-d!"

Toscanini did not return to Rome until 1920. He did conduct the works of the composer who "represents the lofty Germany" all through the war, performing the Ninth Symphony
a few months after the cannons were stored away. At a rehearsal for this performance, an unfortunate incident occurred
which has been contradictorily reported. The testimony of
Annibale Pastore, a teacher of philosophy and psychology at
Turin University, who witnessed the scene, sounds believable. He testified to what he called "the external fact" as well
as "the internal fact, more important."

The external fact.

> In the Finale, when the tremendous cry of the chorus rises
> to its greatest height, Toscanini is a flame of exultation
> and frenzy. Suddenly, three hard knocks of the baton ar-
> rest the orchestra. I see that the Maestro is turning to one
> of the second violinists seated in the second row. He
> screams at him: "What are you scratching here? Two
> inches with your bow!" And he hurls at him the folded
> handkerchief with which he has been fanning himself.
>
> The violinist answers, "I am playing, not scratching. And
> you, why did you throw that handkerchief at me?"
>
> Toscanini, still trembling all over, continues: "I am giving
> everything and you give nothing. You ought to give—
> with your bow."
>
> Saying this, and still vibrating with excitement . . . he
> jumps down from the podium and goes over to the second
> row of the second violin section.
>
> The second violinist insists, "I did all I could—and you
> are a boor." Toscanini: "You don't say? And with *this*."
> And with a nervous gesture of his baton he slams at the
> man's bow. The bow breaks and part of it hits the violin-
> ist in the forehead. The violinist goes toward Toscanini.

The other members of the orchestra and the soloists hold him back. I could no longer see clearly what was happening. I heard indistinct voices, voices of the chorus screaming, "Out! Out!"

A companion guides the violinist out of the orchestra. Near the pit exit close to the violas, he turns and screams at Toscanini, "You are not a maestro, you are a scoundrel!" The rehearsal is interrupted, the stage is cleared. So is the pit. There is general confusion. . . .

The next day, which was a Friday afternoon, Toscanini enters as in a dream without looking at anybody. He ascends the podium. He says to begin at the *primo tempo* of the second part of the letter P. . . . Then, sweeping the whole orchestra with his glance, Toscanini notices the presence of the second violinist. He descends eagerly from his pedestal and he goes over and shakes his hand.

The internal fact, more important.

The Maestro was not in a normal mental condition. It was evident that he was in the throes of the "holy furor" which invades the spirits of artists and exalts them to such a degree that their normal personality is extinguished. The enormous proportions which the musical *pathos* assumes in Toscanini are evident to all, even to those who are not psychologists. . . .

The aesthetic monomania reaches in Toscanini such violence that he cannot properly be judged and he is not responsible for actions in moments of aesthetic excitement. . . . Toscanini is as innocent as a child. His gesture is not intentionally immoral, it is simply involuntary and amoral. [*Il teatro contemporaneo,* 1920, No. 10]

Mr. Pastore's testimony may not pass the test of modern psychological theory; it served well enough, however, that when the violinist sued Toscanini, it gave the court the excuse to judge Toscanini guiltless. The violinist's wound proved to be slight and was cured in ten days. Toscanini voluntarily sent him the money to cover his medical expenses. All the same, the rumor persisted that Toscanini had blinded the man.

2

By the end of 1919 he was weary of what he considered idleness. He had accepted conducting engagements in Rome and Padua, but these were in the nature of guest conducting. He lacked a home, a center.

La Scala did have one short season, in the autumn of 1918. For it he prepared a performance of *Mefistofele*, in honor of Boito, but six months dead. Previous to that the opera house remained closed, as it did the year after. The dust gathered silently. The paint chipped off. The stage machinery rusted. To deprive the Milanese of their opera was almost as bad as depriving them of their risotto. Protest meetings were held, with cries of "Shame!" "Shame!" The *Corriere della Sera* spoke of "cultural disgrace"; under the editorship of Luigi Albertini—"one of the greatest liberal minds since Cavour"— the newspaper hardly let a day go by without agitating the cause of the Scala. The sleeping beauty had to be reawakened, though it had become a questionable beauty. The municipal government began to work on a plan by which the old theater could be adapted to new times, to serve a larger and less aristocratic public. The plan, worked out after several false moves, was to form La Scala into an independent organization, the Ente Autonomo della Scala. The box-holders relinquished their proprietary interests, a campaign for voluntary contributions was inaugurated among the citizens, and, no doubt most important, a tax was levied on all amusement enterprises, such as cinemas, sports events, theaters, the money to be spent on the opera house.

Firmly financed, the work of rehabilitation could begin. Toscanini, who had been consulted on every move, was approached by the Municipal Administration. At the meeting of July 9, 1920, Toscanini was offered: (1) directorship with complete and absolute authority; (2) an administrative assistant to help him in scheduling, contracts, and other work. This was

Angelo Scandiani, a very able man who later chose as his as-sistant Anita Colombo. Eventually she became Toscanini's secretary (really, more than a secretary) and for a time La Scala's manager.

What it amounted to was that Toscanini now had under his care a theater of his own.

His first consideration was devoted to the physical improve-ment of the auditorium and the installation of modern stage machinery. He met with architects and builders: they said that the work would take a year and a half. In the interim he would build an orchestra worthy of La Scala. He called musicians from all parts of Italy; they came, they auditioned, he lis-tened and relistened, he balanced one choir against the other; and finally he got together an orchestra in which the second violins were as good as the first violins and the trombone as fluid as the flute. He rehearsed the orchestra for a full month. They made their debut in Milan and the critic from the *Corriere* greeted them, "How Toscanini was able to form an orchestral entity of such excellence can only be explained by the organiz-ing ability of this illustrious musician." Offers to hear this orchestra flew in from near and far. They toured Italy and then embarked for a tour of the United States, the purpose of which was obviously to make postwar propaganda for Italy, and the cost of which was partly underwritten by Italy and partly by the U.S. government, which put a special train at their dis-posal. They arrived in New York on December 13, 1920, and, before appearing publicly, went to Camden, New Jersey. There Toscanini made his first recordings. For him it was sheer tor-ture: a cramped room, a reduced orchestra, the necessity to re-peat over and over again, and no piece longer than four and one-half minutes. They recorded, among other compositions, the Minuet and Finale of Mozart's E-flat Major Symphony: it is astonishing how bad the record is. An orchestra could not be adequately captured on wax, though that year Caruso made his final and beautiful record, the *Crucifixus* of Rossini's *Petite Messe*. From that session Toscanini carried away a hatred of recording which took him years to overcome.

On December 28 Toscanini entered the Metropolitan Opera, the house he had quitted five years before. A war lay between, a Europe changed, the world became more complicated—six days previously the Brussels conference had settled Germany's reparations, a little more than a month previously the Russian counterrevolution had ended, Prohibition had come to the United States that year, and Harding had been elected—but it all did not seem to matter that night. Richard Aldrich wrote in the *New York Times* (December 29, 1920):

> There was a tumult of welcome last evening for Arturo Toscanini when he appeared at the Metropolitan Opera House for the first time since he left it at the close of the operatic season of 1914–15. The welcome was given in applause and cheers by an audience that filled the Opera House to its utmost capacity behind the railings as well as in every seat on floor and galleries and in the boxes. It was an audience not only of a popular character, but also one largely of music lovers, including many distinguished musicians.

Yet, while Aldrich had nothing but high praise for Toscanini, he did not find the orchestra all that good. It is probable that the orchestra did not show itself at its best, tired as it was from the voyage and the recording session. The tour which followed and which comprised fifty-nine concerts in forty-one American and Canadian cities proved in every aspect triumphal. In Topeka, or in Boston, in Tulsa, or in Providence, people traveled many miles to come and hear Beethoven, Mozart, Verdi, Debussy, and they came bearing that special love and buoyed by that special excitement he could communicate. They brought gifts, often useless and encumbering gifts, silver forks, loving cups, hand-stitched pillows, and a live goose. The goose was refused, the other gifts stored in the baggage car, eventually to be distributed among the members of the orchestra. Toscanini had planned to end the tour in March. But the demand was so great that he decided to give additional concerts: instead of the three concerts scheduled for New York he gave ten, two of which were played at the Hippodrome, each attended by eight thousand listeners.

When he and the orchestra were ready to embark (April 3, 1921), several thousands came to the dock to wave flags and to shout "*Arrivederci!*" The orchestra played "The Star-Spangled Banner."

3

He spent the summer getting ready for the new Scala. He had to engage singers, choristers, stage crews, and supervise the creation of new scenery. He was in the theater every day from early morning till late at night. Once when he was displeased by an ugly backdrop, he ordered it repainted that night, the performance being only a few days off, and then stayed with the scene-painters all night. Two million lire had been raised by the new tax, but this sum was contingent on the house operating in 1921–1922, after so many years of silence. The house was not ready, the reconstruction but partly finished, but he knew that he *had* to open,* since it was unthinkable to forego so large a sum.

He limited the first season's repertoire to ten works, five of which he would conduct himself: *Falstaff, Rigoletto, Boris, Mefistofele, Meistersinger;* the other five were assigned to Ettore Panizza: *Parsifal,* Puccini's *Triptych, Barber of Seville, Wally,* Wolf-Ferrari's *I Quattro Rusteghi.*

There followed eight years of a renaissance, eight years during which every night when the house lights dimmed a first night could be expected. There were no "repetitions," no evenings when the tension lessened, no occasion when an old dish such as *Lucia* was served on an inexpensive platter by an incompetent servant. Even when Toscanini was not conducting his inspiration was present, as was often he himself. The men who presently joined La Scala, conductors such as Guarnieri, Gui, Votto, Santini, were almost as impatient of routine as he. They were like a band of archeologists who after a long journey came upon great sculptures in a tropical forest, except that these sculptures were known in every lineament and the discoveries were rediscoveries. Every season the repertoire was expanded—there were failures of course, Boito's *Nerone* being one of them—and every season fresh talent sought. Toscanini

---

* Later he regretted that he did. Once La Scala was reopened, the reconstruction was never completed.

called the revolutionary designer, Adolphe Appia, to stage *Tristan* in 1924, and Galileo Chini to stage *Turandot* in 1926.

The Scala of those years could be defined simply: it was an institution permeated by ardor.

Finally, in 1929, Toscanini took the entire complex abroad. They went to Vienna and Berlin; it was the first time in 150 years that La Scala had performed outside its own walls.* Austria's and Germany's stellar musicians, stage directors, critics, scholars, actors, producers invaded the performances: Max Schillings, Max Reinhardt, Erich Kleiber, Bruno Walter, Leo Blech, Karl Elmendorff, Siegfried Wagner, Furtwängler, Klemperer, the musicologists Oscar Bie, Julius Korngold, and Paul Bekker, the historian Alfred Einstein—they were all there. The essays, dissertations, commentaries gushed forth in elongated sentences. The pundits whose attitude toward Italian opera had long been supercilious and patronizing now recanted, while the Northern public cheered with Southern fervor. Einstein summed up the quality of the performances in five words: "Greatest discipline becomes greatest freedom."

4

Once it had grown to maturity, the New York Philharmonic Orchestra was never less than competent. Yet it had experienced sharp differences in quality. Mahler was followed by Josef Stransky, which was rather like replacing a Jefferson by a Coolidge. Stransky remained as the head for years, until the Napoleonic Willem Mengelberg came along. Talkative—endlessly talkative—conceited, stocky and strong, he was a virtuoso conductor, and in the music he loved, that of Strauss, Mahler, Beethoven, he achieved highly individualized and dramatic performances. "His lapses try one sorely, but his virtues are magnificent," wrote Lawrence Gilman. For two seasons Willem van Hoogstraten shared the leadership with Mengelberg. I listened to Hoogstraten often, at the summer concerts

* With one exception: they have given one performance in Paris of Spontini's *La Vestale* in 1909, for the benefit of the sufferers from an earthquake in Calabria.

in Lewisohn Stadium, sitting on the twenty-five-cent stone seats. He was handsome and "acted" the music, and the musicians played as they pleased. Later Stravinsky and Furtwängler came as guest conductors, still later Fritz Reiner, Thomas Beecham, Bernardino Molinari, Clemens Krauss, Bruno Walter, Ossip Gabrilowitsch, Otto Klemperer—all of them knowing that the New York Philharmonic had been shaped by Mengelberg into a paramount orchestra.

Mengelberg was difficult to get along with and proved no great box-office magnet. In 1925 Clarence H. Mackay, president of the Philharmonic Society, decided to make Toscanini an offer. He sent Max Smith to Milan to negotiate. Toscanini and he talked it over. Toscanini was tempted, first because he knew the worth of the Philharmonic Orchestra, superior to any in Italy, second because he was becoming more and more interested in symphonic music, third because he had enjoyed the open friendliness of the American people who, though a few of them indulged in back-slapping familiarity, responded with unfatigued enjoyment, fourth because his own relationship with the Fascists and his personal relations with Mussolini had worsened. The last consideration weighed as importantly as the others. Yet he did not want to leave La Scala: there lay his duty and his affection. Smith suggested that Toscanini might work out a timetable which would allow him to reach both worlds. But would it not be a terrible load to carry? An amount of work which would undermine his friend's constitution? Here Smith mistook the nature of an artist. The terrible load is *not* working, *not* performing. Arthur Rubinstein in his eighties gave a series of ten recitals in Carnegie Hall, within a short span of time, and after the tenth he felt fresher than before the first. Pablo Casals said that what kept him alive so very long was the opportunity to draw the bow across the cello. By and large it is not the summer, spent near a mountain lake, which refreshes the artist but the winter, spent in an overheated concert hall.

Toscanini worked out a plan by which he could retain the artistic administration of the Scala, while absenting himself for six weeks to become guest conductor of the Philharmonic. He made his debut on January 14, 1926, his program consisting of Haydn's Symphony No. 101, Sibelius's *Swan of Tuonela*, Siegfried's Death and Funeral Music from *Götterdämmerung*, Weber's Overture to *Euryanthe*, and a novelty for New York, Respighi's *The Pines of Rome*. Respighi's wife, Elsa, recalled that the success of the piece was such that "for the only time in my life I burst into tears from too much joy."

By the middle of February he had recrossed the ocean, was back at the Scala, and prepared the Italian premiere of Debussy's "Martyrdom of Saint Sebastian"; all together he conducted fifty-two Scala performances that season.

That summer he conducted *Falstaff*—the opera of operas which to him represented the elixir of Mediterranean laughter, though its action was laid on the bank of the Thames— he performed what he called "the comedy of pure intoxication" in appropriate surroundings, in the little theater of Busseto. In the registry of that tiny town on the plain of Parma, then under French domination, Carlo Verdi recorded in 1813 the birth of a male child by the name of Joseph Fortunin François, who later was dubbed plain "Giuseppe." In its theater, so intimate that every word and inflection could make its mark, Toscanini twice presented *Falstaff*. When he was very old he dreamed of returning there to do it once more; it was too late.

About *Falstaff*, he had made a little discovery which had moved him to tears. Puzzled about a point in the score, he asked the Ricordi firm to let him have Verdi's original manuscript for study. He had consulted it several times before. This time, leafing through it, he caught a sheet of paper which fell out. It was in Verdi's handwriting; Verdi had placed it between the final pages. Verdi had written, "All is finished! Go, go, old John. . . . Find your way as best you can. . . . Diverting rascal, eternally true, under different masks in every time, in every place!! Go . . . go. . . . Walk, walk. . . . Farewell." It was, in a special sense, Verdi's farewell note to life. With Ricordi's permission Toscanini kept the sheet—he couldn't think of parting with it. Was it not strange that nobody had found that piece of paper before, not even he, closely though he had examined the manuscript?

5

His connection with the Philharmonic became closer. After two seasons as guest conductor, he became associate conductor with Mengelberg. That double regime lasted only briefly. In the spring of 1928, the Philharmonic and the New York Symphony merged and Toscanini became the man in charge; he remained so till the end of 1936.

Mengelberg loathed Toscanini. As he made no secret of any of his feelings, so volubly did he speak of "that Italian stickler." Jealousy made him unreasonable. I still have in my mind's eye the picture of the little man, fiery red in the face, hair flying, whispering audibly furious disapproval of the orchestra, and that during a public concert. Toscanini, on his part, did not have much respect for him. In later years he told the story of how Mengelberg tried to instruct him in German music: "Mengelberg—he talked and talked and talked. He showed me at great length how to conduct the *Coriolanus* Overture. He had got the right interpretation from an old conductor who had got it from Beethoven. I said, 'I got it straight from Beethoven, by reading the score.' "

Mengelberg's portrait could have been painted by Brueghel, Toscanini's by Titian. The two pictures could not have been placed side by side. The New York public soon and decisively decided. Mengelberg left.* Though in the second season illness forced Toscanini to restrict his appearances to three—he was suffering from weakness of the legs and bursitis of the arms, a conductor's occupational disease—he quickly became the most famous figure of America's musical life. To many thousands who listened, more or less attentively, to the radio on Sunday afternoons, his name served as a symbol, though they pronounced it Tosca*ninni*. Was this identification too inclusive?

* Mengelberg's later history is a sad one. In 1930 he returned to Amsterdam, claiming that Toscanini had plotted against him. He again conducted the Concertgebouw orchestra, sided with the Nazis against his native country, took a position in the Reichsmusikkammer, conducted in Germany during the war, and in 1945 was barred by the Netherlands Honors Council from further participation in the musical life of the country. He died in Switzerland in 1951, eighty years old and half-forgotten.

Was it a hero-worship which threw too bright a light on the interpreter and too dim a light on the composer? Perhaps so. Yet music is a sleeping Snow White—existing for most only as undecipherable and inert signs on ruled paper—until the interpreter awakens her. That is both music's blessing and its curse. A blessing, because passing through the brain of an interposed artist, it emerges in a dozen possible shapes and colors. A curse, because those signs are vulnerable to abuse. Toscanini, after listening to a bad performance, once wrote to a friend, "Blessed are the arts that do not need interpreters. They cannot be victimized by mountebanks, as it happens very often to the Divine Art of Music."

The eleven seasons in which Toscanini conducted 450 concerts with the Philharmonic represent a span of years which appeared to America first as the best of times, then to turn into the worst of times, then slowly to grope toward an uneasy light. When Toscanini closed his first season on April 4, 1926, America's chief problem seemed to be the flood of illegal liquor inundating the country and carrying crime in every keg. When he closed the second season—with Brahms's *Requiem,* on April 3, 1927—Lindbergh was preparing to fly. When he left for the summer in 1929, prosperity was overswarming the innocent; when he returned in October, panic had invaded the suburb and depression was scattering the pink slips of unemployment. Misery caused a change of philosophy; the ideal of "success" became tarnished. Neither Horatio Alger nor J. P. Morgan was the hero any longer. People began to search for things which cannot disappear as fast as money. They looked for better values. During the depression the arts benefited, though economically they were hurt. Ticket sales decreased; even for Toscanini concerts there were empty seats on some Sunday afternoons. Yet a more vigorous artistic life began, the WPA helping in spite of all its inefficiencies. The Philharmonic commenced its regular Sunday afternoon broadcasts in 1930 over CBS, the Metropolitan on Saturdays from 1931 on. When the country began to recover in 1933 concert attendance almost immediately showed a sharp rise, though the Philharmonic, hard-pressed financially, had to make an appeal to the radio audience in 1934. They promised anybody who sent a contribu-

tion a picture of Toscanini. He thought that "undignified"—
but he lent himself to it. Not for one moment, however, did he
have to economize or decrease rehearsal time—as if he would!

What marvels did he not accomplish with an orchestra which
he formed into so ductile an instrument that it could plead like
a Duse or storm like a Bernhardt! It was the old story: the
Philharmonic ascended to a level which it could never reach
again. His programs were "conventional" enough, if by conventional we mean the works acknowledged as being enduring:
several Beethoven cycles (he played the Ninth in his second
season, the soloists being Rethberg, Louise Homer, Crooks, and
Fraser Gange), Brahms cycles, a great deal of Wagner, Mozart, Haydn, Schubert, Strauss, Debussy, Berlioz, the Verdi
Requiem (with Rethberg, Matzenauer, Mario Chamlee, and
Pinza, January 15, 1931), a few concertos with soloists such
as Heifetz, Horowitz, Serkin, Casadesus; here and there he
brought to the surface the bubbles of a Rossini overture, more
rarely compositions by contemporary Italians, still more rarely
American music, though he did perform pieces by Schelling,
Chasins, Hanson's Romantic Symphony, and the premiere of
Wagenaar's Symphony No. 2. The last work began to irritate
him with its seemingly senseless dissonances and on the last
page of his copy of the score, according to Howard Taubman
in *The Maestro,* he wrote a concluding C major chord and
noted under it in red ink, "My Chord. Arturo Toscanini."

In 1930 he took the Philharmonic on a European tour. It
was the year in which the International Apple Shippers' Association, foreseeing a bumper crop, conceived the idea of selling apples to unemployed men at wholesale prices and on
credit—and presently one could buy an apple at a corner stand
for five cents. The Philharmonic management foresaw that the
deficit of the European tour would amount to more than the
cost of four million apples, more than $200,000. All the same,
and in spite of the poor economic conditions, they approved
the plan and raised the money. It was a gesture toward a Europe as plagued as America, a denial of the old accusation of
American commercialism, a prideful demonstration of musical
excellence—and Toscanini wanted it very badly. On May 3,
1930, the tour opened at the Opéra with the usual "*tout Paris*"

audience—ninety-five clucking sensation-seekers in evening regalia to five music-lovers—who heard the *Eroica*, the Brahms *Haydn Variations*, Mendelssohn's Nocturne and Scherzo from *A Midsummer Night's Dream*, and the Prelude and Love-Death from *Tristan*. From Paris the orchestra proceeded on the large circuit: Zurich, Milan, Turin, Rome, Florence, Munich, Vienna, Budapest, Prague, Leipzig, Dresden, Berlin, Brussels, London: twenty-three concerts within one month. Audiences marveled: here was a new sound, almost a shocking sound, a clarity and suppleness which was alien to their tradition. Not by accident did Toscanini include the Mendelssohn music in eleven of the twenty-three programs, while in two others he played the "Queen Mab" Scherzo by Berlioz. The precision of those skipping and shimmering strings—one could not believe it even as one heard it, and a few said it was "too perfect." In Vienna and London the greatest ovations were offered to the orchestra. A former music critic, Bernard Shaw, had asked Ernest Newman, "Tell me about this man Toscanini—is he sober, honest, and industrious?" Interviewed after the first London concert, Shaw said, "It was a good concert."

In one of the Paris concerts Toscanini played Ravel's *Bolero*. Ravel was present. The piece, as usual, provoked excited applause. Ravel did not rise from his seat to acknowledge the audience's clamor. That little incident was responsible for one of the ubiquitous Toscanini-anecdotes, told and retold in books and articles.* Ravel was supposed to have objected to the tempo at which Toscanini conducted the *Bolero* as being too fast. Toscanini was supposed to have answered, "If I play it any slower, I'll *never* get through with it." I questioned Toscanini about this: he never said any such thing, nor did Ravel complain about the tempo. That the anecdote is a journalistic fabrication is indicated as well by a letter Ravel wrote to Toscanini:

> Montfort L'Amaury
> September 19, 1930

My dear friend:

I learned recently that people were talking about an "af-

* For example in the biography by Andrea della Corte or the one by Mario Labroca and Virgilio Boccardi.

fair Toscanini-Ravel." No doubt you would ignore the matter, though the newspapers wrote about it. It appears that my refusal to stand up and acknowledge the applause at the Opéra was prompted by my desire to reprove you for not adopting the exact tempo of the *Bolero*.

In point of fact I have always believed that when an author takes no part in a performance, he must disclaim for himself an ovation which should be reserved for the interpreter or the work or for both.

Unfortunately I was badly placed—or should I say too well placed?—for my abstention to pass unnoticed. However, to make sure that my attitude left no room for doubt, I turned toward you, applauding gratefully.

Ah, well! Mischief makes a better story and a more sensational tale than truth.

I can only hope that you will continue to believe in the admiration and profound friendship of your

Maurice Ravel

During the eleven years of his Philharmonic tenure the New York critics had a difficult time. It is difficult to keep praising, and what new can be said of still another performance of Beethoven's Seventh? Sometimes the critics seemed like King Gama—"Isn't your life extremely flat/With nothing whatever to grumble at!"

Olin Downes wrote on April 27, 1936, near the end of the final season:

The greatest demonstration this writer has ever seen in a concert auditorium was tendered Arturo Toscanini when he finished his program with the New York Philharmonic-Symphony Orchestra yesterday afternoon in Carnegie Hall.

Before the cheers and applause of an audience of some 3,500 persons who stood and refused to move for about a quarter of an hour, Mr. Toscanini, obviously overcome, was helpless. Under no circumstances would he have made a speech, but if he had attempted such a thing it would have been impossible. He could only come back and forth from the wings, bow, wave his arms in a futile attempt to

153

express his appreciation and return back stage and come out again and again.

While this was going on people not only stamped but flung programs from the balconies until finally the conductor, who had repeatedly called the orchestra to its feet, made another signal and the men followed him from the stage. Usually this is the end of a Toscanini demonstration, but it did not have that effect yesterday. He had to appear several more times before the crowd would leave the hall.

The public thus registered its opinion of a conductor who has led the Philharmonic-Symphony now for eleven seasons and whose hold on the public, in this city which has been the graveyard of so many conductors, has not weakened in that period.

He played Mozart's G Minor Symphony at that concert and his conception of that symphony differed radically from that of other conductors, notably Bruno Walter's. He did not think of it as a happy, tripping piece, its first theme gaily swaying. He played that theme as a dark and impatient question. "Mozart is serious when he uses the key of G Minor, and dramatic. See *Don Giovanni*," he said. He told the orchestra, "Mozart is no boy in short pants."

Downes wrote:

The glorious symphony is often played. Almost never is its full beauty and significance encompassed. We doubt whether Mr. Toscanini himself ever came as near perfection in its reading as he did on this occasion. It was as if he were attempting, with the last ounce of strength and genius in him, to leave with his last Sunday afternoon audience a supreme memory of beauty and also, in departing, to make final obeisance before Mozart by laying this laurel wreath at the foot of his score.

The notes of the symphony are relatively simple of execution. The secret of its ineffable song is almost uncapturable. This writer has listened, like many others, a great many times to the G minor. He wishes to say that he heard it for the first time in ideal essence yesterday. . . .

This was achievement which it had taken a lifetime of study by a man of genius to bring to pass. We do not sufficiently understand or value what that means. We could not sufficiently exalt the vision and the heroic will required to accomplish such a thing. It is what is meant by art. . . .
[*New York Times*, April 21, 1936]

6

A performer travels to perform. Only seldom does he linger in a city long enough to visit a museum or walk in its parks or probe its virtues and faults. His peregrinations resemble those hurried tourist tours—"If today is Tuesday, this must be Belgium." He knows the best way in and out of a city, his grasp of the timetable being as firm as that of a travel agent. His routine is more or less unvarying: the ceremonious arrival, the visit to the hall (testing piano and acoustics), the preparation for the concert, the local interviews, the concert itself, the after-concert supper (occasionally enjoyable, more often an awful bore), sleep, away the next day. Some artists carry with them an "iron ration" should they find themselves late at night without anything that they like to eat; Rubinstein used to travel with a salami and a jar of strawberry jam.

Toscanini loved to travel and his voyages were less frantic than those of other artists. In later years he was fascinated by planes, though they were never fast enough for him. He had no fear of flying and was delighted when the captain invited him to the cockpit; he asked the purpose of every switch and button. He understood none of it.

For the 1930 Philharmonic tour a special train was put at their disposal. He enjoyed every minute of it, walking through the train, chatting with the musicians, listening to their jokes, watching the poker hands, marveling when they didn't look at the scenery, and, in short, acting like the benevolent headmaster of a boarding school.

The tour finished, he faced the fulfillment of a wish he had harbored for years, the opportunity of opportunities, the chance to conduct Wagner at Bayreuth. After the death of

Cosima, Siegfried, who was less of a traditionalist than his mother, had invited him, an Italian, to the podium where hitherto only German *Kapellmeister* had officiated. He went, filled with the fervor of faith, the humility of devotion. He found an orchestra self-important, heavy, clumpy, many members with high-sounding titles and ill-sounding intonation. He suffered and ran out of the rehearsals, holding his ears. Then he went back and began again, correcting errors of long standing by having the manuscripts brought over from Villa Wahnfried; he would berate, yell, "No, no, no!" (the musicians nicknamed him "Toscanono"), fly into the open, march three times around the theater, calm down and come back, implore, plead, exacerbate the musicians once more. He recalled later that he would have given up the task gladly and turned his back forever on this landlocked theater had it not been that Bayreuth was Bayreuth. He persevered and the results were *Tristan* performances sweeping in passion and engulfing in beauty and *Tannhäuser* performances, while less successful than *Tristan*, of vivid eloquence. Winifred Wagner (Siegfried died in August) pleaded with Toscanini to return the next year on his own terms, the most important of which was the promise of a thorough house-cleaning of the orchestra.

Ernest Newman, most eminent of Wagnerites, went to Bayreuth to hear *Tristan*. He wrote:

> It is astonishing what light is often thrown on a work by a study of the markings alone, astonishing, we may cynically put it, how much composers know about the works they have composed.
>
> I had a blinding light thrown on this simple but too often forgotten truth during Toscanini's performance of "Tristan" at Bayreuth last summer. I thought I knew that work from end to end and from outside to inside; but I was amazed to find, here and there, a passage coming on me as a new revelation and going through me like a dagger stroke. What, I asked myself, has Toscanini done here? I took a mental note of the passages, and looked them up in the orchestra score when I got home. Then I found that

156

all, or practically all, that he had done was to play the notes just as Wagner directs them to be played.

Newman goes on to discuss the passage in the first act when Isolde tells Brangäne of the moment when the wounded Tristan, helpless in her power, looks at her and she is unable to execute the revenge she had planned:

A musical friend to whom I played the passage on the piano as nearly as I could in Toscanini's way declared that he had heard "Tristan" fifty times, but had never noticed that passage before. Nor had I, particularly. Yet all that Toscanini did was to realize what Wagner has marked in the score! The melody is given not to the violins but to the violas; the violins are underneath these. The viola marking is *weich* (soft, smooth). The dotted contrabass notes are marked *sehr weich*. The cello part (here shown as the tenor) is marked *sehr zart* (very tenderly, delicately, sensitively). All that Toscanini did was to play the passage as Wagner conceived it: he got just the right strength and the right colour out of the violas at the top and the contrabasses at the bottom; he gave a strange significance to the cutting-off of the bass notes; and above all he gave us that curious succession of slurs following dots in the cellos as I had never heard it before. The total effect was indescribable: I shall remember it and thrill to it to my dying day; there was nothing in the whole marvelous work that surpassed it for poignancy.
Yet it goes without saying that Toscanini *must* have done something more than merely play with the right time-durations, the right nuances, and the right colour a few bars that in most performances are passed over as being of no particular significance. What, then, was that something more? I take it to have been the imagination of Toscanini piercing to the very heart of Wagner's poetic meaning in the passage, the genius of this poetic perception translating itself into a certain delicacy and intimacy of handling, and this again passing over by the sheer magnetism of genius into the players.

157

In 1935 he conducted for the first time for the radio audience of America. General Motors sponsored a series of concerts and he agreed to lead one. He chose Lotte Lehmann as soloist. She had auditioned for him and he at once recognized her unique quality. If there ever existed the artistic personification of what is lovable in a woman, if there ever existed in real life the sweetness of Cordelia seasoned by Portia's wit, it was she. She was one of those artists who prove an irritation to those who have not heard her, because those of us who *have* heard and seen her compare subsequent impersonators of the roles she played to our ideal, annoying those born too late. Off the stage she was a plain enough woman, not conventionally comely; but on the stage she was whatever she wanted to be, her face as expressive as her voice, a soaring Sieglinde, a Marschallin filled to the fingertips with charm, an Elsa who could imagine the miracle. It was she, too, who showed in her Lieder recitals how beautiful the German language can be.

On the day of the first Toscanini rehearsal with the orchestra, by ill luck she got her monthly period. In the taxi she cursed her fate and envied all the people in the streets who seemed to be calmly going about their business, while she knew that now she had to sing, and sing her best, and could not. Her companion urged her to tell Toscanini the truth. She was ashamed to do it. Her friend said, "If you won't, I will." So she did. At once he had a chair brought for her, made her sit down, and told her to take it easy. She needn't exert herself for him—he knew her capabilities.

With this first concert began a close friendship. He was then almost sixty-eight years old, but he fell in love with her with the fervor of a young man. Whether they were lovers I do not know. He used to phone her almost every day wherever she was—a voluntary exile from Hitler, she eventually made her home in California—and he sent her orchids several times a week. She traveled, he traveled, but there was always the phone, and wherever he might be he thought of her and there were long confidences to be exchanged.

His journeys would have challenged the energies of a man twenty years younger, but he didn't know what fatigue was. Was it not only his work but his infatuations which kept him

young? Considering only the years from the end of the Philharmonic tour to the year he terminated his stewardship of
the New York orchestra (1930 to 1936), the chronology of
Toscanini's voyages represents a testimonial to the artistic will:

1930	July–August	Bayreuth	*Tristan, Tannhäuser*
	October	New York	Philharmonic
	November–December	Philadelphia	Philadelphia Orchestra
1931	January	New York	Philharmonic
	February–April	Philadelphia and New York	Philadelphia Orchestra and Philharmonic
	May	Bologna	Martucci celebration
	July–August	Bayreuth	*Tristan, Parsifal*
	November–December	New York	Philharmonic
1932	(Resting in the early part of the year because of illness)		
	April	New York	Philharmonic benefit for unemployed musicians: Ninth Symphony and *Parsifal* excerpts
	June	Paris	Debussy celebration
	October–November	New York	Philharmonic
1933	March–April	New York	Philharmonic (Beethoven cycle)
	June	Paris	Four concerts, Walther Staram Orchestra
	October	Paris	Two concerts (Wagner)
	November–December	Stockholm	Stockholm Orchestra
	November–December	Copenhagen	Two concerts
1934	January–April	New York	Philharmonic
	June	Paris	Two concerts
	November	Vienna	Two concerts, Vienna Philharmonic
1935	January–April	New York	Philharmonic
	February	New York	General Motors broadcast with Lehmann
	May–June	Paris	Six concerts
	July–August	Salzburg	*Falstaff* and *Fidelio*
	August	Salzburg	Concert, Vienna Philharmonic
	October	Vienna	Two concerts: one performance, Verdi *Requiem*, to commemorate the murdered Dollfuss

159

	November	Paris	Four concerts, Orchestra Staram
	December	Brussels	One concert
1936	January	Monte Carlo	One concert
	January–April	New York	Final season, Philharmonic
	April 29	New York	Farewell charity concert, Philharmonic
	May	Paris	Two concerts to raise funds for a Saint-Saëns monument
	July–August	Salzburg	*Fidelio, Falstaff, Meistersinger*
	July–August	Salzburg	Two concerts, Vienna Philharmonic
	September	Vienna	*Fidelio* (Salzburg performance); three concerts, Vienna Philharmonic, including *Missa Solemnis*
	December	Paris	Three concerts
	December	Tel Aviv	First tour, special Israeli orchestra

7

"Nothing in the world is inconsequential," wrote Schiller. Nothing in music was inconsequential to Toscanini. He remarked once, "It is relatively easy to take care of the masterpieces; the weaker music needs extra care." With some awe and much delight Chotzinoff told me the story of the benefit he had organized for the Chatham Square Music School, a nonprofit school for young musicians located in a poor section of New York. He had marshaled an extraordinary array of talent, including such luminaries as Heifetz, Horowitz, Tibbett, Milstein, for the occasion, but in the last minute, screwing his courage to the sticking point, he approached his friend Toscanini and asked him if he would conduct one number—just for the fun of it. Toscanini at once consented, and an impromptu "Children's Orchestra" was formed, consisting of such "children" as Heifetz, Adolf Busch, Ed Bachmann, Nathan Milstein, and Mischa Mischakoff in the violin section, Carlton Cooley and William Primrose among the violas, Emanuel Feuermann, Alfred Wallenstein, and Frank Miller among the cellists. They were to play the kind of music which used to

160

be scratched by a ship's band at teatime: "*Loin du Bal*," Strauss's "Tritsch-tratsch Polka," "The Skater's Waltz," and Mozart's little caprice, "A Musical Joke." A cinch, wasn't it? Toscanini came and began to rehearse as if the music had been the *Götterdämmerung*. For more than three hours he worked with this group of great artists until they played together well and truly, the balances just right, each note in its place. In a crescendo-decrescendo passage of the Mozart number he made the boys in the band rise to their feet and sink back again, exactly in time to the music. It was late at night when he got through, and the amateur actors who were to perform the skits and songs (including Chotzinoff) now felt that whatever *they* did would come as a bad letdown, and that the Toscanini part of the program ought to be enlarged to a full evening, everything else canceled. "Nonsense," said Toscanini, "let's see what you can do." They sent out for sandwiches. He sat in the first row and watched while they performed for him. They finished as dawn broke over the Lower East Side; he approved the show. Everybody crawled home dead tired, everybody except Toscanini.

That evening he was the first in the theater. He had been fitted—rather, ill-fitted—with a frayed schoolmaster's coat several sizes too large for him and with a long and not entirely clean handkerchief trailing from his back pocket.

After the performance, the schoolmaster was frantically cheered by the standing audience. He refused to take a curtain call without his "children." *

The Chatham Square Music School concert is only one example of the many occasions on which Toscanini gave his services to a cause. The chronology above indicates this. It indicates as well that his travels, his changes of locale, may have been partly prompted by a form of restlessness, perhaps a distant heritage from some Italian trouper of long ago, wandering from village to village with his guitar. More than once, at least in his youth and middle years, he felt a tugging toward the distance. In his last two years with the Philharmonic he grew restive. As Europe darkened, as Hitler's and Mussolini's pow-

---

* In his book *Toscanini, An Intimate Portrait,* Chotzinoff gives further details of this memorable evening.

161

ers oozed over the continent, his own mood darkened. Sometimes he shut himself up for a whole day, refusing to eat, refusing to talk, refusing even to look at music, but listening to the news and cursing. He was discontented with the Philharmonic's pleading for financial support, and was offended—or pretended to be—when the orchestra's board of directors chose Beecham as a guest conductor without consulting him. Other minor irritations were used by him, unreasonably, to tell himself that he had had enough. He said so to Clarence H. Mackay, the chairman of the board. But then he dropped the matter. Bruno Zirato, one of New York's well-known and well-liked personalities, a giant of a man, hearty, good-natured, and with a voice which never dropped below a fortissimo, was then on the executive staff of the orchestra. He had long ago been Caruso's secretary and had known Toscanini for years. Now, in February, 1936, he approached Toscanini to discuss with him terms for the following season. Perhaps Zirato waited too long, Toscanini having arrived in January. At any rate, Toscanini said No. Zirato, shocked, ran to Mackay and Mackay called on Toscanini for a further conference. Toscanini again said No. Zirato proposed, if the Maestro was tired, would he consider resting a year and returning the season after? That would be Toscanini's fiftieth anniversary as a conductor. The Philharmonic Society would offer him the opportunity to conduct one or two operas of his choice—Verdi or Wagner, whatever he wanted and with whatever cast he chose. It was a cleverly calculated temptation, but Saint Anthony resisted. The answer was still No.

There are indications that Toscanini regretted his decision. Yet, burrowing into contradiction, the more they pleaded, the less he could give in. When the resignation was announced, letters from every part of the country arrived by the bushel, some at Carnegie Hall, some at the Hotel Astor. Gentle or insistent, the letters came too late. A special farewell concert was announced for April 29. The program, as might have been expected, was devoted to Beethoven and Wagner:

Beethoven: *Leonore* Overture No. 1
   Violin Concerto (Jascha Heifetz)

Wagner: *Meistersinger* Overture
Siegfried Idyl
Prelude and Finale, *Tristan und Isolde*
Ride of the Valkyries

I was present at the leave-taking, having rushed to Carnegie Hall as soon as the special concert, nonsubscription, was announced. After standing in line for three hours, I was able to buy two tickets in the last row of the dress circle. I would not have traded them for the gold of the Indies.

Only 140 standing-room tickets were available. On the day of the concert, a line began to form at 7:30 in the morning. The people waited all day and one unknown benefactor treated them to doughnuts and coffee. By 8:16 P.M., when the sale of the standing room ceased, the crowd had swollen to five thousand; they refused to accept the verdict of "no more," broke ranks, and threatened to storm the hall. Mounted patrolmen cleared the sidewalk, carefully yet firmly; even the horses seemed to feel sympathy.

Orchestra seats had been priced at ten dollars apiece, the lower boxes at two hundred dollars apiece. Toscanini had stipulated that the proceeds of the concert were to be divided among all those who had worked with him at the Philharmonic. That meant not only the members of the orchestra, but also the doormen, the ushers, the telephone operators, the stenographers, etc.

Among the farewell gifts offered to Toscanini was a letter by Beethoven, presented by the directors of the Symphony. The letter was written in 1814, the year of the Vienna Congress, the year of the zenith of Beethoven's fame, when the third version of *Fidelio* proved a great success. Beethoven was feeling benign:

> It will give me great pleasure, my esteemed R., to set your poem to music and to bring it to you myself in the near future. I can hardly say whether it will be heavenly because I am only earthly, but I shall try my best to come as near to your very exaggerated estimate of me as possible. Your friend and servant, Beethoven.

The R was Johann Baptist Rupprecht, a successful businessman and a Sunday poet. Beethoven set one of his poems to music on two occasions. Toscanini was overjoyed with the gift. He did not need the translation which had been furnished with the original, but deciphered the German and said, "No, no, he was not earthly, he *was* heavenly."

The end of the concert was marred by a sorry incident. We in the audience had jumped to our feet and begun to cheer and shout when—nobody knew from where—a photographer appeared, dashed to the stage, and set off a flash directly in front of Toscanini. Toscanini, frightened, raised his arm to cover his eyes and ran off, policemen jumped on the stage, one chased after the photographer, who was in full flight, and took the camera away from him. Toscanini had stumbled backstage and did not return. Instead, Maurice Van Praag, the personnel manager of the orchestra, came out and said, "Mr. Toscanini was almost blinded by that flash. He cannot take any bows, he is sorry. He asks me to say that he loves you all."

Howard Taubman, reminiscing about the event years later in his book *The Maestro*, wrote:

> I remember the evening well. I hurried back to the office of the *New York Times* to write a report of the event and was getting ready to go home shortly after midnight. Telephones began to ring throughout the office. Was it true, the question was asked repeatedly, that Toscanini had gone blind? News reports on the radio had said so, and the town was filled with wild rumors. The night managing editor got hold of me and said, "I want you to go and check personally, and you're not to go home until you've seen Toscanini for yourself."
> Toscanini, I knew, was giving a farewell party for the men of the orchestra at the Hotel Astor. I went over reluctantly, knowing that these affairs were private and thinking that I would not be welcome. I rode up to the Astor roof and managed to get in. The party was gay, indeed. The maestro had provided food and drink, and the orchestra players thronged the room.

This did not look like a wake for a man stricken with blindness. At the end of the room I saw Toscanini. He was seated on a sofa flanked by a couple of attractive girls who worked in the offices of the Philharmonic-Symphony, and was chatting with animation. He was not blind. His eyes, weak and myopic, had been blinded by the flash, but it had been momentary. He could have returned for further bows after a few minutes, but he had been so angry that he had refused.

Now he was cheerful and friendly. He did not wish to talk about the photographer, and he did not care to say much about the years he had spent with the Philharmonic. He had agreed some weeks before to go to Palestine in the fall to help launch a new orchestra made up in large part of refugees from Nazi Germany, and this project was uppermost in his mind. He had no desire to grow sentimental about the past; he was thinking of the future. Over and over he said, "*Andiamo in Palestina.*"

Among the farewell greetings one came from President Roosevelt, thanking Toscanini "for all that you have done for music during your stay among us."

It was the end of a great era. When John Barbirolli arrived the following season, he found an exhausted orchestra and a public unwilling to grant him the sympathetic warmth to which his ability entitled him. They treated him coldly because they remembered former fires.

CHAPTER SIX

"I HAVE LOST THREE COUNTRIES"

"FREEDOM in a democracy is the glory of the State, and, therefore, in a democracy only will the freeman of nature deign to dwell."

Though Toscanini had not read all of Plato's *Republic*, these famous words he knew well; he had copied them on a large sheet of paper. He was as bitterly opposed to any form of tyranny as he was opposed to flabby chords, as fervid in his admiration of the paladins of democracy—from Franklin to Victor Hugo to Mazzini—as he was in his admiration of Debussy. There was no middle ground: a head of state was either "great" or "a scoundrel." But, as he kept asserting, he was a musician, a leader of an orchestra, not a leader guiding communities toward the light. If through his actions he finally became a lantern at which the Italian people glanced in hope, he became so because he acted by his emotions, not by political ratiocination. He wished to take no practical part in politics and he thought his beloved Verdi had made a mistake when he had consented to become a member of Parliament. In the post-Mussolini days, in 1949, Toscanini was offered the honor of becoming a senator of the new Italian state. He declined the honor. Long ago, at the inception of the Fascist party, he had made an exception: he thought Mussolini, whom he then admired, would be able to weld the disunited Italians, governed by a namby-pamby king, into sturdiness. Toscanini's name appears sixth in an early list of "candidates" under the Fascist symbol. But even before the "March on Rome" in 1922 Toscanini had resigned from the party and year after year Mussolini had become more unsympathetic to him. The lack of sympathy turned into hatred as Mussolini became Il Duce and began to tear civil liberties to shreds.

In 1924 Mussolini decreed that all Italian theaters were to display prominently photographs of himself and the King. La Scala ignored the request. The directive was repeated—and again ignored. Finally members of the Milan Municipality called on Toscanini—no doubt on pressure from Rome—and asked if he would obey the decree. After all, it was so unimportant a gesture; it was easier to give in than to fight it. One has a mental image of these serious gentlemen in morning coat and striped trousers lined up before Toscanini, timidly trying to placate the ogre. His answer was brief: "As long as I am the director of La Scala, there won't be any pictures of the King or Mussolini shown. Not anywhere in this theater!" Of course Mussolini heard about this.

Later Mussolini summoned Toscanini for an interview. Toscanini felt that he had to go to protect the fate of La Scala. Mussolini received him in his huge office, kept him standing—rarely did Mussolini ask a visitor to take a seat—and went through his neo-Napoleonic gestures, striding up and down, hands crossed behind his back, head thrown back, and shouting all the time. The Scala, Mussolini said, was an insubordinate institution, led by a stubborn and recalcitrant apostate who had not the faintest notion of all the great and wonderful things which the Fascists were accomplishing for the Italian people. He, Il Duce, was getting sick and tired of the troubles in Milan. "In all friendliness," he was warning Toscanini. The tirade lasted the better part of an hour. Toscanini did not utter a single word. He just stood. Then he was dismissed.

The refusal to play the *"Giovinezza"* at the premiere of *Turandot* was repeated during the tour of the New York Philharmonic. The Princess of Piedmont was present at the concert in Turin (May 10, 1930). Traditionally, the "Royal March" which served as the national anthem had to be played when a member of the ruling family attended a public function. But Mussolini had given orders that the "Royal March" was invariably to be followed by the *"Giovinezza."* Toscanini was willing to play the "Royal March," but he once more refused to play the Fascist song. What was to be done? Local officials conferred, scratched their heads, sprinted and scampered about, until they came up with a proposal which Toscanini accepted. The orchestra assembled, Toscanini ascended the podium, stood with arms folded, while a town band, obviously ill at ease, materialized on the stage; they huddled on the side and, blowing ineptly but loud, they played both selections, while Toscanini remained motionless; then with a sigh of relief which was visible if not audible, they slunk off. The concert began.

In spite of this obvious insult, Mussolini did nothing. He waited.

He did not have long to wait. The critical occasion came precisely one year later.

Giuseppe Martucci (1856–1909) was a composer, teacher, and conductor who in the early days had befriended Toscanini. The older man—Martucci was eleven years older than Toscanini—had introduced the younger to much contemporary music; Martucci was a great Wagner enthusiast and conducted *Tristan* in 1888 in Bologna. Toscanini never forgot the debt he owed his friend and frequently conducted his music, which was eclectic, pleasant, but never of major stature. Now, for a seventy-fifth birthday celebration, the city of Bologna scheduled two commemorative concerts. Toscanini joyfully agreed to conduct them, and the dates were fixed for the first weeks in May, 1931. A postponement became necessary when Toscanini suffered an attack of bursitis. The first concert was rescheduled for May 14, a date which, unbeknownst to Toscanini, coincided with a Fascist celebration. It was a "Fair of the Province of Littoria," and for it no less a bigwig than Count Costanzo Ciano, Communications Minister, had come from Rome as Mussolini's representative. He was accompanied by Leandro Arpinati, Under-Secretary of the Ministry of the Interior. Since both of them had to be invited to attend the concert, and both of them had to officiate at an official dinner before the concert, Toscanini was asked to postpone the hour of starting from the planned 9:15 p.m. to a little after 10:00 p.m. Surprisingly, Toscanini consented, stipulating only that there were to be no official political demonstrations inside the hall to "distort the music into a show." As it turned out, neither Ciano nor Arpinati nor any of the local officials appeared; they stayed at the banquet, probably on purpose. Toscanini arrived with his family by car at about 9:30 p.m. At the stage door he was accosted by a group of young Fascists. They had been waiting for him. One of them asked, "Are you going to play the *'Giovinezza'?"* On receiving an unequivocal No a few hurled themselves on Toscanini, hit him in the face, and succeeded in administering several blows at his body, before he could be pushed back into the car and driven away. The carabinieri then chased the mob. An announcement was made from the stage that Toscanini had been suddenly taken ill. The concert was canceled. The audience went home muttering.

Several clues indicate that the incident had been engineered. In the afternoon, the Prefect of Bologna had made two suggestions: first, that the concertmaster conduct the hymns, or second, that a band be hired to play the prescribed music outside the theater at the moment of the arrival of the officials.* Toscanini agreed to the second of these proposals; *Arpinati vetoed it.* At the same time a rumor was launched in the city that "Toscanini showed himself obstinate." Arpinati, deciding not to attend the concert, thought that Toscanini "ought to be left to his own devices." It is more than probable that he and some of the other Bolognese officials foresaw the possibility of a hostile demonstration in a city fermenting with Fascist yeast and encouraged or welcomed such a manifestation. At least they did nothing to prevent the incident.

Toscanini was not seriously hurt. His back pained him and his cheek was swollen. He and the family were driven back to the Hotel Brun, where they were staying. A mob of about 200 Fascists surrounded the hotel, shouting insults and threats.

* These facts have been researched by Franco Serpa, who published an article on the Bologna scandal in the *Nuova Rivista Musicale Italiana* (January, 1970). He exhumed as well several of the documents cited in this chapter.

169

Toscanini paced up and down his rooms and had to be restrained from appearing at the window and telling the milling crowd what he thought of them. Presently Ottorino Respighi joined the Toscaninis; he was a Bolognese, well respected in the city, and had no difficulty making his way through the crowd. About midnight a deputation, headed by Mario Ghinelli, the Secretary of the Bologna Fascist party (who might have been the instigator of the demonstration), was announced; they wished to speak to somebody in the family. Carla went downstairs. She would not do, they wanted a man. Respighi went down. To him Ghinelli said that he would urge Toscanini to leave Bologna before dawn. He, Ghinelli, would guarantee that Toscanini could depart undisturbed, but if he stayed he would not be responsible for what might happen. Respighi went back upstairs with the message. Was it a trap? Carla and Wally were afraid it might be. Toscanini brushed them aside; he would leave, come what may. Let them set a trap—he didn't care. At 1:15 A.M. they went downstairs, drove off, and arrived in Milan at dawn.

At about the time of Toscanini's departure from Bologna, Giuseppe Guadagnini, head of the local police, telegraphed to the "Ministry of the Interior, Dept. of Security" in Rome:

> In Cipher
> Very Urgent
> Bologna, May 15, 1931, 1:30 A.M.

08200. Last night Communal Theater concert was to take place conducted by Maestro Toscanini in presence of LL. EE. Ciano and Arpinati STOP Above-mentioned Maestro was requested to play patriotic hymns at beginning of concert but informed us he could not acquiesce for artistic reasons and in spite urging by me and other authorities refused request sharply STOP Fact awoke indignation Fascist circle and population as soon as refusal known STOP Police had taken measures to prevent incidents STOP Nevertheless while Maestro alighted automobile about 10:00 P.M. and got ready to enter theater stage entrance was surrounded by several Fascists who asked him if he would play Royal March and at his curt refusal was hit in the face by blows by an unknown person STOP Concert was postponed motivating indisposition Maestro STOP Fascist demonstration organized by three persons invaded central streets meeting under windows Hotel Brun where Maestro is staying. Remained some minutes singing national hymns STOP No other incident STOP At midnight city reassumed normal aspect. Respectfully

Prefect Guadagnini

This was, evidently, not quite the truth. Guadagnini then telegraphed the head of the Government Press Service in Rome, suggesting that "Press not publish incident occurred Maestro Toscanini entrance Communal Theater of Bologna and reasons postponement commemorative concert Martucci STOP Have taken care of local newspapers."

These telegrams were followed by long "promemorias" commenting on every detail. That these were brought to Mussolini's attention is proved by the fact that several bear the stamp with which he used to mark the acts read by him. An official version of the incident was printed in the Italian newspapers, soft-pedaling the matter. But the foreign press all over the world burst into headlines: "Incident at Bologna—From our own Correspondent," wrote the London *Times;* "*Toscanini Misshandelt,*" read the Viennese ; "*M. Mussolini osera-t-il déporter Toscanini?*" read the Parisians. The distribution of these foreign newspapers was forbidden in Italy; nevertheless some were smuggled in. The Italian papers countered with anti-Toscanini diatribes: Toscanini was "a monster" and the people "should have spat in his face." How come, asked a Rome paper, that Toscanini was willing to play the British and American national anthems in London with the New York Philharmonic, but not the Italian ones? Were the Italian hymns of less artistic value? One paper, *Il Popolo d'Italia,* doubted that Toscanini was worthy of commemorating Martucci:

One must ask oneself if Toscanini is the proper man for a Martucci celebration, when one considers that recently he has been traveling up and down Italy with a foreign or-

ganization and foreign programs, showing toward the
genius of his own country a condescension which leads one
to conclude that it would be better simply to ignore the
Maestro . . .

Another official organ, the *Assalto,* wrote:

Bellini, Verdi, Rossini, who surely possessed a bit more
imagination than our executor of concerts, would have
laughed at a religiosity which is all that pure and sublime.
One need only read the biography of Rossini by Stendhal
to convince oneself that genius is made of a different
metal.*

Our Maestro, who is not a Rossini, realizes—being crafty
and alert—that the canons of religious purity could be
used to nourish his fame. . . . Toscanini puts on the face
of an ascetic to impress the ladies in the front rows of the
stalls, invents the half-light, interrupts a performance because a penny dropped in the hall, and swears in the name
of Art not to play the Royal March. He appropriates
Wilde's motto, "A king may stoop to pick up the brush
of an artist." He raises the baton like Wotan's spear.
With the story of "not corrupting the religious atmosphere" he succeeds finally in carving for himself a political niche. From mystic saint he becomes the saintly war-
rior . . . complete in tails and patent-leather shoes.

In Bologna the illustrious secular apostle found a public
which trusts in a religion stronger than his: the religion of
the state. Mystic or non-mystic, the Fascists of Bologna
asked Maestro Toscanini, up to now an Italian citizen by
birth and civil status, to respect that which every other
citizen of the realm respects.

As has been reported, he responded to the invitation of
the authorities and the Fascists with a repeated and in-
solent denial.

The scandal would not die down. Protests continued to reach
Il Duce's office. Koussevitzky, scheduled to conduct a series of

---

* Not a good suggestion. Stendhal's biography is notoriously faulty, woven
almost entirely of whole cloth.

concerts in Milan, canceled and sent an open letter to the Scala calling the incident "an unheard of and unprecedented outrage." It is clear that because of the protests Mussolini was not certain how to proceed. He was not yet strong enough to disdain foreign opinion. What was to be done with this obstinate and adamant antagonist, so inconveniently famous? On May 18, during a concert at the Scala, some young people in the gallery shouted, "Viva Toscanini!"; nine were arrested. A group of Fascists went to the Via Durini, sang songs, howled insults, and broke a few windows. The police did not interfere. They then marched to the Galleria and dispersed without doing much harm.

Toscanini's passport was taken away from him. His house was placed under twenty-four-hour surveillance. A list was made of all visitors, among them the composers Giordano, Casella, and Pizzetti, the conductors Votto ("morally irreproachable but has ideas contrary to the regime"), Panizza, and Reiner, the cellist Piatigorsky. Incoming and outcoming mail was opened. The telephone was tapped and conversations recorded stenographically. One of these stenographic reports still exists.* It is of a conversation between Toscanini and a "Signora Ada," otherwise unidentified, but probably Ada Mainardi, wife of the cellist Enrico Mainardi:

No. 4938   Milan, October 19, 1935, Year XIII
                  [Thirteenth year since the "March on
                  Rome"]

Intercepted from 5:45 P.M., Oct. 10, 1935

Telephone number 75512 (TOSCANINI Maestro Arturo). Himself at the telephone.

To telephone number X, Signora Ada

ADA: Did you know they have prohibited the sale
              of foreign newspapers?
TOSCANINI: A real obscenity to plunge a country into
              such conditions! It is unheard of that a person can't read the newspaper he wants and

* It belongs to a later period, to 1935. The telephone was still tapped four years after Bologna.

173

that he has to believe what *they* print. It's just incredible. And it isn't even smart because all that does is to raise further doubts. To constrain a people like this—with a rope around their throats!

A: And a bandage around their eyes!

T: We must only read and know what they want us to know. There has to be only one head. This is no longer living!

A: It's horrible! Worse than Russia! Already some days ago the newsstands received instructions not to display foreign papers.

T: Then, those measures against the newspapers edited by our friends—

A: Evidently, they are planning something.

T: No. It's just that the population has to be kept in complete ignorance.

A: One feels suffocated.

T: I can't wait to go away. I can't stand it any longer. These things kill me . . . to see people become slaves in this way! One speaks of black slaves—we are the white slaves.

A: Don't say you want to go away. I, too, if you didn't hold me back, I would leave tomorrow. I'd go back to Germany. There, too, they have a government very similar to this one, but at least since it isn't my country certain things would wound me less and I could live calmly.

T: I hate to hear this. I'd even abandon my house here and go away to breathe free air. Here they throttle you. . . . One has to think the way that fathead thinks. I have never thought like him and I never will! I never thought the way he does. Only for one moment I was weak and now I am ashamed. You have to read only *his* newspaper!—because one can say that in Italy we now have only one newspaper.

A: They ought to admit foreign journals.

T: Certainly! It would be better policy. With this system our position is put in an even worse light. One comes

to believe that the others tell the truth and we tell only
lies. There are still some people who use their brains.
You can't put thought into prison. These days with
all the means we have, the radio, etc., they can't in-
carcerate thought. That system hasn't been invented
yet—put thought into prison.

A: However, in Russia they block and obliterate all the
news they don't want people to hear—

T: We have arrived at the bottom rung of the ladder. . . .
And still, there are people who feel nothing, and live
on, just like that. For me it is suffering which anni-
hilates me.

At the bottom of this transcript some official noted in pencil:
"This proves what we already know: that Toscanini is intransigent [*irriducibile*]."

2

Toscanini, still unwell, wanted to go to Switzerland for a cure,
before beginning his summer's work in Bayreuth. He asked
that his passport be returned. At first the Milan office was
instructed to "mark time" and not to answer the request. Apparently Mussolini then thought this might be too drastic a
measure. The Prefect of Milan was instructed by telegram
on June 3, 1931, that "Only to Toscanini passport can be returned. Members of his family are not (repeat, not) to have
passport. Confirm." The next day the order was again changed
to include the family.

They left. He would not again conduct in his native country until after Mussolini's death. He lost Italy.

He went to Bayreuth, his arm still giving him trouble. He
did not spare himself, though sometimes the pain would become
so excruciating that he would conduct with his left arm, the
right arm hanging at his side. He could endure it for the privilege of leading *Parsifal.*

Two years later he had lost Germany.

The Vienna Philharmonic is a "cooperative" orchestra,
meaning that for their concerts they choose their own conduc-

175

tors; these concerts are undertaken in addition to playing at the Opera, where the orchestra is regularly employed. When in 1933 the orchestra elected Hugo Burghauser as their chairman, Burghauser, being young and ambitious, conceived the idea of inviting Toscanini. Nobody much believed that Toscanini would accept the invitation, because like Figaro's his services were in demand here, there, everywhere. Burghauser wrote him an eloquent letter, and what was more important than eloquence, suggested that he conduct works which had long been considered "specialties" of that proud organization, such as the Beethoven Seventh, the Mozart "Haffner" Symphony, and the Brahms *Haydn Variations.* These compositions were "Viennese music," which meant simply that they had been created by men who had made their way from Salzburg, Bonn, and Hamburg to live and work in the Imperial City. Burghauser thought that playing Viennese music in Vienna with a Viennese orchestra might tempt Toscanini. It did. Toscanini accepted, stipulating that the number of rehearsals was to be "unlimited," determined solely by himself. He came—and it was love at first sound. He needed only four rehearsals. The orchestra, which in the past had often shown itself conceited and self-satisfied, having played under all sorts of conductors under all sorts of conditions, and believing that they knew all there was to know about this repertoire, now behaved as docilely as conservatory students. Rosé, the famous and venerable concertmaster, said, "He has given me back my youth." Toscanini called them *miei cari,* "my dears."

The audiences sought in the music surcease from the menace of the cyclops living near them. The Viennese, so often heedless of reality, denied the existence of Polyphemus, who was preparing to crush them under a huge rock. And already there were a few Austrians who preferred living in a Nazi cave to living in a state split into internal factions, undermined by constant party squabbles, and enfeebled by economic depressions. One attempt at preserving the existence of Austria was being made in the years of the concerts: in 1933 Chancellor Engelbert Dollfuss dissolved all Austrian political parties and established in their place the "Fatherland Front." It was designed to rally the factions around the Austrian flag and to assure Austrian independence. It failed eventually, being insufficiently supported by the trade unions. Yet Hitler at once saw that Dollfuss, the dynamic little peasant whom the Nazis called the *"Millimetternich,"* represented a danger to his scheme of annexation. Dollfuss had to be got rid of. The plot was hatched in Munich by four of Hitler's "Austrian specialists." (Three of the four were Germans.) On July 25, 1934, Dollfuss was murdered in his Chancellory and left to bleed to death. The assassination had the effect of awakening Austrian conscience, though only for a time.

Kurt von Schuschnigg succeeded Dollfuss; he was a dedicated and honest man, but lacking in popular appeal and political glamour. Perhaps he was too much of an intellectual to be a good politician. Yet he managed to hold on for four years, till the Anschluss. Schuschnigg, who loved music and was to be found at the Vienna Opera many an evening, was a great admirer of Toscanini's. He asked Toscanini to conduct a concert commemorating the murdered Dollfuss. Toscanini at once consented and chose the Verdi *Requiem*. At the end of the concert Schuschnigg gave Toscanini, in the name of the Austrian government, a copy of the first edition of the score of *Fidelio* with corrections in Beethoven's handwriting. That was in October, 1934.

By that time he had visited Salzburg, had there conducted concerts with Lotte Lehmann as soloist, and had been asked to return and direct opera performances at the Salzburg Festival of 1935. Bruno Walter, Schuschnigg, and Toscanini discussed the repertoire: Toscanini proposed *Fidelio* with Lehmann and *Falstaff* with Stabile.

An Austria about to die saluted music. Yet even in that supposedly taintless realm, jealousy, envy, and political machinations existed subcutaneously beneath the idealism. Typically Viennese: how often has Vienna chased its great men away—and later named streets after them!

Clemens Krauss was the Director of the Vienna Opera. As such he had the legal right to determine the repertoire for Vienna and Salzburg. As soon as Toscanini's intention of performing *Falstaff* became known, Krauss scheduled a revival of *Falstaff* in German in Vienna under his direction. It was ob-

177

viously a move of "anything you can do I can do just as well." New scenery was to be built and the same scenery was to be used in Salzburg, to save money. In the third act, after Falstaff's ordeal of being "thrown into the Thames and cooled, glowing hot," Falstaff is to be discovered sitting outside the inn "at dusk," as specified by Boito's and Verdi's stage directions. In Vienna they staged the scene *inside* the inn, with Falstaff discovered under a mass of bedclothes. Toscanini and Burghauser happened to be walking through the Opera while the scene was being rehearsed. Hearing the familiar music, Toscanini took out his pince-nez and glanced at the stage. "Burghauser," he said quietly, "if they give me that scenery in Salzburg I do not conduct." Schuschnigg heard about this and in the end he had to overrule Krauss, deciding that Toscanini should have his own staging. Shortly after, Krauss left for Berlin, taking with him the singers loyal to him and crippling the operations of the Vienna Opera.

A peculiar little incident occurred even previous to the Krauss jealousy-move. Toscanini walked over from the Hotel Bristol to the Opera to begin rehearsals for the Verdi *Requiem*. The porter at the stage door stopped him. "What do you want?" Toscanini, astonished, replied he had a rehearsal. The porter answered, "I don't know you. No unauthorized person is allowed in here." Toscanini turned and went back to the hotel. After a while they wondered where he was and Burghauser ran to the Bristol, where he found Toscanini in a hot fury. Eventually the matter was straightened out, but Burghauser was by no means sure whether the incident was due to stupidity or to planned spite.

All the same, these cabals remained tiny flyspecks; ignoring them, what remained for artists and public in the Vienna concerts and the three summers of Salzburg Festivals was a lucent and unblemished miracle.

Mozart's city, Salzburg—Alexander Humboldt, the explorer, called it one of the three most beautiful cities he had visited. It does seem like a treasure chest, with its baroque churches, its spendthrift castles, its imaginative open squares, its seductive intimate streets, its ostentatious green river—all of it guarded by the surrounding mountains, against which the clouds bump and spill their load of rain. In Salzburg, "the rain, it raineth every day" and everything smells fresh. As to its being "the city of Mozart," all that happened was that Mozart was born there, felt miserable there, and got away as soon as he could. The city has used him as a tourist temptation, birthplace, skull (probably fake), uniform, and other appurtenances piously preserved. His face stares at you from every shop window, from the chocolate and marzipan drops called "*Mozart Kugeln*," and from innumerable postal cards. But Salzburg is a Mozart town only when a great artist or a scholar serves Mozart.

The Salzburg Festival was conceived by Max Reinhardt and Hugo Hofmannsthal and they *were* able to attract great artists. The atmosphere was right, the ambition was right, the devotion was right, and the public who came to experience such diverse offerings as *Everyman* and the Mozart *Requiem* was right. Eventually Salzburg got to be too popular; it was turned into a status symbol, the place to go to, the thing to do. The dirndl costumes and the Tyrolean waistcoats with the silver buttons became ever more elaborate and more expensive, and the concierge at the Goldene Hirsch became well-to-do by selling black-market tickets. Still, enough true lovers of music and the theater did come, especially in the days prior to World War II, to mark the occasions as true festivals.

The flags were flying at curtain time and the Salzburgians stood on the bridge which leads across the Salzach River to watch the parade of guests making their way to the Riding School, which then served as the opera house. They watched and seemed friendly and hospitable, *gemütlich* and easy. Virtually none of the visitors knew that some of these friendly people, when they left the bridge, went to a meeting in a dingy room decked with swastikas.

Toscanini was supremely happy that first year at Salzburg and equally so the second year. He conducted the opera he loved so greatly. Conducted? It is not the word for it, as he began rehearsals in the summer of 1935. There was no accent, no button on a jacket, no gesture of a hand, no piece of stage furniture which escaped his attention. Yet *Falstaff*, superbly played by the Vienna Philharmonic, nearly came to nothing

179

the first time Toscanini saw the set for Act III, Scene 1. There it was, the indoor set from Vienna, fobbed off at Salzburg. Toscanini was sitting in the auditorium, he jumped up as if stung by a bee, and he ran for the door, the scene-painter, stage manager, and a bunch of assistants in pursuit. They caught up with him. What was the matter? *"Vergogna, vergogna!"* he spluttered. "Don't you read the text? Nobody here knows nothing. No-thing! It is a place for ignoramuses. Read Boito!! Read Verdi!! . . . I go." He ran to his car and drove around the countryside for an hour. When he got home a letter was waiting for him from the Intendant of the Festival: a new set had been started. It would be correct and would be ready the next day.

Barring that incident, all circumstances flowed together to make the Festival in a special sense "harmonious."

> He had wonderful instruments, the beauty of the Vienna Philharmonic at its very peak, an audience which had traveled far with bated breath, singers unequaled for the tasks he gave them. The baroque town itself contributed its own evocation. And then, finally, I believe that the actual sense of gathering doom—the grim shadow of Hitler—may have intensified the keenness, the exaltation, of the work done there, and our own reception of it. Such things are so intangible that it would not do to insist on them, and yet we all know they exist. We were more or less obeying the injunction of the Prophet Mohammed—Upon Whom Be Peace!—in living each day as if it might be our last. [Vincent Sheehan: *First and Last Love*]

What incredible performances they were! As long as I live I shall not forget the sound of the horns at the beginning of the last scene of *Falstaff*, nor understand how he achieved the delicacy of the orchestral postlude of the preceding scene, where the notes seemed to be the purest thing that exists on earth. For the Fugue at the end he called the singers together at every single performance during the intermission—just to make sure—"Singers forget." In *Fidelio* Lehmann seemed to fulfill Beethoven's imagination: she gave us the woman of whom he dreamed, who perhaps could never have existed, but was nevertheless a truthful creation, in a truth which rises above verisimilitude. Who could ever forget her cry, "Kill his wife first!"? Who could forget Toscanini's pacing of the "Nameless joy!" duet in the dungeon scene? When after that scene Toscanini plunged without pause into the Third *Leonore,* people couldn't bear it; they moaned as if in pain. It was raining that August night in Salzburg and it was cold. But when the curtain rose on the last scene, the sunshine of the music warmed your skin and you listened in hope to a promise which has not been fulfilled.

Thomas Mann was present at that Festival and wrote Alfred A. Knopf of the "glorious impressions, especially the *Fidelio* . . . Today there is something particularly stirring about the humanity of this work, and we all agreed that *Fidelio* is virtually made to be the festival opera for the day of liberation from the second-rate Pizarros under whom we now groan" (November 8, 1935).

Asked the next year why he chose Charles Kullmann, a young and relatively unknown American tenor, to sing Walther von Stolzing, Toscanini answered, "Because he hasn't got a paunch." Toscanini freed *Die Meistersinger* of *embonpoint,* made it nimble, turned it into a comedy of youth triumphant, unloosened the fun, wiped the veil off its often obscured radiance, apportioning in exquisite equilibrium the fragrance of St. John's Eve and the splendor of St. John's Day. He gave it uncut and the long work seemed shorter than ever before.

In the following Festival, that of 1937, he added *The Magic Flute* to the three other operas. To this work, considered by some as an arcane treatise of philosophy and by others as a somewhat lopsided combination of childish fun and Masonic ritual, to this work which German conductors have always clutched as their special prerogative, Toscanini brought an interpretation which caused much controversy in the Salzburg coffee houses. Freeing it of Sunday sermon solemnity, he gave it with prevailingly fast and winged tempos, a weightless fantasy. Alexander Kipnis, who sang Sarastro, thought the pace much too fast. Others agreed with him. I found it enchanting. Jarmila Novotna, a beautiful girl and an intelligent artist, was a particularly charming and light-hearted Papagena, and

Toscanini, seventy years old, immediately became captivated by her. (It was an admiration which lasted some years; when Novotna appeared in New York in 1944 in Offenbach's *Helen Goes to Troy*, Toscanini used to come to previews, sit in the first row, and watch her.)

Though Mozart was still there and Verdi and Wagner, Toscanini was no longer quite so happy in Salzburg that last season. Once again he felt as if the smell of the political sty was seeping into the theater. He was furious when he learned that Furtwängler had been engaged to conduct the Ninth Symphony. Furtwängler to him was a Nazi. He was a Nazi because he had remained in Germany, even though he might not have endorsed Hitler's methods. That meant that Furtwängler was a man to be despised. Toscanini had once recommended him as his successor with the New York Philharmonic, but now he wanted nothing more to do with him. When they met, as was unavoidable in Salzburg, he demonstratively turned his back on Furtwängler. The German conductor experienced the tragedy of compromise, a tragedy no less sad because it was lax: a marvelous musician and a weak man, Furtwängler tried ineffectually to help some of the persecuted musicians, yet was not strong enough to dare a clean break with the Nazis. He lived out his life in the pallor of uncertainty. It must be said, however, that the division between these two men was caused not by ideological differences alone: Toscanini found Furtwängler's personality unsympathetic—and made no secret of it—while Furtwängler, outwardly polite, was jealous of Toscanini. "When Toscanini dies, I shall be the world's most famous conductor," he once said to a friend. He never made it.

The Salzburg performances were to be broadcast to Germany, in exchange for which the Bayreuth Festival would be transmitted to Austria. But performances conducted by Bruno Walter, a Jew, would not be accepted by the German radio. That was all Toscanini had to hear: he vetoed the whole plan. The Nazis retaliated by forbidding German singers to appear in Salzburg. It didn't make that much difference: Lehmann, a "pure Aryan" and a German, had previously declared that under no circumstances would she sing in the new Reich.

Within Austria itself Hitler had by now made many converts, and Salzburg was one of the focal points of the Austrian Nazi party. The men with the swastika armband began to stride into the open.

Toscanini decided not to return. When he announced this, a shock ran through the musical world of Austria. Bruno Walter, not seeing what was happening because he did not want to see, pleaded:

Paris, June 1, 1937

Dearest friend Toscanini:

I am terribly worried and agitated by what I heard. I can't imagine a Salzburg without you. Salzburg needs you, we all need you. I'm sure you have your very good reasons. But I'm equally sure that the fault of Kerber [Erwin Kerber, director of the Festival] or somebody else's is ascribable solely to the Austrian "laisser aller" which, while not excusable, certainly does not reflect any bad faith nor any lack of comprehension or respect toward you.

I beg you with all my heart to let me know what needs to be done to satisfy you, and I will assume the responsibility to see that it is done.

Tomorrow, Tuesday, I am terribly busy. But Wednesday afternoon I can make myself free to visit you, and learn your wishes.

You know better than I—remember last summer!—that Salzburg is perhaps the last non-political spot left where art still has a roof over its head. Don't go away from there—I repeat, we need you!

I greet you in true friendship.

Your faithful
Bruno Walter

What a sad letter! In reply Toscanini begged Walter to get out of Austria himself. On March 4, 1938, Toscanini had planned a benefit concert at Carnegie Hall for the Salzburg Festival. On February 16 (before the Anschluss) he changed the beneficiaries, three quarters of the receipts to go to the Unemployed Musicians Fund, one quarter to the *Casa di Riposo*, the home for indigent musicians founded by Verdi.

Anybody who did not agree with the change in beneficiaries could have his money refunded. Not one ticket was returned.

Exactly one week after the concert, Schuschnigg was forced to resign, and the radio announced the formation of an Austrian National-Socialist Government. The next day Hitler's troops swarmed over Mozart's city. Toscanini had scheduled a rehearsal with the NBC for that day. He began the rehearsal, but after a few minutes he exploded because of some trifling offense that one of the musicians had committed, stopped the rehearsal, locked himself in his dressing room—and wept.

3

He said that he had lost three countries: Germany, Italy, and Russia where he had never been. In point of fact he had lost four, counting Austria. He addressed himself now all the more actively to the insulted and the injured.

Bronislaw Hubermann, the violinist, took the lead in forming an orchestra in turbulent Palestine. In the winter of 1936 he went to New York to ask Toscanini to conduct a benefit concert in New York to raise money for the orchestra. Toscanini considered it, replied that there were other means of raising money, and that he would do better: he would come to Palestine, he would brave the voyage to a country to him unknown and disturbed by Arab sniping, he would stay long enough to train the orchestra and conduct a series of concerts. He would do this without one penny of compensation. At that Albert Einstein wrote him from Princeton:

Princeton, March 1, 1936

Honored Maestro!
I feel the need to express to you how much I admire and honor you. You are not only the incomparable interpreter of the world's musical literature, whose performances have earned the highest approbation, you are as well a man who has shown the greatest dignity in the fight against the fascist criminals. I feel a deep sense of gratitude for the

aid you have promised to the newly to be founded Pales-
tinian Orchestra, aid which is of immeasurable value.

The fact that a man such as yourself is living among us
compensates one for the many disappointments which one
continuously experiences with the *species minorum gen-
tium*.

With love and high admiration
    I greet you—

A. Einstein

He went. He stayed for more than a month. "I want to get
things going right," he said. Which means that he rehearsed
the orchestra—partly constituted of famous Jewish musicians,
partly of uncertain youngsters—without a trace of sentimentality. The first time he jumped on the podium, the assembled
musicians expected some kind of greeting, some few welcoming
words to mark so extraordinary a gathering. He said,
"Brahms." And off he went into Brahms's Second. What a
man's antecedents were was unimportant, as was his personal,
often pitiful, history. Here he had to play. If he didn't "put
blood" he was an "imbecile," an "old man."

The people feted him as if he were King David, whose name
means "well-beloved." The workmen employed in finishing the
hall in Tel Aviv left off their work to sit quietly, listen to the
rehearsals, and then take up their chisels and brushes and work
far into the night. Mothers carrying their children stood waiting outside the hall to get a glimpse of him. When his automobile carried him back to the hotel, the streets were lined with
people cheering. A mother gave birth to girl twins: she named
one "Tosca" and the other "Nini." The wealthier offered three,
four, five times the price of a ticket for any of the concerts—
there were three each in Tel Aviv, Jerusalem, and Haifa—then
one in Cairo—but almost nobody would part with a ticket.
Hundreds who couldn't get into the concerts stood outside
near the windows to try to hear *something*.

Toscanini wanted to see everything. What artists seldom do,
he did: he became in Berenson's phrase "The Passionate Sight-
seer." He who was nearing seventy ran around like a boy on his
first European hostel excursion. He went to Bethlehem and to

185

Nazareth. He visited a kibbutz. He was invited to a Passover feast, sat through a Seder, and had the ceremony translated for him. Chaim Weizmann, future president of Israel, had put his armored car at Toscanini's disposal; at his orders the car was preceded and followed by several police cars. One day the car arrived at the hotel two minutes late. Toscanini was no longer there; he had decided to walk. The car caught up with him but he waved it away. Arrived safely at the hall, Toscanini laughed and said to the chauffeur: "Shalom. Next time be punctual." On the day of one of the concerts Toscanini disappeared. They searched for him with mounting anxiety. He returned in the afternoon, radiant. He had been to see the Dead Sea, all by himself.

He returned in 1938, though both Hubermann and Weizmann had told him that conditions had worsened, tension tightened, the danger of an Arab attack become more possible. He went all the same, though he was more circumspect on the second visit. The warnings were not idle: only by luck did Toscanini and Carla escape a bomb thrown at their car. The government made him a present of an orange grove, and for years after a basket of oranges would arrive on his birthday. He left, using an Italian hydroplane. The musicians had given him a banquet at the King David Hotel. Asked to say something, he said, "Thank you all, my dears. I was happy here. Don't be satisfied with yourselves."

The voyages to Palestine represented more than musical events. To the world, or at least that part of the world still capable of sane thought, they affixed a seal of approval on the idea of a Jewish state in Palestine.

In these years (1938 and 1939) he supported as well the Lucerne Festival, where Adolf Busch had formed a group of musicians who were either fugitives from Hitler or Mussolini or decided to be so, though they need not have been. (The Busch brothers, Fritz and Adolf, left Germany voluntarily.) Adolf acted as concertmaster, Toscanini's brother-in-law Enrico Polo was in the string section, as select an aggregate of musicians as could be found anywhere in the world. (Somebody counted twenty-three Stradivari, Guarneri, and Amati instruments in that section.) Ansermet selected the woodwinds and brass. Bruno Walter, Fritz Busch, and Ansermet conducted some of the concerts. The city of Lucerne offered Toscanini a villa at Kastanienbaum, near Triebschen, for his stay. Once again he refused a fee: the tickets were high-priced and all of the income was to be spent to support the musicians. The city government did everything possible to treat the concerts tenderly: while the music played, the steamers on Lake Lucerne stopped, cars were detoured from nearby roads, and even the cows in the pastures were deprived of their bells.

Here, then, was a Festival in every sense devotional. He conducted, among other compositions, Mozart's G Minor Symphony, Mendelssohn's Fifth, Beethoven's Second and Seventh, Brahms's Third,* the Verdi *Requiem*, the Brahms Violin Concerto with Adolf Busch, and the Brahms Second Piano Concerto in an incandescent performance by Horowitz. That concert (August 29, 1939) was to be the last he would conduct in Europe—till after World War II. Though all in that audience must have carried along with their delight a heavy measure of dole, none knew, certainly not the numerous diplomats present, that a world war would begin in five days.

At Triebschen, Wagner's and Cosima's villa, he performed the *Siegfried Idyll* in Wagner's original scoring for sixteen instruments, as it had been played as a birthday surprise for Cosima when she arose on Christmas morning, 1870. Toscanini conducted it twice, once in the garden of the Villa Triebschen and once, just for a few friends, in the room in which Siegfried Wagner was born. Among these few friends were Wagner's daughter Eva and his step-daughter Daniela. Defying their sister-in-law's policy they came to Switzerland. After the performance, the two old ladies kissed Toscanini and begged him to return some day, any day. He shook his head and turned silently away. He was never to see them again, not them, not Bayreuth.

Neither the German nor the Italian newspapers took much

* I was sitting in the organ loft behind the orchestra and therefore it was one of the few occasions when I could see Toscanini's face directly in front of me. To this day I remember the exaltation of his mien during the last movement of the Brahms Third.

notice of the man who, according to governmental policy, was making rebellious noises next door. But one paper did, the *Regina fascista* of Cremona, headlining its article, "The Honorific Jew":

Toscanini directed in Wagner's honor a concert in the Triebschen Museum. Even the Swiss press found words of censure for this gentleman, who simply because he knows how to conduct an orchestra, thinks himself entitled to act like a lout.

When two ladies—not Jewish—offered him a bouquet at the end of the first part he threw down his baton and fled the podium. [That may be true: he hated the custom and used to say, "Flowers are for women and corpses!"]

More significant is the fact that "the great democrat," after declaring that he wished to give a concert for the people without touching a cent, fixed the prices shockingly high: 22.55 Swiss francs a seat. [Actually the best seats cost more, 55 francs.] At those prices no plain man could attend. It is true that he was not paid, but he asked for 100 free tickets and free lodging for himself, his family, and numerous Jews who accompanied him. [Of course, untrue.]

The unselfishness of Toscanini cost the organizers of the concert 6000 Swiss francs, a sum, which when one adds the cost of the gifts offered to him, rose to 40,000 Italian lire. Some bargain!—as they would say in Rome.

Since Toscanini did all this in the spirit of pure antiFascism, we wanted to find out who were the Italians who betook themselves there. . . . This was not difficult and we are in the possession of the license numbers of the Italian cars.

So that nobody should think we are bluffing, we now invite our comrades in Milan and Florence and Rome to identify the proprietors of the automobiles carrying the following license numbers: [A list of these numbers follows]

Loathing the web of politics, Toscanini nevertheless became enmeshed. His own nature would not let him act otherwise. It was all very well to say that art existed independent of politics—he himself had said so—but he could not bear the stench of liberty's decay. Other artists could: Richard Strauss said that he had been a composer and conductor under the Kaiser, that he had done his work under the Weimar Republic, that he was quite willing to serve the Third Reich, and that should Communism come to Germany he would become a commissar. He felt he could do more good if he stayed. Toscanini could not stay.

CHAPTER SEVEN

HOW DID HE DO IT?

⸻

IT is impossible to explain Toscanini's methods systematically. He had no method. His way of making music was personal unto himself. The conductors who imitated his "style" of conducting arrived at nothing better than projecting an embarrassing *déjà vu* image, or rather, a *déjà entendu*. In Schiller's *Wallenstein* one of the soldiers says to the self-important sergeant, "The way he [Wallenstein] clears his throat and the way he spits, that you have managed to mimic. But his genius—" Some artists deed their methods to pupils or followers, and with success. A connection can be perceived between Leopold Auer and his pupil Heifetz, and less directly between Liszt and Horowitz, between Nikisch and Bruno Walter, between Schnabel and Serkin, between Rachmaninoff and Moiseiwitsch. There was an "Auer method," a "Schnabel doctrine," features of which could be taught, *were* taught, and passed to younger artists. The Toscanini style could hardly be didactically limned; he himself would have been the last person to attempt to do such a thing had he been asked to do so. That he did exercise a profound influence on the art of conducting is obvious. He brought to bear a corrective on the excessive romanticism of interpretation. He arrested the business of tearing a passion to tatters. He inhibited other conductors—not all—from swinging a spangled cloak over inexact playing. Instilling new respect for the text, George Szell said, he forced other conductors to rethink the problems of interpretation. That part of the legacy was beneficent. On the other hand, because he was the observ'd of all observers, he provoked imitation. Lacking his probity and balance, other conductors thought that the goal to perfection lay on the road of despotism. It was a tempting road to follow: the Napoleonic complex propels a conductor easily. But it wouldn't work: the musicians wouldn't tolerate it. The conductor as martinet has now gone out of fashion. Toscanini's creed of fidelity to the text induced certain other conductors to become pedants, parsing the script without ministering to the poetry.

Though Toscanini would agree that there can be nothing final about interpretation, he cast a long-lasting spell. To this day he represents to many of us the high-water mark. Winthrop Sargeant, in describing a concert by Georg Solti and the Chicago Symphony, wrote recently, "Nothing like this had been heard since the days of Toscanini" (*The New Yorker*, May 24, 1974).

How did he do it?

We could speak of his "baton technique." The term denotes the skill of signaling to the orchestra the rhythm and dynamics of the music, as well as balancing the components of polyphonic structures, subduing this strand, emphasizing that one, etc. Features of baton technique can be taught, but fundamentally it is an inborn gift. Toscanini's baton technique was obviously more than adequate for the task, but other conductors possess baton technique as good as or technically better than his. Erich Leinsdorf's technique is impeccable—but often the soul is absent. On the other hand, musicians will tell you that Koussevitzky's technique was unclear. What difference? He was a great conductor.

Toscanini thought that discussion of baton technique was futile. Milton Katims wanted to become a conductor and Toscanini supported his ambition. Katims told me that the two discussed musical problems many, many times but only once did Toscanini attempt to give him some suggestions on technique. They were in his room, Toscanini picked up his baton and began to demonstrate. Suddenly he caught sight of himself in a mirror. "Isn't this a silly thing for a grown man to be doing!" he exclaimed laughingly, and threw down the baton.

Katims, who by this time has had long experience as a conductor and who has long pondered the question, is sure that Toscanini could not have demonstrated his technique—it was that instinctive. Nor could Katims ever explain to himself how Toscanini drew what he wanted from the orchestra. Sitting for years directly in front of Toscanini, the mystery still remained. Katims said to me, "The viola is not the most important member of the string section and the role it plays is often not easily discernible. Yet somehow or other, by means I still do not understand, he made me play the right line. How? How did he get it across to me? Was it through his hand, his elbow, his arm, his shoulder? I do not know."

If we cannot elucidate his technique, can we come a little closer to defining him through an imagined chart?

If we were to construct a diagram of his musical personality, we could indicate two dotted lines, one leading from the printed page into him, the other leading from him outward to the instruments of the orchestra. The line going inward would denote that he ingested music until it became part of his blood. It isn't just that he knew the composition by heart.* It isn't just that he learned it so thoroughly that he never forgot it. It isn't just that he possessed so wide a genealogical view that he would place the composition in the exactly right context. It isn't just his understanding—an intuitive understanding—of the work's purpose and the composer's intention. It was rather a passion as intense as a love-embrace. Somehow a sexual element flowed with it.

The line leading outward would denote his ability to convey his passion to the men sitting in front of him.

Of course his memory helped him, and there are no end of instances which attest to its retentiveness. The most famous of these anecdotes has been told in various versions. I believe the one reported by the violinist Augusto Rossi to be correct: it

---

* It has been estimated that he knew by heart every note of every instrument of about 250 symphonic works and the words and music of about 100 operas, besides a quantity of chamber music, piano music, cello and violin pieces, and songs.

was in St. Louis, just before the start of the concert, that the second bassoonist, Umberto Ventura, came to Toscanini. He was in great agitation. He had just discovered that the key for the lowest note on his instrument was broken; he couldn't use it. What was to be done? Toscanini, shading his eyes, thought for a moment and then said, "It is all right—that note does not occur in tonight's concert."

He thought he would like to have the strings of the NBC play the slow movement of Joachim Raff's Quartet No. 5. The libraries and music stores of New York were searched for a score of the Quartet. None could be found, the piece having fallen out of favor. Toscanini, who had probably not seen the music for decades, let alone played it, wrote the entire movement down, with all the dynamic marks. Much later Bachmann, a collector of musical curiosities, found a copy. They checked it against the Toscanini manuscript: Toscanini had made exactly one error. (Told by Howard Taubman.)

The same Bachmann remembered that once they were playing a game, with Steinberg present. Toscanini said, "Play any excerpt from any of the standard operas or symphonies. Stop when I tell you to stop, but don't take your hands off the piano." Steinberg played. After a few bars Toscanini said, "Stop . . . That is from *Siegfried* Act III, Scene I, bars so and so. The note played by the fifth finger of your left hand is for the bassoon, the second finger clarinet and oboe—" and so on, going through the entire scoring.

I was reading a biography of Rossini and learned that he had composed two endings for his *Otello*, one tragic as in Shakespeare, the other a "happy end," where Othello and Desdemona are reconciled and sing a duet. Rossini's *Otello* is, and surely was at the time, an almost forgotten opera. I happened to mention the curious double ending to Toscanini that night at dinner. He said, "Of course." And he went to the piano and played *both* endings.

In Vienna once Toscanini, in a friendly challenge, wrote out from memory the part the second bassoon plays in the second act of *Die Meistersinger*. He wrote it faultlessly.

Retention of minutiae is an attribute of the interpretive artist; it lies at the base of performance, and it can be trained.

Toscanini's astonishing feats were not unique. Bülow's memory was equally precise: he conducted the first performance of *Tristan* entirely without the score and on his first American tour he played 139 concerts without the music on the piano, this at a time when playing from memory had not as yet become the custom. Otto Jahn in his biography of Mozart tells an anecdote now become standard history: Gregorio Allegri's *Miserere* was considered the exclusive property of the Vatican Choir and was so highly prized that no one was allowed to copy it, "on pain of excommunication." Mozart heard it once, went home, wrote the whole thing down from memory, went back, heard it a second time, made a few corrections scribbling secretly in his hat, and performed it later at a gathering at which the papal singer Christofori was present, who confirmed the absolute correctness of Mozart's "theft." (The incident worried Mozart's mother and sister; they thought he had committed a great sin. Wolfgang and Leopold laughed.)

Obviously the ability to remember is no guarantee of performing excellence. *The Oxford Companion to Music* gives the record of a

> Mr. Napoleon Bird, barber of Stockport, Cheshire, who in 1894 won the World's Record for what has been called "Pianofortitude" by publicly playing for forty-four hours without repeating a composition; from 11 p.m. to 3 a.m. he played dance music for hundreds of couples, and, during the subsequent forty hours, whenever any vocalist or instrumentalist appeared and asked to be accompanied, the mere statement of the title of the piece and the key required were sufficient.

Phenomenal though Toscanini's memory was, he did not rely on it. He conducted no concert without once again, for the seventieth time, taking the scores of the program and reading through them as carefully as if he were examining them for the first time. He often did this in bed, the night before. At every rehearsal the score was there, just in case he wanted to confirm a point or refer to a letter or number, printed in the score for the convenience of conductor and orchestra. He did not bother to learn these by heart. (Mitropoulos did.)

194

His memory was strengthened by what I may call the "mind's ear," meaning the ability to hear a composition by reading it. That ability is essential to a conductor, but Toscanini possessed it to an amazing degree. He had but to glance at a page of complex music, his glance seemingly casual, and he heard the page both horizontally and vertically in his imagination. He appeared to be riffling through a new score at top speed and one, two, three could decide whether he liked it and what were its weaknesses. To put it differently, his eyes translated into sound as quickly as those expert translators at the United Nations transpose from one language to another.

There was nothing wrong with what is usually called the sense of hearing. He could hear the slightest false intonation amidst an orchestral turmoil. He could hear subtle differences in the quality of sound, produced by some hidden supporting instrument. Josef Gingold, one of the violinists in the NBC Symphony, recalled:

> There was a contemporary piece—I can't remember what
> —that he programmed, tried once, and took off: he
> couldn't take it; it was too dissonant for him. He came to
> that rehearsal knowing the piece by memory; and as we
> were reading it we came to a terrific discord: it was so dis-
> sonant that we actually had to look at the fingerboard to
> see where our notes were. And he stopped: "Eh, *terzo
> corno!* Third horn! *Re!* I didn't hear!" The man had had
> a few bars' rest and had cleaned his horn, and hadn't been
> able to get it up again in time to come in. Toscanini
> couldn't see that far, and didn't see that the man wasn't
> playing, but he heard that the D was missing. [B. H.
> Haggin, *The Toscanini Musicians Knew*]

He could hear the minutest shading not only in what was being played but how it sounded. He would have the orchestra play a chord, stop, think, then tell them to adjust it—a touch more of the first trombone, a shade less of the clarinet—play it again, and it would emerge in clear eloquence and so solidly constructed, so truly a chord, that one could not drive the blade of a knife between the notes.

Gregor Piatigorsky told me of the time when he began to work on Castelnuovo-Tedesco's Cello Concerto. They rehearsed first at the Hotel Astor, where Toscanini then lived. Piatigorsky sat at the far end of the room, Toscanini sat at the piano. The next day they repeated the rehearsal. At a certain passage Toscanini said, "That is better—to use the third finger is better." Piatigorsky was dumbfounded: how could Toscanini possibly know that he had changed the fingering? It was certain he could not see it. Piatigorsky asked, "How do you know I changed the fingering from yesterday?" "I heard it," answered Toscanini.

Eminent though these abilities were, they were not what set him apart. He was unique because his relationship to the orchestra was unique.

An orchestra is a heterogeneous community with two communal feelings: first, everyone is glad to be employed and part of a group; and second, nobody is satisfied. Some are disappointed because they didn't get to be soloists, some are disappointed that they didn't get to be first-desk men, almost all chafe under the anonymity which has necessarily been forced upon them—the second violinists ought to be first violinists if justice prevailed—and almost all think that they could do better standing on the podium than the dubious master who happens to be standing there. But with Toscanini—that was different. No player thought that he could do as well. Not one.

The force he exercised transgressed respect for his knowledge and technique. It was a hypnotic force, a spell laid by a necromancer. His talisman was love. They loved him. Even when they hated him they loved him. He made them play better than they thought they could play. He made their task seem the most important enterprise in the world. An approving glance from him wiped out the anonymity. The harnessing of the atom seemed inconsequential compared to making music. The second flute felt as indispensable as the first cellist. When he yelled and was cruel they not only forgave him, they suffered with his suffering. They sweated not only because they were forced to sweat but because *he* sweated. I knew a viola player who was famed for his stinginess. "When I play under Toscanini," he told me, "I feel like giving my check back." To be sure he immediately recoiled in horror to add, "What am I saying?"

The incantation lay in his eyes. In a hundred-piece orchestra each musician was convinced that Toscanini was looking directly at him. His eyes anticipated the problem the player was going to meet the next instant; the glance indicated the quality of the musical expression required, while the stick held the rhythm and the left hand controlled volume and dynamics. Hugo Burghauser, who played bassoon in the Vienna Philharmonic before coming to New York, and who was not only one of the most experienced but one of the most thoughtful musicians I have known, said:

> This was perhaps, in the work situation, his greatest ability: to show unmistakably, unfailingly, even to a musician of medium-caliber mind, what is going to happen. And another almost unheard-of ability, which some of the *best* conductors did *not* possess: when he was conducting, especially in a performance, in a medium tempo, say an *Allegretto* or an *Andante*—about half a bar before the occurrence of a detail in the music you saw already on his face and in his gesture what he was coming to and would want. This was extraordinary: the parallel conducting of what was going on now and what was coming the next moment, so that the musician felt he was being guided through the polyphonic complexity of the music, like Theseus led by Ariadne's thread through the labyrinth. It was an entirely unheard-of ability, almost like the clairvoyance of a seer. [B. H. Haggin, *The Toscanini Musicians Knew*]

Toscanini often moved the baton close to his eyes to force the men to observe his eyes, but that I am sure was an unconscious, not a deliberate, gesture. The eyes exhorted and commanded, they foresaw, and every player was as aware of them as of the movement of the stick. One was reminded of those paintings in which the artist by some trick manages to make the Apostle's glance follow you as you walk past.

He came to the rehearsal with every detail clearly established in his mind. He didn't say, "Let us try how it sounds played

197

this way or the other," though he himself was to the last willing to experiment; he didn't give vague instructions, he didn't make speeches—how musicians hate talking conductors!—he did not indulge in mysticism, his verbal communication being short and businesslike.

Most of the time what you heard from him was "*Piano*" . . . "Together" . . . "Short" . . . "*Forte*" . . . "Staccato" . . . "Long, the note" . . . "*Crescendo, tutti*" . . . "*Animando*" . . . "Together" . . . "Sing! *Cantando*" . . . "Free." And always the demand, "Play with feeling." Even a pianissimo had to contain the warm juice of life, however delicately whispered. On the other end of the dynamic scale, in a fortissimo, he required the last measure of strength a player could summon.

Verbal instruction and instruction through the movement of the baton went together. No waste motion was to be observed in his beat:

Almost never does it contain an ambiguous or superfluous movement. And never does it contain a deliberately studied one. Functional down to the last crook of the little finger, it deals with the momentary exigencies of split seconds, expressing not general ideas of loudness or softness, but an endless chain of subtle warnings and encouragements concerning the immediate course of the musical flow. Occasionally Toscanini, desiring an emotional, luscious quality of tone, will place the middle finger of his left hand against his breast and vibrate it like a cellist vibrating on a string. An unconscious relic of the time when Toscanini was himself a cellist, it is his only standardized, predictable gesture. [Winthrop Sargeant: *Geniuses, Goddesses and People*]

He hated anything to remain unclear. Every performance of *La Mer* was agony in his brain; he heard something in certain passages for the woodwinds which he could not pull to the surface. He tried and tried but he never succeeded in satisfying himself. Perhaps that is why he played it so often. Perhaps he overscrubbed one or two shadowy pieces, yet in most music the cleanliness helped to give the listener the impression that he was hearing the familiar work newly, in a "premiere." He invited the audience to a voyage of discovery.

Above all, Toscanini loathed "noodling," the playing of a run by approximation instead of articulation. An example of "noodling" can be heard in the ordinary performance of the third movement, the March, of Tchaikovsky's *Pathétique*. When Toscanini played *all* the notes, and in inexorable rhythm, the audience could not contain itself and had to burst into applause. Nicolas Moldavan, who was one of the world's foremost viola players (he played in the Flonzaley and Coolidge Quartets before joining the NBC), explained this to me: "Other conductors sweep the dirt under the carpet. Toscanini lifts the carpet up and sweeps the dirt out."

Though, as I have said, he most often launched single words at the players, sometimes he would expand. Examples:

To the first violins in the Overture to the last act of *Traviata*: "Can't you read what it says there?" . . . "It says *dolente*, Maestro." . . . "Then weep, *weep* in God's name."

To the cymbalist in the Prelude to *Lohengrin*: "No! Too heavy! In this moment Lohengrin draws his sword from the sheath. Think of this. A *light* stroke!"

At the beginning of the scherzo of the Schubert C Major Symphony, which he could not get right: "Let's forget about Schubert as a sad man, eaten up by disease, desperate, hungry in Vienna. He was young, he liked fun, he liked company, he sang, he drank wine, he ogled the girls . . ." Pause. "And if he didn't he ought to have." The orchestra laughed and the beginning came out light and impudent.

To the BBC Orchestra in the Overture of *Die Meistersinger* at the first statement of the Prize Song: "Violins, play soft, soft—as if you said [whisper] 'I love you.'"

To the NBC contrabasses in the recitative of the last movement of the Ninth Symphony: "Together, *Corpo di un Dio, together*, at letter *N. N* like Napoleon. If he had been a contrabass he would have been an idiot, too."

To the NBC in *La Bohème*: "You play this as if it were Wagner. You play everything as if it is written by Wagner. Except Wagner—Accompany, accompany, go with the singers." (As I have noted, it is not true that he gave singers no

199

time to "breathe." He just did not let them hold on to climactic notes until the melodic line was pulled out of shape and their breath gave out.)

To the trumpets: "This must sound far away. Not too far— Brooklyn."

I made some notes during one of the rehearsals of the Ninth Symphony. He rehearsed the first movement for one hour and a half, playing the beginning six times to get the horns to sound mysterious. There was no philosophizing—merely *"accento"* . . . *"tenuto"* . . . "play *sforzando"* . . . "separate the notes" . . . "no *crescendo"* . . . "sing," etc. At the first *ritardando* he rehearsed the woodwinds seven times to make it sound "tired." But once the remark "So beautiful!" escaped him. Then he said, "Not so bad" to the orchestra, which was followed by, "I am never satisfied with *this* passage [bars 171 to 173]. Never—ne-ver!" At the coda he said to the low strings, "Like the sea." In the hour and a half not a hundred words were spoken.

A famous anecdote illustrating how well he could demonstrate the quality of sound he wanted is sometimes told about a passage in Debussy's *Iberia* and sometimes about a passage in Strauss's *Salome's Dance*. He tried to get the trombones to play with a smooth sheen. After talking to them and cursing at them and not getting what he wanted, he pulled a silk handkerchief from his pocket, unfolded it, and dropping it, allowed it to flutter gently to the floor.

At the beginning of the *Siegfried Idyll: "Ruhig bewegt*, but *bello,"* quoting Wagner's tempo indication in the two words and adding his own comment—using three languages for four words.

Two characteristics contributed to the impression that the last performance was an interpretation glistening with new-bathed freshness. The first was his sense of rhythm. The pulse of music was with Toscanini always flowing, virile, strong, never slack, and steady within a dozen subtle variations. He achieved it without words, though he would occasionally say, "Go, go, go!" or "Take a breath" or "Don't sleep" or "Look at me! Look at me!" or "Take your time, there is time." The music swayed in continuous motion, a motion which remained fundamentally steadfast within the movement of a symphony. The heart of the composition did not suffer palpitations, its life remained healthy. Yet the nightingale was always alive, never a mechanical one. You lived with it. What Mozart wrote to his father about the Overture to *The Abduction from the Seraglio* applied here: "I doubt whether anyone, even if his previous night has been a sleepless one, could go to sleep over it."

The second characteristic: There were no false or premature climaxes. A major symphonic composition is as progressively constructed as a play. It contains, speaking nontechnically, an exposition, a climactic scene, and a dénouement. Now, it is easy for an orchestra to make a lot of climactic noise when the score is marked fortissimo. But one fortissimo differs from another fortissimo, and if you shoot off all you have too early, the listener is instinctively disappointed later on. One can observe this sense of construction in such diverse compositions as the *Siegfried* threnody, or a Rossini overture, or the first movement of the *Eroica*, all of which contain several peaks, but only one climax. Toscanini, with his "dramatic ear," knew when the climax came. He held something in reserve. He did not anticipate. He knew at the downbeat of the first bar where he was going to come out when the curtain fell.

That concept of the whole, the ability to weld even episodic music into a unity, is one of the touchstones of the great interpreter. Artur Schnabel showed it when he played the Beethoven Sonatas. Goethe's saying that "architecture is frozen music" can be turned to say that music is flowing architecture.

2

His belief that opera needs equal attention in its dramatic (or linguistic) as in its musical aspect has been mentioned earlier. But something more can be said of the procedure. He began with the words. "First the music, then the words" (*Prima la musica, poi le parole*), is the title of an opera by Salieri, from which Richard Strauss fashioned *Capriccio*. There the precedence of the music is challenged. Toscanini built from the words to the music. When he first got together his cast for *Falstaff*, said Mariano Stabile, he made them all speak their parts, accompanied by a piano, the object being to clarify whether "we understood the character we were supposed to portray."

He even urged the violinists to "study the text, to recite the words" of an opera so that they would shape their phrasing to the cadence of the words, but whether they did so is a moot question. To him *le parole* were as important as *la musica*. To the chorus singing "*Immenso Ftha*" in *Aida*, he said, "Immenso—two m's, three m's, four m's." He tried to show Richard Tucker how to say the line (marked "with greatest agitation and surprise"), "*Tu! . . . Amonasro! . . . tu! . . . il Re?*" (You are Amonasro, you the King?) He twisted the word *Re* to an open sound, and the effect was like the ground sliding from under you. Naturally, he was less sure of diction in Wagner's operas, but even in Bayreuth he corrected, or better he heightened, the phrasing of German singers, saying, "I don't speak German, but when I conduct I speak all languages." He wanted the German words pronounced "melodiously," the voice colored to an appropriate dark sound in dark vowels, as in "*Ruhe*" (rest) or "*Öde*" (desert), or a joyous sound in open vowels, as in the word "*Meistersinger*." He caricatured singers who crunched or rasped or caterwauled the words, imitating them in a kind of double-talk German. Dramatic emphasis could not be achieved by sputtering: "Wagner is a musician. He wants you to sing!"

Even the spoken dialogue of opera did not elude his attention. In the dungeon scene of *Fidelio*, after Florestan is saved and just before the Florestan-Leonore duet, there is a bit of dialogue, usually given as: *

FLORESTAN: *O meine Leonore! Was has du für mich getan?*

LEONORE: *Nichts, mein Florestan!*

(FLORESTAN: Oh, my Leonore—what have you done for me?

* Various versions exist.

LEONORE: Nothing, my Florestan!)

Toscanini conducted without his eyeglasses. At the rehearsal in Salzburg, just before Lehmann was to speak the line, he reached into his breast pocket, took out his glasses, and looked at her. When she said "*Nichts*," simply, almost tonelessly, but putting a world of tenderness into the monosyllable, he silently took off his glasses and continued. It was a sign of approval to be treasured forever.

Yet in the *Fidelio* NBC-broadcast, he used singers whose German was far from perfect. It was a curious error of judgment.

In preparing an opera he used to rehearse the orchestra without the singers and in those rehearsals he "sang" all the roles. At the NBC rehearsals, working with an orchestra unfamiliar with operatic scores, he gave the musicians all the words, to show them what was happening. He sang and declaimed in an old man's croaking voice, but with a force and a conviction and a skill of characterization which made one realize that had he not become a conductor he might have become a great actor. He could imagine himself into each character and limn that character by declamation. His favorite "role" was Otello; even when the singer Ramon Vinay came to rehearse, Toscanini would rarely let him finish Otello's dying speech: he loved it so much, he couldn't bear not finishing it himself.

A few of us possess a rehearsal tape of *Traviata*, without the singers. Toscanini reads the letter which Giorgio Germont has written Violetta and which promises her lover's return. It is spoken to the accompaniment of a solo violin. I must have heard in my life twenty-five different Violettas, good and bad. Never, never have I heard one whose reading of the letter moved me as did Toscanini's, so unexaggerated, so without a trace of hamming, each word consonant with the accompaniment, so heart-breaking. Not even Licia Albanese, who sang the part with Toscanini and who was a superb Violetta, could read it as he read it. He taught her how to read the signature "Giorgio Germont," letting her voice sink to a level of hopelessness and without taking a breath connecting the two words to the cry, "*E tardi*" ("It is late"). This leads into Violetta's "*Addio del passato*" and, Albanese remembers, as they were rehearsing Violetta's farewell to the past, she looked at him and saw that his eyes were filled with tears.

In Shakespeare's *Othello*, after the quarrel incited by Iago, Othello emerges to inquire what "frights the isle from her propriety" (Act II, Scene 3). He turns to Iago:

> OTHELLO: Honest Iago, that look'st dead with griev-
> ing, Speak, who began this? On thy love,
> I charge thee.
> IAGO: I do not know . . .

Boito in the opera uses the lines almost verbatim, compressing them somewhat:

> OTELLO: Onesto Iago, per quell' amor che tu mi
> porti, parla.
> IAGO: Non so . . .

"*Non so*" is even more compressed than "I do not know."

At a piano rehearsal in Riverdale, Toscanini at the piano, the baritone Valdengo arrived at "*Non so*." Toscanini closed the lid of the piano, looked at Valdengo, and said, "I am very sorry you were ever born" . . . Dead pause. "Come to think of it, I am sorry *I* was born, to have to sit here and suffer. You do not understand Iago, you do not understand Verdi, you do not understand Shakespeare. You understand no-thing. Have you ever thought about what kind of a man Iago is?"

He thereupon launched on a detailed analysis of Iago's character. It so happened that for an essay I was writing I had a short time previously made a fresh study of the play, in the course of which I had read several books on the subject, including *Shakespearean Tragedy* by A. C. Bradley, still considered by scholars one of the seminal commentaries on Shakespeare. Bradley, in his dissection of Iago, writes:

> Nothing could be less like Iago than the melodramatic villain so often substituted for him on the stage, a person whom everyone in the theatre knows for a scoundrel at the first glance . . .

"Honest" is the word that springs to the lips of everyone who speaks of him. It is applied to him some fifteen times in the play, not to mention some half-dozen where he employs it, in derision, of himself. . . .

It is to be observed, first, that Iago was able to find a certain relief from the discomfort of hypocrisy in those caustic or cynical speeches which, being misinterpreted, only heightened confidence in his honesty. They acted as a safety-valve, very much as Hamlet's pretended insanity did. Next, I would infer from the entire success of his hypocrisy—what may also be inferred on other grounds, and is of great importance—that he was by no means a man of strong feelings and passions, like Richard, but decidedly cold by temperament. Even so, his self-control was wonderful, but there never was in him any violent storm to be controlled. Thirdly, I would suggest that Iago, though thoroughly selfish and unfeeling, was not by nature malignant, nor even morose, but that, on the contrary, he had a superficial good-nature, the kind of good-nature that wins popularity and is often taken as the sign, not of a good digestion, but of a good heart. . . .

These are but brief excerpts from a long and illuminating analysis—Bradley was as fascinated by Iago as his predecessors were, because "Evil has nowhere else been portrayed with such mastery." His sketch of the character is miles removed from the Desperate Desmond who often lurches from the left corner to the right corner, and differs as well from the view that Iago was driven by a "love of evil for evil's sake" which other critics have assumed and which explains nothing.

Toscanini's exposition of Iago, given that morning to an astonished baritone, followed Bradley's analysis so closely that one would have concluded that Toscanini had studied Bradley assiduously. He had not. He had not read him. He had not even heard of Bradley. The coincidence sprang from Toscanini's intuition, that mysterious kinship of understanding that an artist can bring to another artist, and which, needless to say, was here nourished by a complete knowledge of the play and by the meditation of years. It was a miraculous demonstration, a proof of the highest achievement of which the interpretative artist is capable.

After Toscanini finished with Iago he said, "Walter, please bring me *Hamlet*." He thumbed the pages rapidly until he arrived at Hamlet's exhortation to the players. He read it to Valdengo, who still didn't quite know what was happening to him.

All this took the better part of an hour. Then Toscanini said: "Now sing '*Non so.*'" The result can be heard on the record.

He went into similar details with Vinay, the Otello. The sad part is that once escaped from that unique baton, Valdengo or Vinay or most of the others slid back into mannerisms and tricks which *they* thought effective and which were merely vainglorious. Little of Toscanini remained in them.

He knew it, too. He was aware of his impermanence. He knew he was not immortal. For his eightieth birthday Sarnoff had given him a clock which was guaranteed to run for fifty years without winding. At the presentation, he looked around at the guests, most of them elderly, and said, "Just think, when this clock will need winding, I'll be the only one around here to wind it." But to the orchestra he said, "Verdi will live forever. But I? I will be dead like all the rest. I'll never conduct orchestras again. And the worst of it is"—and here a twinkle lit up his glance—"they will play badly, *badly*."

3

The attempt to sketch Toscanini by dwelling on anecdotes, on his rages, his excoriations—a procedure which is rather like describing a tree by the gnarls of its trunk—or the attempt to document his memory, ear, knowledge, does not penetrate to the heart of the mystery. Something else was involved.

That something else was his affinity to the orchestra, and the orchestra to him, a profound apposition, an emotional alliance. I have said that the men, in whom resistance was as ingrained as is the resistance of son to father, loved him. "Our Old Man truly loved us all!" wrote Samuel Antek, which also means the reverse. Why did they love him? Out of respect? Admiration? For his integrity? Yes—but more because they knew him to be an unhappy man. He could laugh and joke; but only very rarely, they knew, did he experience the sense of fulfillment which is the true gratification of the true artist. The most famous of conductors was a failure to himself. He could not find the solution to the problem of interpretation, as he conceived the problem to be. He could not make them play all of what he heard when he read the score. When he whipped them he whipped himself. When he yelled at them he was yelling at himself. Not always, of course, but often enough. He saw himself as the advocate of the composer, pleading the composer's cause, not his own. Like "the noblest Roman of them all" he was motivated by "a general honest thought." All too often, he felt, the advocate stuttered and the honest thought came out falsely.

W. J. Turner, a sensitive critic and author of an excellent biography of Mozart, remarked that as he observed Toscanini he was reminded of Berlioz's saying, "Do you think I make music for my pleasure?" Turner writes, "I am certain that it is not a pleasure for Toscanini to conduct, but rather that he suffers."

The orchestra sensed his unhappiness and wanted to help him. It was not alone, I believe, the tremendous tension he created which produced those unique performances, not the fear or the "psychology of crisis," though they contributed; it was his reaching beyond a possible reach which the men, being themselves artists, understood and for which they tried to lift him. They went beyond "safety" to attempt to come near an ultimate goal he had set for himself. Such is the kindness that prevails among kindred spirits.

To an extent which struck listeners as extraordinary he *was* able to project his ideas—see Burghauser. But it was not complete enough for him; he remained perturbed. The solution he sought eluded him. It was good enough, all the same, for a cooperation which has existed between few artists, a rapport which one could without hyperbole call awesome. Of that Burghauser tells an incident:

207

Toscanini happened to conduct with us *Pictures at an Exhibition* by Moussorgsky-Ravel in Budapest, after we had produced it in Vienna; and it happened that he started —instead of *Tuileries—Bydlo.* I say "started": I mean he gave the down-beat for *Bydlo.* And a phenomenon occurred which not one of us, and hardly Toscanini himself, ever experienced: *not one musician started to play!* It was ghost-like, a little like a nightmare: Toscanini conducted in the air, and not one sound occurred! Toscanini, for a tenth of a second, was flabbergasted and stony-faced: how come nobody plays? But in another tenth of a second he realized that instead of *Tuileries* he had conducted the beginning of *Bydlo,* which was very different in dynamic character. And with an almost undiscernible nod, he gave the right dynamic sign for the beginning of *Tuileries,* and then the orchestra, most harmoniously, as if nothing had happened, started to play. Afterwards he said: "This is the greatest compliment an orchestra can pay me: I make a mistake, and the orchestra at once realizes I am wrong." Why? Because his *Zeichengebung,* his gesture for communication and conducting, is so unmistakable in its one possible meaning that you cannot take it as meaning anything else; and you say: "Sorry; he's mistaken; I don't play." But that a *hundred people* should have this immediate mental contact—this happened with no other conductor in my fifty years of playing. [B. H. Haggin, *The Toscanini Musicians Knew*]

What Burghauser calls "mental contact" was a contact of feeling. That contact reached the last man of the orchestra, carried as much by what Toscanini could *not* accomplish as by what he did accomplish. They were united both by triumph and by failure.

The touch of discontent, the knowledge, however mute, that realization falls short of intention, represents both the blessing and the curse of the artist. Because Toscanini struggled fiercely the men struggled with him.

CHAPTER EIGHT

HOW TO BE YOUNG AT SEVENTY

WHEN he was seventy-one, Renoir, immobilized in hands and legs by arthritis, began a second career: he became a sculptor, employing a young assistant to serve him as a pair of hands. Goethe in his seventies worked on *Faust*, which he was not to finish till his death at eighty-three. Voltaire at seventy made his contribution to the *Dictionnaire Philosophique*, Michelangelo drew the plans for Rome's Campidoglio at seventy-one, Wordsworth published "Poems chiefly of Early and Late years" at seventy-two, Freud wrote *Civilization and Its Discontents* at seventy-three, and Verdi finished *Otello* at seventy-four.

We expect that creative minds, nourished by the double experience of life and experiment, produce to the last. Interpreters have shorter spans of usefulness: their task requires bodily strength. The body refuses: fingers have a way of becoming stiff, vocal cords of drying out, and ears of losing accuracy. Singers have the shortest career, because their musical instrument is their body. Not long ago I listened again to the old recording of the first act of *Die Walküre*, with Bruno Walter, Melchior, and Lehmann. Once again—how many times had I heard it!—I fell under its spell. I wrote Lehmann a note which she answered:

Words fail me to tell you how happy and proud your message made me. Thank you so very much. I listen very seldom to any of my records, but the first act of *Walküre* is one of my favorites. I can never listen without tears. This is the tragedy of an artist: I would do everything so much better today, now, that it is too late. . . .

Your very old (almost 85!) friend

Lotte

Yes, that is often the fate of the artist: feeling deepens, prowess flattens.

Pianists have the longest careers. Rubinstein played with glorious gusto in his eighties, and Liszt, though he announced he had retired, still made flamboyant appearances in his seventies. Conductors seem to be endowed with especially long life; perhaps all that arm-waving is healthful exercise. Bruno Walter lived to be eighty-six, Reiner seventy-five, Weingartner seventy-nine, Walter Damrosch eighty-eight; Sir George Smart, who aided Beethoven and Mendelssohn, reached the age of ninety-one.

Yet that a conductor should at an advanced age take up the challenge of training a new orchestra and assume the responsibility of leading in a series of concerts an orchestra created for him, that is a thrust of optimism probably unique in musical history. Toscanini agreed to it at seventy, after a half century of conducting. He would try his best for as long as he could. But even he could not have imagined that "as long" would turn out to be seventeen years.

It was David Sarnoff, head of NBC and RCA, who conceived the idea of bringing Toscanini back to the United States and to offer his music-making to every home in which stood what Sarnoff had originally called "a little black box." There were then some thirty million radios in America. Later statistical estimates established that at most only 10 percent of these were tuned to the Toscanini broadcast. *Only?* That 10 percent represented more than seven million people,* a vast audience, more people than had listened to a Beethoven symphony in all

---

* I am being conservative. Claims have been made for a much larger audience.

of its performances in all the world in all the years since its premiere. How closely they listened one cannot guess. The evidence of the letters suggests that enough listened attentively to bring joy to many a Middlesex village and farm. Sarnoff asked Samuel Chotzinoff, Toscanini's good friend, to go to Milan, where Toscanini, feeling old, had "retired," to tell Toscanini that "NBC would build him a great orchestra," that "America was hoping for his return," that "it was useless for him to talk about his being old," and that "his music would reach millions over the radio." With little hope that he would succeed in his mission, Chotzinoff cabled Toscanini, who was in Egypt:

Toscanini
Hotel Cataract
Assuan, Egypt
Dearest Maestro Unexpected musical developments in America present a situation of tremendous possibilities stop I have all the facts and would like to lay them before you personally so you may decide whether you are interested stop If you can see me I will sail for Europe immediately and meet you at any place convenient to you stop My visit would be personal and confidential and involves neither you nor me in any responsibility or commitment Please telegraph me collect Love

Chotzinoff

In his book *An Intimate Portrait* Chotzinoff tells how he waited in Milan for two depressing weeks, not letting slip a single hint of the reason he was there, until he found Toscanini in a good mood, how he then put forth his arguments with all the eloquence he could muster, but that the final touch which persuaded Toscanini was a newspaper clipping which told that during a Philharmonic broadcast a flock of canaries in a living room had started to sing along with the last movement of the Ninth Symphony. If canaries could be inspired by "mechanical" music over the radio, people could be inspired. Toscanini suddenly said, "Why not?"

Wasting no time, Chotzinoff, on receiving the great news,

rushed to phone Sarnoff. Wasting no time, Sarnoff at once sent a cable (February 3, 1937) confirming the agreement which had been discussed with Toscanini. The long cable ends with:

> You may assure Maestro that we will welcome him with open arms and do everything within our power to make his visit and performances memorable and happy for him and his family as well as for his many friends and admirers in America. Warmest regards . . .
>
> David Sarnoff

Chotzinoff relates how he borrowed an old typewriter and wrote out a simple contract on a plain sheet of paper which Toscanini signed without reading. Here is a copy of the contract:

> The National Broadcasting Company of America, represented legally in these negotiations by Samuel Chotzinoff, and Arturo Toscanini do hereby enter into and accept the following agreement:
>
> 1. Maestro Arturo Toscanini agrees to conduct exclusively from N.B.C. studios New York for broadcasting over its radio networks ten symphonic performances during a period of ten weeks beginning December 1937; and to perform no other engagements in United States between now and expiration of that period, except under N.B.C. auspices.
>
> 2. N.B.C. will furnish and Maestro Toscanini will rehearse and direct for these programs its orchestra known as N.B.C. Symphony Orchestra.
>
> 3. N.B.C. agrees to furnish first class orchestra for these programs subject to Maestro Toscanini's approval.
>
> 4. These programs shall be sponsored only by N.B.C. or R.C.A. or by wholly owned members of R.C.A. family.
>
> 5. N.B.C. agrees to pay Maestro Toscanini for foregoing concerts total sum of forty thousand American dollars, plus the amount of American income tax payable by Maestro Toscanini on this sum.
>
> 6. N.B.C. agrees to furnish its orchestra free for two

benefit concerts in Carnegie Hall; N.B.C. to have the right
to broadcast these benefit concerts.

(signed)

Arturo Toscanini

Samuel Chotzinoff

(Representing N.B.C. of America)

Milan, Italy, Feb. 4, 1937

The same evening Sarnoff was again on the phone. A stenographic report of the conversation has been preserved; I think
it shows how carefully Sarnoff handled the matter:

Telephone conversation with
Samuel Chotzinoff on February
4, 1937, at Milan, Italy.

MR. SARNOFF: I congratulate you, Chotzie!

MR. CHOTZINOFF: Thank you, David.

MR. SARNOFF: I think it is a magnificent job you have done, and I send you congratulations and love.

MR. CHOTZINOFF: Thank you very much.

MR. SARNOFF: The contract, I suppose, has been signed exactly in the way I telegraphed it to you?

MR. CHOTZINOFF: Yes, it has been.

MR. SARNOFF: If you want to have it witnessed, you can have the American Consul General at Milan witness it for you.

MR. CHOTZINOFF: Do you think it is necessary to do that?

MR. SARNOFF: No, it is not necessary, but you could just have it witnessed.

MR. CHOTZINOFF: Do you think it would be better to do that? I think it is perfectly all right just the way it is.

MR. SARNOFF: All right, then. This means, I suppose, that he will begin the concerts in December?

MR. CHOTZINOFF: Yes.

MR. SARNOFF: When will he come to New York?

213

MR. CHOTZINOFF : He gets through in Palestine about the middle of December, and that means he will come to New York about the third week in December.

MR. SARNOFF : When will he have time to rehearse the orchestra, then?

MR. CHOTZINOFF : He will just need about four rehearsals. But of course it all depends upon what kind of shape the orchestra is in.

MR. SARNOFF : Then the actual concerts can begin the end of December?

MR. CHOTZINOFF : Yes. Yes, he will be in New York the third week in December, and four rehearsals will be all he will need.

MR. SARNOFF : What is this idea about Rodzinski?

MR. CHOTZINOFF : Because he likes him very much. He likes Rodzinski very well, and he thinks he would be happier if Rodzinski will choose the orchestra for him.

MR. SARNOFF : As a matter of fact, Rodzinski is having luncheon with me next Tuesday.

MR. CHOTZINOFF : Rodzinski sent Maestro a wire asking him for this thing, but even before that Maestro spoke to me about it.

MR. SARNOFF : Then shall I discuss it with Rodzinski?

MR. CHOTZINOFF : Why not?

MR. SARNOFF : Then you want me to discuss it with him?

MR. CHOTZINOFF : Yes, and ask him if he will do it. And David, Maestro thinks it better be given to the papers tonight. What about David Stern? Will you give him the first chance?

MR. SARNOFF : We think it would be better to make it a general release, and let all the papers have it. Do you think that is all right?

MR. CHOTZINOFF : Yes, you make the release, but make it very dignified.

MR. SARNOFF: Would you prefer that I get up a release and telegraph it to you before I release it?

MR. CHOTZINOFF: No, it will be all right for you to release it.

MR. SARNOFF: We will have to wait until tomorrow, anyhow, it is too late tonight. If we want to get your okeh on it, it would delay it another day.

MR. CHOTZINOFF: No, you are to do it, but you make it very dignified.

MR. SARNOFF: All right, if you want to leave it to me, I will make up a release tomorrow and have it in the papers on Saturday.

MR. CHOTZINOFF: Say something about the fact that he is thrilled to play to an audience of twenty-five million people.

MR. SARNOFF: I will make it a dignified statement, just say that NBC and RCA have invited Maestro to come here and perform a series of concerts which will be given the latter part of the year, and this is for the benefit of the radio audiences. I will only speak about the concerts on the air.

MR. CHOTZINOFF: Yes, that is right.

MR. SARNOFF: Then you leave it to me, and I will see that a dignified statement will be released Saturday morning. It would be very nice if you would ask Maestro to send me a telegram, saying something to the effect that he is glad to accept my invitation and glad to make this arrangement. You help him word a telegram and send it to me and I will release it.

Then you are leaving on the 11th?

MR. CHOTZINOFF: Yes; and I think this is the greatest scoop of the century.

MR. SARNOFF: Don't you think it was wise to have telegraphed this contract as I did?

MR. CHOTZINOFF: Yes, I do. I will leave here on the 10th, and will be in New York on the 17th. Be very careful about the wording of the publicity. There has been a lot of dirty work here, I will tell about it when I see you. Pauline [his wife] has been a great help.

MR. SARNOFF: Tell the Maestro I look forward to seeing him, and will make the release from here the first thing on Saturday—it will be in the Saturday papers.

MR. CHOTZINOFF: This will be a big blow to Wally.*

MR. SARNOFF: I am sorry, but we can't help that.

MR. CHOTZINOFF: And Maestro couldn't help it either.

MR. SARNOFF: No.

MR. CHOTZINOFF: Then I can tell him you will get Rodzinski?

MR. SARNOFF: Yes, but we will wait until you get back to arrange the details. I will tell Rodzinski Tuesday.

Though he and Carla and the Chotzinoffs were the only four people who knew the terms of the contract, the *Corriere della Sera* carried the whole story with full details, including the fee, the next morning, indicating how efficiently the Fascists were spying on everything pertaining to him. How they found out Chotzinoff does not say. But with the telephone conversations and the cables back and forth it took no great detective ability for the Fascist officials to learn the facts and to give them to the newspapers, as a spite move.

As to how it all happened, indubitably Chotzinoff told the essential story correctly, though perhaps he titivated some details for romantic decoration. I don't believe that Toscanini had no idea why Chotzinoff had come to Milan—see the cable of January 14. I doubt as well the story of the decisive role played by the canaries: Toscanini was not as naïve as all that.

---

* I assume she wanted her father to return to the New York Philharmonic.

It is more probable that, whether he said so or not, two considerations convinced Toscanini, the first being the many letters he had received from the radio audience at the Philharmonic broadcasts, some of which he had read and valued; the second, that for him life without conducting was an impossibility, as life without the exercise of their art is death for most artists. How clearly that appears when one reads a letter, written to Wally, fourteen years later when Toscanini was eighty-four!

[New York] October 3, 1951

My dearest Wally:

. . . I am as I always am, well in the eyes of others, unwell to myself. I am longing to see my old house in the Via Durini! But how can I? I have the need to work, and in Italy I cannot. Only here do I find the right ambience. And I must work, otherwise life becomes unbearable. I made two records. I was able to do them with about three and a half hours of rehearsal. Howe [his doctor] took my blood pressure afterwards—122 over 80. I was not in the least tired. Next Friday I have another rehearsal. Beethoven: Second Symphony. Overture to *Don Pasquale*. You see your old father went to work and with enthusiasm . . .

Once the die was cast, Toscanini wrote Sarnoff and at once began discussing the formation of the orchestra. Sarnoff answered:

RADIO CORPORATION OF AMERICA

February 24, 1937

Maestro Arturo Toscanini,
20 Via Durini,
Milan, Italy.

My dear Maestro:

First, let me thank you most cordially for the kind letter you wrote me by your own hand on February 8th. It was delivered to me by our mutual friend, Chotzinoff, promptly upon his return home.

217

I greatly appreciate your thoughtfulness in writing me and share all the sentiments you have expressed.

This being my first privilege of a direct communication to you, I should like to take this opportunity once more to tell you how happy you have made me and my colleagues by your decision to accept the invitation I extended to you. This joy is not confined to those of us who have the honor to be associated with the Radio Corporation of America and its National Broadcasting Company. The satisfaction is nation-wide, as you will note from a folder of newspaper clippings which I have mailed to you under separate cover today. These newspaper comments followed the public announcement I made of your expected return to America in December of this year.

In addition to the newspaper comments on the subject, I have also received many letters and telegrams from persons in various parts of the country expressing their delight in the anticipation of hearing the radio concerts which you will conduct. The letters are too numerous to send along to you in total, but I have selected a few which are typical of those which I have received, and I send them to you herewith. I am sure you will be touched, as I am, by the sincerity of these communications and by the fact that young people, as well as old folk, found joy in the announcement of your expected visit to our country.

I am particularly thankful to you for having taken the trouble to outline to me your views as to the composition of an orchestra suitable for the purpose we both have in mind. You may feel assured that your views and wishes in the matter will be given the most careful consideration. At the moment, we are discussing this subject with Chotzinoff, and you may expect within the next few weeks to hear from us more definitely as to the progress we hope to make in this direction.

To have gained your confidence is a triumph; to retain it will be a privilege. I can assure you of my best efforts to merit both.

With my affectionate greetings to you and my cordial respects to Madame Toscanini, believe me

Sincerely yours,
David Sarnoff

What Sarnoff wrote was the truth, if anything understated. Excitement, all over the country, ran high. Praise was heaped on praise. Editorials and articles, letters and telegrams abounded. Let one letter serve as an example for the hundreds that arrived:

Dear Mr. Sarnoff:

May an insignificant high school student be allowed to congratulate you and offer sincere thanks and appreciation? I read in the Times Saturday morning of your signing of Signor Toscanini while I was riding to New York on the train, and the good passengers around me must have thought I was slightly insane, judging by the delighted chuckles and gasps I emitted.

I seriously believe that American music lovers owe you a great debt. Personally, I am trembling in anticipation. My only fear is that the concerts will be in a studio, with admission by special pass only. If the concerts are to be public, I want to put in a request for a pair of seats right now, no matter what the price.

It would be ingenuous to suppose that the munificent fee (munificent for those days) did not offer a temptation. Yet before Toscanini finally accepted, contract or no contract, the men in New York lived through anxious moments. Somebody cabled Toscanini that, because of the expense the new orchestra entailed, NBC was causing some employees to lose their jobs. Toscanini swallowed this story without probing it, perhaps because it gave him psychological backing for a hesitancy he was beginning to feel. He cabled asking to be left off from his obligation; under no circumstances would he be the cause of firing the most minor employee. The author of the canard was never found, but it took endless letters, telephone calls, and cables to convince him that the cable had been a vicious falsehood, and to assure him that, far from letting people out, NBC was taking people on to handle the details connected with the broadcasts. It was touch-and-go for a long time. Finally, when word came that Toscanini had actually embarked on the *Ile de France*, that it was "go," everybody including Sarnoff heaved a sigh of relief. It was unlikely that even Toscanini would manage to have the ship turned round in mid-ocean.

Sarnoff's decision was a brave and admirable one, all the braver because neither the bankers, nor the stockholders to whom he was responsible, nor his executives at NBC were in accord with it. The boys at NBC thought it sheer madness, to fill an hour and a half of time with "that long-hair stuff nobody wants," a program no sponsor would consider. G. Washington Hill, president of the American Tobacco Company, then one of the largest advertisers on NBC, said to Sarnoff, "You know what I'd do if I were a major stockholder in your company? I'd fire you! I'd fire you for wasting money on classical music in a mass medium." The boss would not be budged, his resolution fortified—as are most resolutions in business and not in business alone—by an amalgam of reason and emotion, emotion weighing more heavily than reason. Sarnoff was an example of the poor man who, untutored and unschooled, had climbed to the apex of success by his extraordinary and firm vision, daring, and capacity for planning. Working with Marconi and De Forest, he developed a system of communication new to the world. The evolution of that system he did not foresee and, indeed, it did not meet with his approval. He regretted its excessive commercialism. He told me once, "I had hoped that radio and television would bring the peoples of the world into closer communication, that by doing so they would begin to understand one another better—and that they would stop wars. How wrong I was!"

As with many men, his drive for achievement left a hollow in him, a blank page on which he did not know what to write but which he wanted to fill. If the clown wants to play Hamlet, the scientist wants to be an artist, or at least to taste the fruits of artistry. Sarnoff knew nothing about music but longed for it in a fogged search. It was a landscape strange to him, full of pleasing noises which appealed to him because they *were* strange. He sought the acquaintance of artists and was on friendly terms with Josef Hofmann, Mischa Elman, Ania Dorfman, Rosa Ponselle, Jascha Heifetz, John McCormack. To know them gave him greater satisfaction than to know business leaders. When Sarnoff entered a room, you knew that an important personality had entered. He was not in the least humble. He seemed like the manager of a telegraph center to whom secret messages had been entrusted and he tended to make pronouncements to which he expected everybody to listen. He may also have been a communist's idea of a capitalist. His customary attitude was one of "presiding," whether at the head of a conference table or the dinner table at home.

In the presence of artists, though, he became, if not self-effacing, unpresuming. He had met Toscanini and looked up to him. His admiration was not entirely free of the American worship of the superlative, "the best," "the greatest." A survey made by *Fortune* magazine disclosed the amazing fact that 39.9 percent of all the people in the United States (including those of lowest educational level) had heard the name "Toscanini." Of those who heard of him, 71 percent could identify him correctly (January, 1938). Sarnoff, in short, brought Toscanini to America because he himself responded emotionally to music and wanted the most famous interpreter of music.

One need not belittle the idealism which was inherent in the decision by observing that a few shrewd reasons influenced it as well: (1) Saturday night was a wasteland on the radio—the night you went to the movies or to hear Glenn Miller—the time was difficult to sell and NBC needed a sustaining program to fill it. (2) Criticism of "commercial" programs—*Amos 'n' Andy, Edgar Bergen and Charlie McCarthy, John's Other Wife, The Lone Ranger*—was beginning to be voiced more truculently, and it would benefit the profitable network to show that it was willing to act not exclusively for profit. (3) The rival network, CBS, was broadcasting the Philharmonic. (4) NBC was obliged to employ a "house orchestra" for various chores; that orchestra could be, and was, used as the nucleus of the new Toscanini orchestra. The house orchestra numbered

seventy-four players; * of those thirty-one were retained for
the NBC Symphony. The players of the Symphony were con-
tractually obligated to work thirty hours a week: only fifteen
of those hours were allocated to Toscanini rehearsals and concerts. Strictly speaking, it was not true that "NBC would
build him a great orchestra," meaning that the orchestra was
to be reserved for Toscanini's exclusive use.

Nevertheless, it was substantially true, and what was accomplished was prodigious: the creation of a body of ninety-
two players which could vie with the laurel-decked orchestras
of the world. What usually takes years to build was built in
nine months, a homogeneous musical organism. At Toscanini's
request Artur Rodzinski became assistant conductor; it was
he who selected the men by audition, and he who preliminarily
trained the orchestra. Over seven hundred auditions were held.
NBC allowed him to offer top salaries for the men he wanted.
A series of trial-run concerts was broadcast.

Toscanini was still in Milan. One morning soon after his
acceptance he told Carla he had not slept at all the previous
night. What was wrong? "I was worrying over the first program."

2

The first-desk men were of first quality, virtuosi one and all.
Yet one weakness remained: a clarinetist could not be found
who quite matched in excellence the first flutist and the oboist.
He wasn't bad; he was good, but had to be ranked somewhat
below the level of the other woodwinds. Before Toscanini was
due to arrive, some three or four men from NBC went to see
Sarnoff. They wanted his advice: should Toscanini be told
about the clarinetist or should he be left to find out for himself? Sarnoff said, "Problems of that kind are better met head
on. I think he should be told." "Very good," was the reply,
"YOU tell him!"

The *Ile de France* arrived, Sarnoff and his delegation took a

* *Fortune* said in its article that the Musicians Union demanded in a new
contract for the year 1938 that the 74 be increased to 115, and that the 92
men of the NBC Symphony be part of this house orchestra of 115. I could
not find confirmation of such a demand.

boat to meet the ship at quarantine and entered the cabin where Toscanini was waiting. He embraced Sarnoff and said, "Orchestra very good. Clarinetist not so good." Sarnoff looked at his committee and burst out, "Goddamn it, in a big organization *nothing* can ever be kept a secret. Who told him?" A storm of protests followed: nobody had said a word. Sarnoff turned to Toscanini: "How did you know?" . . . "Well, I have a little short-wave radio in my room in Milan and I was listening to a broadcast of the orchestra and I could hear, I could hear." Before the first rehearsal Toscanini asked to see the clarinetist. He said to him, "You are a fine musician, but there are some things you do wrong. Let me show you." He showed him, worked with him; the man remained with the orchestra for the years of its existence, and became one of the world's greatest players of that temperamental instrument. Sarnoff often told the story at executive meetings, saying that it was the mark of a good executive to strengthen the weakest link in his chain.

Next to Studio 8H, NBC had built a small dressing room for Toscanini, and Carla saw to it that his good-luck pictures and mementoes were duly placed there. There he arrived a full hour before the first rehearsal was to begin, sprayed his body and face with eau de cologne, dressed in his rehearsal jacket, and then sat, silent and immobile. Outside on the stage the orchestra assembled, every one dreadfully nervous and therefore making more noise than was necessary, then tuning up and waiting. Ten seconds before the hour, the librarian emerged and clapped his hands loudly. At once there was utter silence, the taut silence of expectancy which lames the muscles. Toscanini walked to the podium, the men rose, he waved the slightest of greetings with his hand, the men sat down, he smiled almost apologetically for the briefest of seconds, his glance darkened, out of his face, pale and drawn, he forced the word "Brahms," down smashed the baton, and as from a hot geyser too long held underground, there spurted forth the first bar of the First Symphony with its six heavy drum beats. He went through the entire first movement without stopping. Then he said, "Not so bad." Several of the men in the orchestra knew Toscanini from previous affiliations and they were not deluded. At once he called, "*Da capo.*" And now he began in earnest:

223

As we in the violin section tore with our bows against our strings, I felt I was being sucked into a roaring maelstrom of sound—every bit of strength and skill called upon and strained into being. Bits of breath, muscle, and blood, never before used, were being drained from me. I sensed, more than I heard, with near disbelief, the new sounds around me. Was this the same music we had been practicing so assiduously for days? Like ships torn from their mooring in a stormy ocean, we bobbed and tossed, responding to these earnest, importuning gestures. With what a new fierce joy we played!

"So! So! So!" he bellowed. *"Cantare! Sostenere!"* His legs were bending slightly as he braced himself for his violent movements, which were becoming larger, more pile-driving, as the music reached its first great climax. *"Cantare! Sostenere!"* I was to hear these words often in the years to come. "Sing! Sustain!" [Samuel Antek, *This was Toscanini*]

Christmas Night, 1937, 10:00 P.M.

The invited audience of a thousand people was constituted of New York's elite of elite. It was as difficult to obtain a ticket as for an infidel to enter Mecca.* At the doors the guests received programs printed on satin; these programs couldn't rattle. (In later concerts cork, and during the war cardboard, were substituted.) Shortly before ten Sarnoff spoke a brief welcome: he was happy, he said, that "our beloved Maestro was coming back to us while he was still a young man." The young man with white hair emerged, cut short the cheers, and the orchestra began Vivaldi's Concerto Grosso in D Minor. This was followed by Mozart's G Minor Symphony and then the Brahms. When the last long-held note of the symphony had ceased at 11:30, not one person in the audience remained in his seat. The noise was like a quake which "shakes the old beldam earth and topples down steeples." Seven times Toscanini, his suit as wet as if it had been held under a shower, had to appear and each time he made the orchestra stand.

* But for subsequent concerts a black market developed and invitational tickets were sold for high prices.

That Christmas night began what was for him the steadiest and, taken all in all, the most fruitful period of his life. He did not tire of the NBC as he had tired of the Scala or the Philharmonic. There were disappointments, there were quarrels, there were frustrations, but these were outweighed by the freedom extended to him, by a public which frequently expressed its love and understanding and by an orchestra which never ceased to worship him. Each player took part in an odyssey and was "by those deep sounds possessed with inward light." At some concerts—of course not always—the light was so strong, the working together so perfect, the execution so near the wish, the inspiration so free that one could have applied Blake's words to each player, of holding "infinity in the palm of your hand, And eternity in an hour."

After such a concert Toscanini sat in his dressing room, his eyes wide open, shaking. He did not believe that what had happened had happened; it seemed improbable. After such a concert one player said to his wife: "Give me a minute to crawl back into my skin." All this was done—and at the "wrong" time. The world began to foam at the mouth and to totter like an epileptic. A man who should have been put into a straitjacket came near to becoming the master of the insane asylum. Chaos had come again. Was this a time for music? Yet he was there, autocrat and servant, giving music to those who could or would listen, and thereby providing a measure of meaning to meaningless disorder.

The NBC project was almost scuttled the following season, after Toscanini had announced that he would be glad to return. While he spent the summer in Italy, the Fascist press accelerated a campaign of vituperation against him: "The government ought to take steps against this enemy of Italian solidarity." Toscanini paid no attention. One day a friend of Walter's, an official at police headquarters in Milan, phoned Walter and arranged to meet him at a bar. Walter went to the meeting and found his friend in a state of nervous fear: after making sure that he could not be overheard, the friend whispered he had come, at some danger to himself, to warn Walter that they had received orders to confiscate his father's passport. Toscanini, said the directive from Rome, "had no reason for leaving Italy." The next day it happened. Toscanini was forced to hand over his and Carla's passports. He insisted that an inquiry be made in Rome as to whether the passports would be returned in time for him to fill his engagement with NBC, for which he was due to leave in a few weeks. Presently Walter was summoned to the police. He was told that the passport *would* be returned if Toscanini would sign a statement promising not to make any derogatory remarks about the regime while abroad. With a heavy heart Walter carried the message home: he knew the answer beforehand. Toscanini bellowed, "That assassin, that fathead! I would not ask him to return my passport if I were to starve the rest of my days."

Walter then phoned Sarnoff. Sarnoff phoned Roosevelt. Roosevelt phoned somebody in the State Department. The State Department phoned the American Ambassador. The American Ambassador called on Mussolini with the message, politely but unmistakably couched, that the President of the United States took a dim view of the incident. Journalists in London and in Switzerland got wind of the affair (or was it leaked on purpose?) and wrote articles denouncing "the political imprisonment of art." Mussolini gave in. (Ciano claimed in his memoirs that it was he who was instrumental in returning Toscanini's passport. That is almost certainly a lie.)

Walter had in the meantime arranged to have a helicopter pick his father up at Lago Maggiore and smuggle him into Switzerland, should the passport not be returned. Toscanini was very disappointed when the plan proved unnecessary; he would have enjoyed a dramatic escape over the top of the Alps. As it was, he left prosaically on the Simplon Express. At the Italian border a minor official caused further confusion, whether by stupidity or malevolence was never made clear: Toscanini was told that he could not continue the journey without special clearance from the Milan police. By the time this was untangled, the connecting train to Cherbourg had left and the next train would not get him there in time to board the *Ile de France*. Walter telephoned the French Line and they immediately agreed to delay the sailing of the ship for four hours. Toscanini arrived, the *Ile de France* departed with him on board—and that was the last Toscanini was to see of Italy until Mussolini was dead.

America was to be his home from then on. In Riverdale, then a sylvan suburb of New York, he bought a Victorian house spacious enough to have suited Galsworthy's Forsyte family. A broad staircase led from a balcony, behind which the bedrooms lay, to the living room, and when friends came Toscanini used to stride down the stairs disdaining the banister, greeting one and all, and finally steering deftly to his favorite chair. Nobody else ever sat on that chair. The dining and living rooms gave on to a terrace; from there the grassy ground descended in a polite slope toward the Hudson River; the garden was planted with tulips and hyacinths, standing in confused array around the trees, like children around soldiers. No other house was visible and one scarcely remembered that one had come there on a road leading past the skyscrapers of Medical Center. The furniture throughout the "Villa Pauline" was comfortable and commonplace. It was the sort of home in which a well-to-do but unimaginative merchant would be at ease, except that in the living room there stood on a side table a porcelain figure of Falstaff, and over it hung an oil painting of Toscanini, and that picture, middling though it was as a painting, drew your attention and made you feel more breathlessly anticipating than you had been when you came in. Then, when you saw Toscanini, you didn't notice the furniture. In his home he was gracious even to a musician he might have crucified at yesterday's rehearsal and never did he act the celebrity. He did not attempt small talk, but he didn't seem to mind the gossip which often swirled around in rivulets; I think he rather enjoyed it. Very soon Goethe or Verdi or Boito entered the conversation.

A cluttered order reigned in his study off the balcony, with innumerable pictorial mementoes and a plethora of gifts from admirers; he knew where every object belonged. A small piano stood in the study, the grand piano in the living room. The walls were lined with cases containing books and scores, many of them inscribed to him. More books, more scores formed the wall of the balcony; when he paced up and down the balcony, he had but to stretch out his hand a little to reach one of these mute companions. In one corner stood a phonograph; Walter showed him many times how to operate it, but the machine always frightened him. Walter and an engineer rigged it up so that all his father had to do was to place the record he wanted on the turntable and push one button. The location of that button was marked by a large white arrow which they had pasted on the machine. Since he slept little, he would often get up in the middle of the night, and then he wanted to listen to chamber music. Suddenly the household would be awakened by a frightful mechanical racket: it was his attempt to set the phonograph in motion.

He was as happy in Riverdale as his own disposition and his grief over the mounting misfortunes of the world allowed him to be. Few artists ever were so carefully tended, few so greatly loved.

He agonized over Hitler's early victories as intensely as he might have suffered had he forgotten a page of the *Eroica*. Even music could not always offer palliation. Stubbornly—one required stubbornness in those days—he held on to the belief in eventual victory. The doubt underneath the belief often made him hit out at those near him, and he refused to avert his gaze from the contemplation of pain, as a man watches a fire which burns his own house.

Possibly to offer him some comfort in renewed work, possibly to get him away from that terrace in Riverdale where for him the green had turned to black, possibly to accede to his wish for motion, as lively in his old age as it had been in his youth, a tour was arranged to take the orchestra to South America. The overt reason for the tour was propaganda, with the blessing of the State Department. On the long sea voyage, watching the ship cutting the waters, watching the play of the waves, Toscanini became calmer. He was curious to know every detail of the ship's working, he stood on the captain's bridge, he crawled into the engine room, he visited the kitchens, and sometimes at night he would watch the passengers dancing. He hovered over his men with new solicitude; from early morning to late at night he was surrounded by musicians discussing the only subject which really interested them. They needed sleep—he didn't, or didn't seem to.

Musicians are often passionate gamblers, as they are often good cardplayers. Bodanzky was an excellent bridge-player, Richard Strauss played skat at all hours. Moisciwitch used to gamble on anything and everything, and carried a miniature roulette wheel in his pocket. On the boat to South America one man was playing the slot machine and of course losing steadily. His friends begged Toscanini to talk to him and make him stop. Toscanini at once went to him, putting on his sternest face. An hour later the two men could be seen alternately feeding half dollars into the machine. Neither hit the jackpot.

While he was on the ship, the news came through that the Germans had entered Paris, France had surrendered, and Pétain was begging for an armistice (June 17, 1940). Toscanini sat in his cabin moaning so piteously that he could be heard in the adjacent cabins. Nothing would assuage his grief; he would neither see his men nor take food. He kept moaning until suddenly Carla appeared at the door of the cabin; in a harsh voice—she who never raised her voice—she called out, "Tosca—Enough!" At once he stopped, fell silent, swayed from side to side, hung his head—and presently the steward brought him something to eat.

3

Till his return from South America, his relation with Sarnoff and NBC continued serene. Then troubles arose, partly caused by an incident in which management acted imprudently and which was magnified out of all proportion by Toscanini. Perhaps, knowing Toscanini, troubles were bound to come. Fault lay on both sides, no doubt. Perhaps his culpability could be condoned, if not pardoned, when one understands that his thrashing about was the symptom of his misery.

The world was breaking to pieces, he was old, his country had shown itself as even more craven than he had believed possible. What use was it to continue the struggle? The letter he wrote on the ship returning from South America sounds an elegiac tone:

[Undated. Written on the S.S. *Uruguay*]

... While writing I feel sad at heart and it will be always so when beautiful things come to an end. But it is a sadness caused by happiness. If I think to our concerts they seem far, far away—they are like dear, sweet memories of times long past. Anyhow, they were beautiful! You have never played so well, so inspired in three seasons that I am with you. We have never been so linked, so all-one, as in these sixteen concerts. We must be proud of what we have done! I can't say which of these concerts has been the best! I only know that the next to the first was better and so on. I hope you will never forget them. Memories of beautiful, dear things are the poetry and the sweet perfume of our existence. Goodbye dearest friends. God bless you all.

Home once more in Riverdale, his mood worsened, as the Luftwaffe began its Blitz on London (September, 1940), Hitler and Mussolini held a grandiloquent meeting at the Brenner Pass (October), and the Germans massacred the Jews of Warsaw (November). At the request of Walt Disney, Sarnoff had invited him to the opening of *Fantasia*. Toscanini replied:

November 8, 1940

I must decline because I do not feel in the spirit to go amongst many people. As you can well understand, this old heart is heavy because of the many sad and tragic happenings in the world today. Please understand dear David.

During the 1940 season he continued his work with NBC. One day, however, the depression burst into open wrath. He was rehearsing the *Missa Solemnis* in Carnegie Hall for a benefit performance. He usually rehearsed for three hours—including intermissions for the orchestra—and he rarely exceeded the allotted time. As a matter of fact, and contrary to general opinion, he knew that overtime was expensive and he felt a sense of responsibility toward the company's money. He possessed

an extraordinary sense of time: over and over again I saw
him stop ten or five seconds, exactly ten or five seconds, before
the three hours of a recording session were up, say "*Basta,*"
and dismiss the orchestra, *without once consulting his watch.*
This time, however, though he was supposed to finish at
6:30 P.M., he went on. Some of the men were due to play in a
commercial program at the NBC studio at 8:00 P.M. Seven
o'clock came, seven fifteen, seven thirty, and he showed no
inclination to stop. The contractor of the orchestra crept at
the last possible moment to the back of the stage and beckoned
to the musicians needed elsewhere to crouch down and sneak
out. That was unbelievably stupid—it was the commercial
program which should have been pulled through with substi-
tutes. Toscanini, his eye and ear concentrated on Beethoven,
at first did not notice the exodus. Suddenly he did. With a
jungle cry of rage he tore his collar, fled from the podium and
ran to his dressing room, where he kicked everything in sight.
Nobody came near him, but after a while they tried to explain
what had happened. He roared that he had not been told the
truth: he did not know of the orchestra having to be at the beck
and call of other engagements. He had been tricked. He had
been insulted. He had been "chea-ted." It was unforgivable!

Eventually he forgave, because he felt like forgiving. His
anger was, of course, justifiable.

Not justifiable was his interference when other conductors
led the orchestra as guests. Since he could not travel during
the war, he used to come to Studio 8H and watch them rehearse. When he liked what he heard—from a Monteux, an
Ansermet, a Bruno Walter—he was all smiles; when he didn't
he scowled and, sitting in one of the back rows, he started to
indicate to the orchestra *his* tempo. He was capable as well of
walking out muttering imprecations. At best his presence in
the hall drove the guest frantic with nervousness. During the
summer of 1941 NBC had engaged a conductor of doubtful
quality to lead a couple of concerts of light music. Toscanini
came and what he heard so infuriated him that he went tearing
down the corridor, shouting, "This is not my orchestra. What
has that man done to my orchestra? He is a disgrace. *Vergogna! Vergogna!*" and meeting one of the NBC executives,

he exploded, "Why didn't you ask *me* to conduct?" He then announced that he would not return to the NBC, that he was through, "finish-ed." Like Achilles in his tent, he buried himself in Riverdale. He would not answer the telephone calls from NBC executives, nor pleas, nor letters. Even David Sarnoff could not mollify him and indeed, as a gesture of revenge, he went to lunch with William Paley, head of CBS, Sarnoff's archcompetitor. Nothing came of this, but Toscanini did not conduct any of the regular NBC Symphony series during the 1941–1942 season. Foreseeing the future, Sarnoff nevertheless decided to keep the orchestra alive. Stokowski conducted it that season. Toscanini could hardly have been indifferent to this move; perhaps it helped eventually to bring him back.

Yet, once more be it said that one must understand his behavior in the light of the horrible news, a grim summer in which the German army reached Leningrad and the German air force rained fire on Moscow. Long before the quarrel with NBC, Toscanini's melancholy and despondency, so directly dependent on the state of the world, had caused him to write to Sarnoff:

April 31 [misdated, should be 30] 1941
My dear Sarnoff:

First of all I have to make my apology for having delayed so many times and for a long while to answer your letter of the February 24th.

If in that time it was hard and painful for me to take a conclusive decision about to accept or not your proposal to conduct next season the NBC orchestra, today things are not at all changed and I feel that I am in the same state of mind as before. However, I have to come to an end making free you and me of the nightmare which weighs upon us since February.

My old age tells me to be high time to withdraw from the militant scene of Art. I am tired and a little exhausted— the dreadful tragedy which tears to pieces unhappy humanity saddens me and makes me crazy and restless:— how can I find peace, heart, wish and strength in order to meet with new responsibility and new work? As for me, it is impossible . . . so that my dear David don't be hesitating any longer and make up at once your plan for the next season. . . . Later on if my state of mind, health and rest will be improved and you will judge my cooperation advantageous enough for the NBC call me and I shall be glad to resume once more my work. Believe me dear Sarnoff I am sad at heart to renounce the joy to conduct that very fine orchestra you formed for me and gave me so great satisfaction!

My deepest gratitude for you will never be lessened. . . . Many and many thanks for the cooperation you gave me in my task as well as the facilities you placed at my disposal.

Affectionately yours

Arturo Toscanini

The letter was written on the day the British were forced to withdraw from Greece. What it meant was No and Yes. Sarnoff understood it. He waited.

Some seven months later, when America had been seriously drawn into the war, and particularly after Pearl Harbor (December 7, 1941), Toscanini resumed his relationship with NBC, to conduct a series of benefit concerts for the U.S. bond drives; the first of them took place the day before Pearl Harbor, the fifth on April 4, 1942, at the time Rommel's Afrikakorps was beginning to meet resistance. Once having resumed, Toscanini found, after all, that the "very fine orchestra" had not been spoiled. From then on his contributions to the war efforts were frequent and joyously given, the Red Cross, Roosevelt Hospital, Child Welfare League, War Orphan Committee, War Bond Drive, Infantile Paralysis Fund being some of the beneficiaries. The two largest concerts were given at Madison Square Garden for the Red Cross, one in May, 1940, and one in May, 1944. For the latter concert the NBC and the New York Philharmonic were combined; he conducted Wagner in the first half and the last act of *Rigoletto* (Warren, Milanov, Peerce, Moscona, Merriman) in the second half. Nearly eighteen thousand people paid more than $100,000 to be there.

During the intermission La Guardia auctioned off Toscanini's baton for $11,000.

In 1942 he gave the American premiere of Shostakovich's Seventh Symphony, most of which had been composed during the siege of Leningrad. Toscanini had followed Russia's fight for life with great sympathy. He rejoiced at the Russian people's tenacity, familiar to him from *War and Peace,* a book he had read three times; he rejoiced when the counteroffensive of Leningrad began (July 28, 1942). He wanted very much to be the first to present the new symphony in the United States. Stokowski, too, wanted to be first. Both being RCA artists and the score being in RCA's possession, a bit of diplomatic juggling had to be practiced: it was decided that Toscanini could give the radio premiere, Stokowski the concert premiere in Philadelphia. The score had been flown over, photographed on microfilm. Toscanini now took an enlarged copy, spent several evenings in bed with it, and learned the long symphony—seventy-three minutes long in Toscanini's performance—by heart. One of the rehearsals took place on a day when New York was being choked by a suffocating heatwave. Even the air-conditioning in Studio 8H could not cope with the thermometer. Toscanini went through the complex symphony—which included a difficult march movement—and at the end he tumbled off the podium and collapsed on the floor near it. A shock of fear went like flash-fire through the players and the few of us who were watching the rehearsal. Had Toscanini suffered a stroke? Had he been prostrated by the heat? We started to run toward him to help him; at this moment he jumped up, impatiently waved away all help, and said, *"Terrible! Da capo*—from the beginning!" And he went through it from the beginning.

Years later he heard a recording of that performance of Shostakovich's Seventh. He wondered, "Did I really learn and conduct such junk?"

4

He had not forgotten Italy. When on July 25, 1943, Mussolini was arrested, he remembered and quoted Mazzini, poet and idealist, who had envisioned Italy "radiant, purified by suffering, moving as an angel of light among the nations that thought her dead." Six days after Mussolini's arrest there appeared two editorials in the *New York Times*. One dealt with the war, the other with an artist:

Six Days in Italy

Every dispatch from Italy adds to the evidence of confusion and uncertainty in that bombed and broken and divided country. There need be no confusion or uncertainty among the United Nations. What has happened during the three weeks since the landings in Sicily and the six days since the overthrow of Mussolini has been a simple sequence of cause and effect.

The obvious major cause was the proven weakness of the Italian Army, arising from its unwillingness to fight any longer at the side of Germany. This feeling was evidently shared by the Italian people. It must have been strengthened by the joint statement of July 16, in which President Roosevelt and Prime Minister Churchill promised Italy "a restoration of national dignity, security and peace" if she would disavow "Nazi Germany and her own false and corrupt leaders." Nine days later Mussolini fell. With him fell the Fascist party and, bag and baggage, the whole power and ideology of Fascism itself . . .

Homage to Toscanini

Arturo Toscanini, a great man as well as a great artist, has a passion for freedom as strong as his passion for music. He loves his native country. He fought for it with distinction in the First World War. Its subjection to the tyranny of Fascism, its disgrace as a puppet of Nazism, wrung his heart . . .

His long generous effort in the United States in behalf of this war for freedom needs no recalling. . . .

At 31 Toscanini reached the summit of conductorship, leadership of the orchestra at La Scala in Milan. According to yesterday's dispatches La Scala, where he was leader at different periods for nineteen years, invites him to come back now that Fascism is crushed. On the theater front the invitations are painted: "Toscanini, we await you"; "Toscanini must open the new season in La Scala." These mute anonymous voices from his old home may well touch the illustrious musician. In their simpler way they say to him what Mr. Roosevelt wrote: "Like all true artists you have recognized throughout your life that art can flourish only where men are free."

That Saturday he went to NBC to plan a special program to be played on the day when the Italian government would sign the armistice with the Allies. It would come any day now. Then he waited. He had to wait five weeks, for him restless and agonizing weeks, during which he was never far from a radio. On September 3, the news came.

The special "freedom" program he conducted was an antique dealer's jumble: the opening movement of Beethoven's Fifth, the "Garibaldi Hymn," and the Overture to *William Tell*. (He loved that overture and when an acquaintance said to him, "Isn't it cheap music?" he answered, "*You* try and compose something as good!" I think he loved it also because he admired Schiller's play with its theme of simple people rising against tyranny.) He ended the concert with "The Star-Spangled Banner." As he conducted it, with a rhythm that no other conductor achieved and which almost succeeded in making the anthem bearable as music, he sang the words.

(Speaking of "The Star-Spangled Banner," Marcia Davenport told a charming anecdote: On the day in 1953 on which Eisenhower was to be inaugurated, she asked if she might come to Riverdale to watch the ceremony on their excellent TV set. Walter invited her to lunch. Toscanini at first thought her request nonsense. "Who wants to watch a thing like that? It's only politics." Then curiosity got the better of his dislike of official functions and he joined them at the TV set. Soon and as it were against his better judgment, he became intrigued by the spectacle, and when Eisenhower appeared he exclaimed, "There he comes, there he comes, now he is arriving." The military band struck up "The Star-Spangled Banner," playing it in the wrong tempo and with bad intonation. Toscanini, scandalized, jumped up, clapped his hands to indicate the right tempo, and shouted, "*Madonna*, why didn't they call me?")

He who protested against "only politics" was now, in Italy's hour of confusion and contrition, moved to make a political statement. In the September 13, 1943, issue of *Life* magazine there appeared an appeal "To the People of America—by Arturo Toscanini." *Life* introduced his words by writing:

With the Italian mainland now under attack the U.S. is being pressed for a solution to the Italian political situation. Thus far, in line with the State Department's chronic emphasis on "expediency," our Italian policy has merely supported the Hitler puppets, the King and Badoglio. The world now watches to see whether the U.S. will dare to take a more positive step in the direction of a democratic postwar future.

In this crisis the editors of LIFE are honored to turn their editorial page over to the great Italian patriot, Arturo Toscanini. . . . Never before has Maestro Toscanini written for publication—not even on his own subject of music. He speaks now because he believes that there is at stake, not only the destiny of Italy, but the worldwide cause of freedom. . . . Mr. Toscanini's world is the world of the arts. An intimate and enthusiastic student of Shakespeare, he applies a quotation from *King Henry VI* to the present Italian King. He is generally recognized, of course, as the greatest living master of music. Here, however, he speaks as a wise, though impassioned patriot, and as a man whose faith in the ideal of human freedom has never wavered.

Here are excerpts from the article:

TO THE PEOPLE OF AMERICA

At this moment when the destiny of Italy depends so largely upon the decision and policy of the United States

Government, I attempt to present a plea for my fellow Italians, addressing it to the American people together with the leader chosen by them, President Franklin Delano Roosevelt, because I think you are well aware of my love for Italy and the United States and my faith and devotion to the ideals of justice and freedom for all peoples of the world.

In presenting this plea I am conscious of the need for all of us to build a just and lasting peace, and that our common aim is to prepare it, and to attain it at the moment required.

I am an old artist who has been among the first to denounce Fascism to the world. I feel and believe that I can act as interpreter of the soul of the Italian people—those people whose voice has been choked for more than 20 years, but, thanks to God, just now is shouting for peace and liberty in the streets and squares of Italy, defying everything, even martial law. . . .

They would like to say: People of America, we are not your enemies and never have been your enemies in the past. We were forced into the role of "enemy" by a vicious and wicked man, Mussolini, who betrayed us for more than 20 years. We never wanted to fight against you, and today we do not want to do it. Only the King of Italy and his bootlicker, Badoglio, both despicable men, are your enemies and want to carry on this war. . . .

Italy will certainly have a revolution as a result of the current war; the Allies will either favor and help it, or hinder it. The Allies' attitude will determine whether the revolution will, or will not, result in an orderly democratic government.

Should this revolution result in an orderly democratic government, as we hope, it will be necessary for the Allies to support all democratic elements currently arrayed against the King and Badoglio, offering to the reborn free Italy—along with the unconditional surrender of the Italian armed forces—equitable peace terms, to include:

Respect for the integrity of the national territory of Italy as it was established before 1922 (the march on Rome) through the strenuous efforts of Italy, France, England, the United States, and their Allies of the first World War. What a crime it would be to separate Sicily and Sardinia, Trieste and Venezia Giulia from Italy! It would be like driving knives into the living flesh of Italy. We shudder just to think of it. . . .

We think, people of America, that these suggestions should be made known independently of the demand for "unconditional surrender" as soon as possible, in order to give to the Italians faith, courage and enthusiasm to act and to fight together with the Allies, and so to save many, many American lives.

We ask that the Allies permit our volunteers to fight against the hated Nazis under the Italian flag with conditions substantially similar to those of the Free French. Thus alone can we Italians visualize the unconditional surrender of our armed forces without injury to our sense of honor. Give us a chance to fight along with you in your just cause which is also our own cause.

In this way, people of America, Italy will become again an element of democratic order among the family of nations.

Do not forget that we Italians have been the first to endure the oppression of a tyrannical gang of criminals, supported by that "fainthearted and degenerate King" of Italy—but that we have never willingly submitted to them. Countless thousands of men and women in Italy shed blood, met imprisonment and death, striving fiercely against that horde of criminals, enduring also the apathy and indifference of the world then full of admiration for Mussolini.

Our own suffering, people of America, gives us the right to ask the Allies that the Italian people must not pay for the guilt of the fascist regime. . . .

Arturo Toscanini

On the day the magazine appeared on the stands, the American Fifth Army landed at Salerno (September 9). On April

12, 1944, the "fainthearted and degenerate King" (Victor Emmanuel II) abdicated. A year after that Mussolini was killed (April 28, 1945), and three days later Hitler's body burned.

5

He continued to contribute to the war effort. He had been offered $250,000 to star in a commercial film and had turned the offer down cold; now he made a film for nothing for the Office of War Information. He conducted Verdi's *The Force of Destiny* Overture and *The Hymn of the Nations*, in which he had changed the words *"Italia patria mia"* to *"Italia tradita"* and to which he had added a quotation from "The Star-Spangled Banner" and the "Internationale." He was immensely proud of that film, and he told everybody about it, but nothing would induce him to look at it. He hated pictures of himself.

"Italia tradita" now began to call him ever more insistently. Would he return? Would he help rebuild artistic Italy? In a short-wave radio broadcast of 1944, members of the Scala orchestra asked that he come to continue "his noble work for Italian art." This broadcast was transmitted to him, though in incomplete form. He answered, Yes, he would come, as soon as Italy would be cleansed:

> All the vestiges of a past of ignominy and treachery must disappear. Justice also demands that the one who gave to the Fascist tyranny all material and moral support, the arms and the legal power to deceive, subjugate, and oppress the Italian people for twenty sorrowful years, be now called upon to answer for his complicity in the crimes perpetrated by the Fascists in his name and for all the violations of the statute which made the Italian people the first victims of Nazi-Fascist terror.
>
> You Milanese, who in 1848 began the revolt against German tyranny, have well deserved to conclude in 1945 this struggle of our Risorgimento.
>
> I shall be happy to return among you as a citizen of a free

240

Italy and not as a subject of the degenerate king and princess of the House of Savoy.

During the night of August 15–16, 1943, fire bombs had fallen on La Scala, destroying most of the galleries, the roof, and much of the stage. But the walls remained standing. Reconstruction of the building had been planned at once but had proceeded haltingly until American money furnished a new impulse. (Toscanini had cabled the management of La Scala, "With all my heart I authorize my daughter Wally Castelbarco to contribute in my name one million lire for the reconstruction of my beloved theater La Scala. I hope to do more in the future.") From October, 1944, the work proceeded rapidly and the building was as good as finished by the end of April, 1946. Hundreds of steel-workers, dozens of engineers, plasterers, painters, electricians, machinists had removed the fallen beams, carried away the charred remains, and had tried lovingly to reproduce the old monument in its ancient splendor. As yet it was only a soundless monument.

In April, 1946, he came. Antonio Ghiringhelli and Greppi, the Mayor of Milan, welcomed him. He could not as yet go to his house in the Via Durini because it had been requisitioned during the war and was just being restored to habitable order. He went to a little house near Crema which he owned but which he never liked. Ghiringhelli went with him, and at once Toscanini began to discuss ideas for the programs, a discussion which lasted far into the night. The Scala wasn't quite ready, either. In a few days he could come and see it, but please, not yet. He waited. After a day or two he lost patience, drove into Milan, and walked into the theater. The auditorium seemed empty, not even a workman appearing to be there; no sound of hammering or sawing disturbed the stillness. The house was dark and he stood in the darkness, perhaps remembering the concerts he had conducted there how many years ago?—sixteen years ago, with the New York Philharmonic. Just then, by one of those incidents which make life improbable, the electricians, hidden in a cubicle, decided to test the new circuits. They turned all the switches on, the auditorium blazed with brightness, and the lights shone on an elegant little man standing in an aisle, who blinked, clapped his hands, said "Good!" turned, and left.

The editor of *Good Housekeeping* magazine, Herbert R. Mayes, asked me to go to Italy to write the story of the reopening of La Scala. The commission represented a wonderful gift to me; he knew my admiration for Toscanini. I have not forgotten that plane trip: it took twenty-seven hours. (I hope the reader will pardon the autobiographical digression.) We landed with a grating noise at Rome's Ciampino Airport on a steel mattress the army had put down. I staggered out of the plane into the sunniest of Easter sunshine. The city smelled of coffee and strawberries. There were no taxis, no buses, no private cars, the only means of transportation being a few trucks on which wooden boards had been placed, and on those boards men and women stood to be carried to their working places. Virtually no store was open, no restaurant, but at many corners women stood selling strawberries and homemade bread. I remember one little stall displaying some misshapen dark bread with a sign, "Ugly, but good." The city had hardly been harmed and now displayed itself with an innocent beauty, the light mirrored on people's faces and reflected from faces to buildings. If a city could be called Arcadian, you could have called Rome so. There was nothing there except life beginning anew, and hope was so pervasive that you could almost touch it.

Somehow I had to make my way to Milan, no planes or trains operating. I did so partly by an army plane, partly by a Canadian jeep, and partly by a taxidriver who had some black-market gasoline. As we drove north through Tuscany, where half the old farmers look like Toscanini, the testimony of destruction became evident: villages burned and torn to jagged bits, houses split in two, deep holes in the road. Yet the fields and the olive trees were still there, and so were the farm women, carrying amphoras on their heads and humming as they walked.

How different was Milan from Rome! Three quarters of it had been destroyed. When you walked in the city you had continuously to adopt as circuitous a route as a drunken man, to avoid the rubble and the debris and the loose bricks which were lying about. Some buildings seemed hale from a distance;

as you approached them, you saw that behind the wall there was nothing, the interior burned out, the wall a stage set. The window frames seemed to be in mourning, with their black borders. Pebbles and gravel still obstructed the main entrances to La Scala. On one door a few faded flowers were fastened with a sign that here a group of anti-Fascists had been executed. Leonardo's statue stood, the pensive face obscured by black soot.

In spirit, too, Milan differed from Rome. Hope seemed less secure, fatigue more attendant. Bribery was rampant, even for a slight service. The Milanese thought it clever to cheat; it was smart to be shifty. There was not enough milk for children, but in the elegant restaurants, most of which had reopened, you could get whipped cream if you were willing to pay the price. The cynicism which was eventually to overspread Italy, the *me ne fregismo,* "I don't give a damn," had its roots in the industrial city.

Seven programs were planned, each to be given twice, three of them conducted by Toscanini, the others by Paul Kletzky, Dimitri Mitropoulos, and Antonio Votto. All the artists donated their services. Orchestra seats for a series cost 15,000 lire (about $75), a considerable sum in 1946. The concerts were sold out, but of course tickets could be obtained on the black market, and on most days one could find two or three men, dressed in shiny black suits, with a few teeth missing and bad breath, standing in front of the opera house offering tickets in conspiratorial tones.

Cynicism and fatigue notwithstanding, the city seethed with excitement over Toscanini's coming. The book stores, of which Milan has so many that it is incomprehensible how they can stay in business, all featured Toscanini biographies, some wretchedly printed and very cheap—"The Return of Arturo Toscanini—10 lire," some more carefully compiled—"The Man of the Day—100 lire." The two leading picture magazines—*Oggi* and *Tempo*—devoted their front covers to him. When he came to the first rehearsal an eight-year-old girl, a pupil of the ballet school, handed him some roses and executed a solemn curtsy. This time he didn't mind the flowers, but when he bent to thank her she ran off at top speed.

Rumors about the orchestra flew about. It was so bad that he would pack up and leave immediately. Walter had brought the violinists some American strings which they needed badly, but that wouldn't help. They could no longer play with the force he required. Some of the musicians were old enough to have played under him many years ago. Well, perhaps he would make allowances, he would be gentle with these men, some of whom had clutched a gun and heard the noise of exploding shells. He had chosen Italian music for the first program, partly because they were familiar with the music, partly to honor the Italian genius. The program included Rossini's *La Gazza Ladra* Overture, a chorus and two dances from his *William Tell*, the prayer from *Mosè*. Then Verdi: *Nabucco* Overture, the *"Va pensiero"* chorus, the Overture to *I Vespri Siciliani* and the *Te Deum*. In the second part the third act of Puccini's *Manon* and Boito's Prologue in Heaven from *Mefistofele*. Among the soloists were Mariano Stabile, Mafalda Favero, Tancredi Pasero, and a young and beautiful soprano, Renata Tebaldi.

Before the concert, the Milanese newspapers—two-page sheets of which there seemed to be a dozen and one seemed to be published every half hour—kept printing stories with such headlines as "Toscanini's Secret," "Latest Facts about La Scala," "The Wizard Returns." Three hours *before* the concert, a newspaper appeared on the front page of which was displayed a huge photograph purporting to be of Toscanini and the orchestra. It was of course a fake. Underneath, one read the banner headline, "Thus Toscanini Reopens Old and Glorious Scala." Since journalists were excluded from rehearsals, one dressed up as a house painter, complete with pail and brush, and pretended to busy himself putting finishing touches to a wall of the auditorium. He then wrote a "human interest" report of the rehearsal.

The orchestra received Toscanini standing, at that first rehearsal on May 3. At once he bade them sit down and launched into the Rossini Overture. He said only, "Light—*very* light," and off they went. It was not light enough. He said (in Italian), "Signori, you've got German boots on . . . This is Rossini. Dry, light, staccato, no vibrato. Look at me! Look at the stick.

Italian. Sunny. Once more." Once more they tried and still once
more. He was not in the least gentle, paying them the compliment of treating them as he did any other orchestra. The
familiar phenomenon, no less astonishing because it was familiar, was enacted once more. Though the orchestra was not
of virtuoso quality, he was able to lift them to virtuosity. The
Overture sprang and hopped and bounced. When it was over,
the musicians broke into bravos. He said, "Not bad. Now
Verdi."

For the first concert, May 11, the rebuilt Scala was ready.
It shone like a new-bought engagement ring and all the lights
were turned on in a city long used to darkness. Everything was
in place: the red carpets laid, the mirrors polished, the floors
waxed, the ushers dressed in black breeches and wearing great
silver chains which made them look like wine stewards of a
French ship. The insignia of the House of Savoy had been
removed from the theater and, at Toscanini's suggestion, a
group of old musicians from the Verdi Home sat in the former
Royal Box. The women of the audience appeared as shining
as the theater. Milan's coiffeurs opened for business at 6:00
A.M. that day. U.S. soldiers had come from nearby and from
as far away as Vienna, traveling by jeep. There were not
enough hotel rooms and the concierges were bribed right and
left.

Italian audiences have a habit of standing until the last
possible moment, greeting their friends with much hand waving
and inspecting one another through oversized opera glasses.
Finally, when the lights dimmed, in a ritual peculiar to the
Scala, where the lights over the loges are extinguished last,
they sat down, only to jump up again to greet Toscanini. They
shouted. He raised his hands for silence and couldn't get it.
He started the Rossini Overture and there ensued such shush-
ing that you would have thought a locomotive was letting off
steam. Then the music quieted them. In the middle of the first
part they stood up again. At the end, after the dramatic *Mefistofele* Prologue, they hailed him with "Bravo, Arturo," feeling
no longer constrained to call him Toscanini. He came out four
times, in spite of a flashlight photographer who aimed but was
only just prevented by Walter from "firing."

The concert was carried by radio throughout Italy. More immediate was its transmittal by loudspeakers to the great square in front of the Dome. There, in the mild night air, stood some twenty thousand people, some of whom had watched the Scala burn three years previously and had seen the night watchman crawl from the theater, white with dust and weeping.

For the second program he chose the Kabalevsky Colas Breugnon Overture, a piece which he particularly enjoyed and which he played and recorded with the NBC; then the Brahms Third, Gershwin's *Un Americano a Parigi* ("*Novità per Italia*"), Respighi's *Fountains of Rome*, and Debussy's *La Mer*. It was a piece of challenging insanity to program *La Mer*, and Ghiringhelli told him so. He insisted, with the result that before the rehearsal was over the floor of his podium was wet all around him, so terribly had he perspired. They had enclosed the podium by a velvet rope. At one moment, when he seemed to despair and didn't know what to do, he looked around helplessly, bent down, and hit his head against the velvet rope.

A month after that, he conducted a Beethoven program, the First and the Ninth.

Toscanini remained in Milan till the end of June, 1946, working to help the orchestra. In 1949, on the anniversary of Verdi's death, he donated $6,000 to the needy musicians of Milan. Yet, much as he loved Italy and firmly though he then hoped for its regeneration, he no longer felt at home in a destroyed city and a morally enfeebled country. He returned to La Scala in 1948 to direct a program of Boito's music, and again briefly in 1949 and 1950, when he led the Verdi *Requiem*. But he was always "a guest," and he observed with increasing bitterness the cleavage between political parties, the in-fighting, the inability of the Italians to govern themselves, the belief that the substance of liberty consisted of slipping an envelope to the policeman. Perhaps what Walter told me one day in Milan was a reflection of his father's mood: "Now we are strangers here." Their real home lay in Riverdale. His true place lay in front of that orchestra which was unequivocally devoted to him, the NBC Symphony.

6

The man in his seventies became the man in his eighties and still he burned. Did the fire in the grate not grow dimmer?

As one reviews the long period with the NBC, and if in this review one is allowed some statistical tolerance, one may observe the flame burning high, then at a little lower intensity, and then, growing hot and strong again, flaunting the natural process of the fire dying out, the embers cooling with age. One could divide the seventeen years into three periods: the first of about three or four years, when the performances were of purest quality; the second three or four, the war years, when certain performances were nervously overdriven; and a final period beginning with the 1946–1947 season and ending before the final 1953–1954 season, eight years when his work acquired new strength, relaxation, warmth, and wisdom. To be sure the division is somewhat artificial and exceptions occurred in each period. Then, too, the differences were relative, relative to the Toscanini standards. Nevertheless, I believe a curve can be traced.

In addition to the state of the body and the nerves, in addition to the interaction between performer and audience which is as shifting as the light in an English dell, in addition to the usual fluctuations which every performer feels and which are responsible for seemingly inexplicable differences in performances, Toscanini was subject to the sway of the world. He may not have known how to turn on a phonograph, nor who or what supplied the electric current, but he was not an ivory-tower artist. He knew what was going on, and where. The anger he felt at the growth of Fascism lay at the pit of his stomach, and the disgust over Hitler's successes entered the core of his work. On the day Mussolini fell he said to the orchestra, "Now we have to play especially well." It was an admonition to himself.

After the unevenness of the war years and beginning in 1946 his spirit seemed to unfold again like the bluebell at the touch of clement air. We heard then certain incomparable performances, such as the *Bohème* in March, 1946, the *Traviata* in

December of the same year, the *Otello* of the following year, the Brahms cycle of 1948, which included a new and astonishing interpretation of the *Haydn Variations*, the *Don Quixote* * of the same year, a *La Mer* in 1950 (in Philadelphia), which of all the performances of that tone poem was the most overwhelming, the *Falstaff* of 1950, a Ninth Symphony of 1952, as well as the Schubert C Major Symphony and the Dvorak *New World*, all of which works seemed to contain new thoughts and new greatness, and in 1953 a towering *Eroica*, the *Missa Solemnis*, and a deeply romantic *Harold in Italy*.

When he played Beethoven's Seventh for the last time, he told the orchestra that he had been up all night studying the score. He now realized that certain details of previous performances were wrong: "I was stupid, you were stupid, only Beethoven was not stupid."

It was of this performance that Olin Downes wrote in the *New York Times* of November 11, 1951:

> . . . We have often heard him play this symphony, but it is not easy to believe that he ever played it before with such beauty, vitality and radiance of tone. . . .

> One knew again that the greatest beauty and the highest morality that the race of man has known is in the music of Beethoven. We heard a reading that in the sense of proportion and style was of the purest classicism. And we felt the divine intoxication and earth-shaking laughter of the Seventh Symphony.

In those final years he did employ a trick with the orchestra. He used to say, "This is the last time I will conduct this piece, the last time. My dear, play it well." Nobody believed him.

By no means everybody agrees with my tripartite division, nor my belief that many of his greatest performances were given with the NBC. George Szell, writing an article for the *Saturday Review* which appeared on Toscanini's birthday (March 25, 1967—ten years and two months after his death), said:

---

* An NBC musician (I have forgotten his name) said to me, "*That* was something we'll never hear again."

Regarding this period, I must say that those who knew
Toscanini only from his performances with the NBC
Orchestra and never heard him with the New York Philharmonic, the Vienna Philharmonic, or the BBC Symphony during those earlier years can have but a very incomplete idea of his real greatness. Not only was Toscanini
then at the very height of his powers, but his collaboration
with those orchestras in public performances with live
audiences seemed to inspire him more. The artificial, anti-
septic atmosphere of Studio 8H with its small, invited
audience; and the NBC Orchestra—which, at its best, was
rather the finest collection of virtuosic players money
could assemble, not an orchestra in the sense of an integrated organism—left more than a little to be desired.

I was fortunate enough to hear Toscanini with the four
orchestras Szell enumerates and I can neither agree to his
intimation of lessened power, nor to the assertion that the
NBC was not "an integrated organism." The superiority of
the long-established orchestras lies to some extent in imagination, as Szell himself proved in superb guest performances,
and the reverse of which one can hear when one listens to a
second-rate conductor officiating at the New York Philharmonic or the Vienna Philharmonic. The latter, especially, sometimes plays like dolts, at other times like heroes. As to the
"small" live audiences in 8H, is one thousand (the capacity
of 8H) small and three thousand large? Anyway, from 1950
on the broadcasts were transferred to Carnegie Hall, with
decidedly large audiences.

Some critics assert that Toscanini's tempos became faster,
more nervous, more pressed, as he grew older. (Example:
Brahms's First Symphony lasted a full minute less in a 1952
performance than in 1937.) "What's a man's age?" wrote
Robert Browning. "He must hurry more, that's all." There is
truth in the statement that in his later years Toscanini tended
to accelerate. Yet one must be careful not to generalize: as
against earlier performances a 1949 *Eroica* was swifter in
tempo but also tauter and more gigantic in concept, while a
Schubert "Unfinished" of the same year proceeded at a calmer

and more serene tempo than before. The *Tristan Prelude and Finale* became in a 1952 performance (recorded) demonstrably slower, taking on new tension and tragic stress. The Schubert C Major Symphony, one of his greatest accomplishments, retains all the power in a 1953 performance that it had seven or eight years previously, but seems less "stern" and somehow more other-worldly.

The propulsion which Toscanini gave to music did not necessarily derive from fast pacing. The timing of his Funeral March of the *Eroica* is nineteen minutes, that of Beecham sixteen, that of Koussevitzky thirteen and one half. The impression of pace came from a continuity of design existing in time and was an impression independent of "real" time—the ticking of a clock—as an impression of space comes from the linear design existing in a painting and is independent of the actual dimensions of the painting. In the tiny Raphael "The Agony in the Garden," in the Metropolitan Museum, a limitless landscape is suggested within a few inches. I have mentioned this continuous tempo design in the previous chapter. Ernst Ansermet commented:

> He refused to underline or bear down on the expression of a detail or of a passage by sacrificing the tempo, and by indulging in the fluctuations and the *rubati* which the romantic interpreters practiced. All the same, his tempo was not mechanical; it was always alive and capable of adapting itself to imperceptible modifications within the large dimensions of the structure. . . . The firmness of the Toscanini tempos served as a lesson to the interpreters of our epoch; the best of them profited by that lesson. In the last years of his life Furtwängler said to me: "I am now convinced that it is possible to give music all the required expressiveness without altering the tempo." [From a lecture held at Florence, June, 1967]

7

In one respect he did follow Browning's direction that he must hurry more. He hurried more by heaping on himself a harder task. More determinedly than ever he stood under the jet of what for him was the fountain of youth, that is the fresh interpretation of familiar large works. As one reviews the programs of the last eight years, one senses the presence of a plan, perhaps but a half-deliberate plan, to turn once again to the greatest products of the musical genius, to present, so to speak, the *Hamlet*s and *Tempest*s of music, rather than the *Coriolanus*es. An indication of the load shouldered late, of the laughing old men out of court, can be found in his programming and recording the Ninth Symphony in 1952 after playing it under the hot television lights in 1948.

He turned as well to the composer with whom, as I have said, he identified himself, and all the more the older he became. In a way that signified a return to the beginning of his career as, with youthful spirit and hard muscles, he braved the additional difficulties with which performances of operas confronted him: the choosing of the singers, the rehearsals with the chorus, the teaching of the music to an orchestra which had not played in the pit, the problems of diction, etc. In short, he held a Verdi festival over an eight-year span:

	Performed	*Toscanini's Age*
La Traviata	1946	79
Otello	1947	80
Aida	1949	82
Falstaff	1950	83
Requiem	1951	84
Un Ballo in Maschera	1954	87

All of these were historic events, but if one were forced to choose just one to take to that desert island, one would, I think, choose *Otello*, both because this work represents in many aspects the crowning glory of Verdi's achievement—"the climax of tragic opera," D. J. Grout called it—and because Toscanini's performance, with an almost perfect cast, represents one of the crowning glories of *his* achievements.

M. R. Ridley, the editor of the *New Temple Shakespeare*, wrote of *Othello:*

It is superb theater, with the severest economy and concentration, and it is by far the most intense of all [of
Shakespeare's plays]. There is no relief, none of that
alternating increase and decrease of strain that is so
clearly marked in the others, none of those periods in
which, even though there is no comic relief, the action
seems for a few moments to stand still while we recover
ourselves. From the moment of the landing in Cyprus
Shakespeare has the fingers of one hand on our pulses and
the fingers of the other on the levers of the rack. It is the
most cruel play he wrote, and the most pitiful.

Concentrated, economical, cruel, pitiful—these are characteristics of the opera as well (Boito did begin the libretto with
the landing in Cyprus), and all of those, all of the "pity of it,"
the heartbreak and beauty as well as the evil and misery, are
contained in Toscanini's performance, from the first upbeat
of the storm to the last lamenting chord. Once again one may
turn to a man like Olin Downes, who found it "not easy to write
of this performance":

It is not easy to write of this performance, for one is writing about some of the greatest music ever written in operatic form, and of performance literally unsurpassable, or
indeed to be equaled in the hearing of any of this generation. And music, unhappily for a poor scribbler, begins
where words stop.

It must be enough to give some of the tangible facts of the
record. They begin, and end, in a sense, with the statement
that by all the evidence and possible deduction therefrom
Mr. Toscanini achieved a reading of this great score
which represented the summit of his own interpretive
powers, if not his interpretive wishes, or dreams, and that
every artist on the stage was at his or her best and completely inspired in achieving the objectives of conductor
and composer. The final act of Verdi's masterpiece must
have been, for even such a perfectionist as Toscanini, as
near the ideal accomplishment as he could conceive. . . .

One exceptional attribute of this occasion, always characteristic of Toscanini when he interprets an opera, must be
recalled: the treatment, by every singer, of the text—the
diction, the communication of the very inner spirit of itself, which puts the burden of the musico-dramatic expression where it belongs, in the mouths of the singers,
on the stage. And that is the fundamental nature of Toscanini's performance. The words were unforgettably ar-
ticulated and their import revealed. . . . [*New York Times,*
December 14, 1947]

It was calculated that some eight million people listened to
the *Otello* broadcast, while some ten million watched the tele-
vised performances of *Aida,* in two parts, in the spring of
1949. "Toscanini" had become a household word in America,
though to most of the people he was still but a sound or a
photograph.

8

It was then that NBC decided to underwrite the costs of a
personal tour, presenting him and the orchestra in the halls
of major cities from the Atlantic to the Pacific. The net cost
of such a plan was calculated at a million dollars; once more
it was David Sarnoff who overrode objections and approved
the plan. Its objectives were twofold: to glorify the reputation
of NBC, and to stimulate the sale of Toscanini recordings.
The record business was just beginning to recover from the
division caused by "the war of the speeds." RCA had intro
duced the new 45 record, while CBS was proclaiming the virtues of the LP, the long-playing record perfected by Dr. Peter
Goldmark, which turned at 33⅓ revolutions per minute. Like
most wars, the war of the speeds was senseless, ruinous to
record dealers, confusing to the public. No good reason existed
why the advantages of the 45 plastic record, thin and un-
breakable, small and handy, could not be utilized in a record
turning at the slower speed and therefore offering a longer
playing time. Yet RCA and CBS fought each other bitterly—
here again emotion, pride, and jealousy, not logic, were involved in making a business decision—and it was only after

that part of the public which liked longer music (as against those who wanted merely the ephemeral "hit" song) had acted out its preference by refusing to buy "classical music" on 45's, that RCA had conceded. Now, in 1950, they were beginning to present their rich treasure of good music on LP's, and for the Toscanini tour, a special series of Toscanini recordings was put on sale.

When Sarnoff approached Toscanini with the idea of a tour, he got a fast "Why not?" The troubadour's instinct awoke at once. To revisit cities where he had not been for thirty years, to see others where he had never been, to feel once again the current which flowed to him from unfamiliar souls, to show of what the orchestra was capable, playing in strange citadels for diverse audiences—these considerations outweighed the fatigue of traveling . . . Two programs would do, they told him, for the entire tour. No, he replied, they would not, the orchestra might get bored, and he was willing to prepare four different programs. After a day or so, he phoned and said "Six." Six it was, but before the repertoire was finally settled, everybody connected with the tour had gone into a tailspin. The scores had to be marked and loaded on the train, the announcements given out, the programs printed in each city— and it was quite possible that before they managed to get Toscanini on the train he would decide that he needed eight programs.

The tour itself was as punctiliously organized as a Chinese calligraphic poem. The special train consisted of twelve Pullman cars: eight were for the musicians and other personnel, one was a combination office and recreation car, one was the dining car, one carried the instruments (about a quarter of a million dollars' worth), one was Toscanini's private car, called, by accident or design, the "Columbus." The "Columbus" had been fitted out with a bedroom, a bath complete with bathtub, a paneled library, a dining room which contained a table seating eight, and a large couch where Walter slept. All the furniture was solid and broad-bottomed, in the old Pullman style. Scores and books and photographs were lying about.

John Royal, a vice-president of NBC, was in charge of the tour; he was a large, choleric man who would have ordered the execution at dawn of any negligent member of the staff, had he been able to do so. There was no need for a firing squad, everybody trying to outguess everybody else as to "what Maestro wanted." The details were handled by Al Walker; he was one of those unimportant important little men without whom the world would be in even worse confusion than it is. Fanatically devoted to Toscanini for many years, he managed to keep secret when he slept or when he ate—he was always around, darting here and there, making sure that the limousine's motor was running as the train arrived, that the supply of clean dress shirts was not running low, the baton placed where it should be, the photographers pleaded with, lied to, and shooed away, the podium set on stage center, the eau de cologne and rock candy put in the dressing room, the kind of cuff buttons which would not fly apart ready before, the rough large towels ready after the concert. He adored "maistro," which he pronounced with a long *i*, and Toscanini, who called him "Wal-kèr," loved him.* Toscanini became friendly as well with the special chef who had been assigned to the train. The chef showed off his skill by preparing chicken à la Maryland for Toscanini, who ate it and praised it. But really what he wanted most of the time was soup and soup again, soup even for breakfast. The chef shook his head. He enjoyed the vistas he saw from the train, he enjoyed the people who came to talk to him when the train stopped, he enjoyed the train itself. Sarnoff had given him a gadget which recorded the speed of the train and he was told that he could tell the driver to go slower or faster. He played with the gadget as a little boy would.

It was on the "Toscanini Train" that 125 people spent forty days and forty nights, clicking off eight thousand miles, across twenty-four states, giving twenty-one concerts, led by one man eighty-three years old. One of his friends who accompanied the train called him "not the oldest man in the room, but the youngest." He was indefatigable; in the middle of the strenuous tour he said, "We ought to give more concerts, have a concert every night, have more music." Now and then he sug-

---

* It may be said to the credit of the "heartless corporation" that NBC kept Walker employed in a sinecure of a post after Toscanini's death and until his own death.

gested that the people would enjoy hearing an encore after the serious program. As usual, he was as punctilious about the encores as about a piece by Mozart. He sent the NBC librarian to the library of William and Mary University to bring him the manuscript of "Dixie." When he rehearsed "Dixie" he indicated a ritard which somehow had been left out of the orchestral parts. "Your own music," he told the orchestra laughingly, "and I have to teach it to you."

He remembered the halls in which he had played many, many years ago, the operas he had conducted in the cities he was now revisiting, and not only the operas but every singer down to the role of the Messenger in *Aida*, and whether he or she had sung well or badly. The only thing he kept forgetting was his eyeglasses. He took them off when he thought about a musical problem, placed them on the chair on which he was sitting, got up to pace the room, sat down again on the chair and—crash went the glasses. Walker had constantly to furnish a fresh pair.

The day of the concert in Atlanta, Toscanini stayed in his room all morning. In the afternoon he wanted to see Atlanta's famous Cyclorama, a huge depiction of the burning of Atlanta. Walker asked Philip Hamburger, a writer *The New Yorker* had assigned to write a report of the tour, to come along. They all got into the car and rode to the Cyclorama in a sudden torrential downpour. Toscanini, who was wearing no hat, jumped out and "almost ran up a long flight of stairs" to the ticket office.

"Oh, oh, oh!" cried a woman taking the tickets at the door. "Maestro Toscanini! We are so honored!" Toscanini nodded briskly and went to the Cyclorama, listened to a fifteen-minute lecture on the battle by a woman, somewhat reluctantly gave the lady at the door his autograph, got into the car and said, "*Molto bene.*" Most of the way back to the hotel he was silent. "Walter," he said suddenly, "what did the lecturer mean when she said 'brother fought brother'? Walter explained to him some aspects of the War Between the States. [*The New Yorker*, May 20, 1950]

He played in good halls and in bad halls, in gymnasiums, arenas, and movie houses. Wherever he played he made no compromises, made no concessions to putative provincial taste —other than playing *Dixie* in the South and *Stars and Stripes Forever* as an encore in Dallas—and required of himself and every man the utmost of dedication and exertion. Over and over again he would call rehearsals, once more to refresh and correct the programs. In Houston the heat was in the nineties, the humidity tropical. Toscanini conducted in his full-dress suit, the audience sat in shirt sleeves. During the Funeral March of the *Eroica*, at one moment his eyes clouded over, his gaze became unsteady, it seemed to the musicians that he was going to faint, prostrated by the heat. The next moment he had overcome the weakness, his body straightened out, his eyes shone, and the beat became more commanding than ever. During the intermission they took off his tailcoat and held it up to dry in front of a big ventilator.

As usual when traveling and when he was not conducting a concert or rehearsing for the next, he became informal, joked with the men, chatted with the people who crowded around him wherever the train stopped. On a free day they spent at Sun Valley, Idaho, he insisted on going up ten-thousand-foot Mount Baldy in the ski lift. The men cheered as he was towed into view; some of them had been afraid to go up in that tow. He said, "I like to try everything." They held a barbecue, the men grabbed pots, pans, kazoos, lids, and formed themselves into the "Sad Symphony Orchestra," and when they asked him to lead them in a burlesque performance of "Stars and Stripes," he answered his "Why not?" and led them. After the tour he gave each member of the orchestra a photograph of himself riding on the ski tow. He inscribed it, "Sweet remembrance of our unforgetable [sic] tour."

All the concerts but one were sold out and most could have been twice sold out. The largest audience attended in Cleveland, twelve thousand people, the second largest in the huge hall in Atlanta. Of their visit to this city Samuel Antek remembered:

As we entered the huge auditorium in the morning for rehearsal, we were greeted by the smell of horses and manure (there had been a horse show a few days before). In the center of the auditorium was a large prizefight ring, erected for the fights that were to take place that night; our own concert was to be played the next night. Workmen were milling about on the stage, building extensions, setting the scene, as it were. We all assembled on the stage for rehearsal. All the noise, hammering, and bustle stopped, of course, when Toscanini came to the stand. After a brief rehearsal, Toscanini stepped off the stand and approached Walter, his son, as the workmen reappeared and began working on the stage. At that moment a foreman of the stagehands walked past, with his hat on his head, and began to set up the railing around the podium. Toscanini stopped abruptly. His face hardened. With a flick of his stick he knocked off the workman's hat. "*Ignorante!*—take off the hat! Is a church here!" The man, struck dumb with amazement, looked about, stared at the prizefight ring, sniffed the manure-saturated air, and looked at the Old Man with perplexed terror. "Yes! *Ignorante!*" rasped the Old Man. "Where is music is a church! Off with the hat, *stupido!*"

In Washington, Truman called on Toscanini after the concert at Constitution Hall. Truman said to him: "I read about the success of your voyage. We ought next year to make a tour together: with my speeches and your music we'll have all of America on our side."

These anecdotes must not obscure the reality of the achievement: he was able to instill a love for music in thousands of people, in a few of whom that love may have remained alive after he was gone. In turn he took from the people their warmth of love, inflaming himself. He took it with thanks.

CHAPTER NINE

"THIS TIME I AM ALMOST SATISFIED"

THE evil eye must have been at work: 1951 began as a bad year for Toscanini and, as usual, troubles came not single spies. The first shock which rolled at him was NBC's decision to turn Studio 8H into a television studio. Radio had become the pale sister of the communications industry, all attention being usurped by the gaudily visible creature, though not visible as yet in the fiery and bilious colors it was later to display, Television. It demanded space, care, expenditure; and NBC's largest studio was given over to the television cameras. Sarnoff himself had lost interest in the "little black box" and turned the research resources of the company toward the large box with the milky eye. Toscanini loved 8H and had come to regard the little room next to it as the tent of his commandment and his shelter after struggle. He felt dispossessed and homeless, all the more so since Sarnoff had proposed to transfer the concerts to Manhattan Center, a shrill and cold hall which he disliked at first hearing.

A wedge was driven into the friendship of the two men. It was soon settled that the concerts would henceforth originate from Carnegie Hall, but for the remaining three years the relationship between the two men did not reassume its former ease. Toscanini never thought that Carnegie Hall was "his" hall, though the orchestra rejoiced at the transfer. There they

could hear one another better than in the dry, unresonant, un-
responsive 8H. Toscanini, however, thought differently: within
the confines of 8H he could hear every nuance of every instrument clearly, and clarity was what he strove for. Yet he accepted Carnegie Hall and there he began the 1951 season,
commemorating the fiftieth anniversary of Verdi's death with
a phenomenal performance of the *Requiem* (later to be used as
the basis for a recording. See page 285) on January 27.
Fedora Barbieri, Herva Nelli, Giuseppe di Stefano, and Cesare
Siepi were the soloists. The Verdi *Requiem* expresses the Chris-
tian view of punishment and absolution in terms of high drama.
Its central section, the *Dies Irae*, comes closer to the concept
of a Signorelli, a Masaccio, a Michelangelo—great dramatists
all—than to Fra Angelico. Toscanini once told me that when
he conducted the *Dies Irae* he envisioned Michelangelo's fresco
of the Last Judgment in the Sistine Chapel, that scene which
Milton, too, saw in his imagination:

> The aged earth aghast
> With terror of that blast
> Shall from the surface to the center shake,
> When, at the world's last session,
> The dreadful Judge in middle air shall spread
> His throne.

Michelangelo filled "the world's last session" with *terribilità:*
the angel blowing the horn, the condemned man who covers
an eye with his hand not daring to gaze at the horrors, the
"Penitent Thief," the messengers flying with the crown of
thorns, the old St. Bartholomew holding in his hand a skin
which may represent the features of the painter, and, above the
turmoil, Christ as judge. Verdi, on his part, filled the Day of
Judgment with music of *terribilità*, a summons to make the
center shake. And Toscanini made it sound as it must have
sounded in Verdi's mind. Who can forget the blasts of those
trumpets or the unison cries of the chorus, wild enough to
make the deaf hear? When has the *Recordare* Duet reached
us with so pure a plea? And who can forget the beauty of the
hushed close, with its promise for peace at last?

* * *

A second grief came: Carla was ill. She had returned to Milan at the first sign of illness, and Wanda and Wally took care of her. Carla had never felt at home in Riverdale, though she never said so, not by a single word. Now she longed to return to the city where she could easily understand the chatter of the people around her. Yet, when she was confined to her bed in the Via Durini, she longed just as much for her absent husband.

He conducted three more concerts, giving no hint of the sadness within him. Though he worked with his usual energy, all was not well, and he developed severe pains in his knee. He looked ashen and now sometimes he would walk to the podium with a limping gait, and sometimes he would hold on to the railing of the podium. The pain was becoming worse and the doctor could not diagnose the cause. He went through the fourth concert (February 17), but then canceled the rest of the season. He sat in the Villa Pauline and called himself "the old man."

Carla, whose health had been improving, suddenly took a turn for the worse. Wally phoned him; that same evening (April 6) he took a plane for Milan. The next day he was at her bedside and he held her hand. She got better almost at once. They were together once more, two old people; he sat and talked to her, and though he could hardly discuss music with her, they remembered together the years at the Scala and their voyages and their dead son and their grandchildren and his fights with Mussolini and was it not incredible that so-and-so, who had been one of Mussolini's ministers, had telephoned to him yesterday and wanted to come and pay his respects? "What did you answer, Tosca?" Carla wanted to know. "I hung up on him." He gave instructions that he was to be called whenever Carla asked for him and, since she slept fitfully, he spent many nights not going to bed but dozing in an armchair near her. He canceled four concerts in May which he had promised the BBC.

At the end of May she sank into a coma. On June 23, 1951, she died peacefully and quietly.

His sorrow, surely not unmixed with self-reproach, had about it an air of resignation. He was alone now, he said, and all he wanted to do was to die. He shut himself up in his room, sitting there in the summer heat of Milan, which can be worse than the summer heat of New York. He would not touch the piano nor listen to records nor turn on the radio. He protested that he could no longer walk; his leg hurt him fearfully. He would die a month from now, in July. No, he would live on to Verdi's age, three years more till he reached eighty-seven, three useless years. After a few weeks he began to go out in the middle of the night, choosing dark streets in the vicinity of the Via Durini. Chotzinoff had come to see him; he and Wally managed finally to get him away to his island by pretending that they could no longer endure the heat of Milan.

Would he conduct again? It seemed doubtful. He remembered a player in the NBC orchestra whom he had kept on for four years after he felt that his usefulness had ceased: he had kept him on because he knew the man had an invalid wife, and he then had arranged a decent pension for him. (All he got for that act of kindness was a nasty letter.) He, Toscanini, did not want to be "kept on."

Suddenly he was confronted with a request from La Scala. Would he make some Verdi records with the Scala Orchestra which would be sold for the benefit of the Verdi Home of Rest? La Scala, the Verdi Home, Verdi's music—he could not refuse. He would try. He would test himself. He would judge himself. He left the Isolino and in the heat of August (6, 7, and 8) he faced the orchestra. The session was kept secret and no one, except the engineers, was to be present. He chose a Suite from *I Vespri Siciliani* and the two *Traviata* Preludes. He started hesitatingly. Five minutes later, perhaps fewer than five minutes, he had become five years younger. His beat was as strong, his command as decisive, his ear as accurate as ever. He forgot the pain in his leg. He rehearsed the whole afternoon, recorded the next evening until very late, and completed the work on the third evening. By the third evening he had become ten years younger. The self-imposed banishment was broken.*

---

* Later he became dissatisfied with these recordings; they were never released commercially.

2

He returned from Italy to Riverdale in September, erect and cured. Late in October he descended, punctual to the second as ever, the thirteen steps from the green room and then up several steps to the stage of Carnegie Hall. The silence of the orchestra represented a question mark, the wildest rumors having flown about, rumors that he had become weak, forgetful, that since Carla's death he was no longer the same. A rail had been built around his podium; it would help the old man to hold on. He saw the rail, gave it one disdainful look, marched up without holding on, greeted the men, and gave the downbeat. A couple of bars later the familiar froggy voice rang out, filling the hall with fury: "Sluggards! . . . Are you sleeping? Sleep at home, not here! . . . Put something! Play with blood!" No song of praise could have been as welcome as this, the accustomed malediction. He gave eight concerts in the fall series.

He was back a month later, at the top of his form, and he remained active during the winter and spring seasons. The critics spoke of "the vigor, ardor and profundity of his interpretations—they have not diminished with the years." His eighty-fifth birthday he wished to mark by once more conducting the Ninth Symphony. How many times before had he played it! I, for one, heard his performances with the NBC in 1938, 1939, 1942, 1945, 1948, and with the New York Philharmonic in 1934 and 1936. It was always difficult for him, very difficult: "Sometimes the orchestra is no good, sometimes the chorus is no good, sometimes the soloists are no good, sometimes I am no good." This time he was not only going to try to do better, but he was going to try to record the work, a task he had not dared before. Two days after the concert, the first of the recording dates was scheduled. John Conly in the *Atlantic Monthly* wrote:

On March 31, 1952, something happened for which music lovers around the world had been waiting for a quarter century. Arturo Toscanini, 85 years and six days old,

263

walked into Carnegie Hall to put on records his incandescent interpretation of Beethoven's Ninth Symphony.

Patently he had rededicated himself all anew to the score, after 50 years' acquaintance with it. Each note sounded as if it might have been written the day before.

He had not been satisfied with the performance and he now re-rehearsed passages before the first take. It was planned to record the symphony, which lasts an hour and five minutes, in two sessions of three hours each, one on Monday, one on Tuesday. As it turned out, overtime was required, so that the total recording time amounted to nine hours. The sessions flowed relatively calmly, though a few *"Poltroni,"* "Go to the hell," "I am astonished—I thought you were an artist," "Play some place else—you don't play for me" were thrown into the stream. He recorded each movement three times on the average, but made eight takes with the soloists—until Eileen Farrell's voice gave out. During playbacks the orchestra and chorus would sit and rest, but Toscanini would listen standing, conducting all the time, and comparing what he heard coming over the loudspeaker with what he intended. In the Scherzo the tympanist did not play "savagely" enough and in the statement of the *"Freude"* melody he kept exhorting basses and celli to "Sing, sing, sing together." It reminded me of some entries in the "Conversation Books," the means by which Beethoven's interlocutors conversed with him. Beethoven's famulus, Schindler, who helped to rehearse sections of the orchestra for the first performance of the Ninth, wrote in the book:

> The recitatives for the double basses are enormously difficult. . . . They cannot execute them in tempo. You can play them with twenty [musicians] but not the way you want.
> How many double basses are to play the recitatives?
> Is it possible? All! In strict tempo that would cause no difficulty. But to play them in a singing style will cost great patience at the rehearsals. If the old Kraus were still living, one would not need to worry, because he was able to conduct twelve basses and they had to do what he wanted.

[Beethoven then proposed to explain to the double-bass players the poetic meaning of the text in order to guide their phrasing. Schindler:] "As if the words were written underneath?" [Beethoven must have replied,] "Exactly so." [Schindler:] "If necessary I will write the words into the parts so that they can learn to 'sing'."

During the mandatory half-hour intermissions, Toscanini would march up to his room, doff his jacket, fan himself, and don a terry-cloth bathrobe. But at the last intermission on Tuesday night he didn't bother but remained in the hall, passed out candy, and told stories to the members of the orchestra who crowded around him. The work was almost done, the giant symphony held fast on magnetic bands. It was as good as he could make it. Yet—at this moment he decided to make the coda of the first movement once more. It was done. He seemed content. He said: "That coda—it is like Dante," and he quoted the lines:

> *Io ritornai dalla santissim' onda*
> *Rifatto si come piante novelle*
> *Rinnovellate di novella fronda,*
> *Puro e disposto a salire alle stelle.*

> (I returned from the holy shadows
> Refreshed like new plants,
> Covered with young leaves,
> Cleansed and prepared to alight to the stars.)

He was quoting poetry—that was a good sign. Everybody, emotionally spent and physically exhausted, heaved a sign of relief and was ready to pack up. Too soon! The beginning of the last movement, that huge orchestral preparation for the choral finale, it was not huge enough, its lines not quite bold and strong enough. Would they play it just once more? "Let us try." He looked at those dog-tired men and said, simply and pleadingly, "With one more drop of blood perhaps we can come a little nearer to what Beethoven wanted." Would they try? Not once, but twice he repeated the final movement up to the entrance of the voice. He left at midnight, after nearly five hours of conducting. One had the impression that he left re-

265

luctantly and would have liked to do the whole thing over again.

The feat becomes the more amazing when one considers that, in addition to playing the weekly concerts, he held twenty recording dates that season, from October to March. In May he left for a rest at the Isolino, only to interrupt it to come back to New York in July and listen to the test pressings of the Ninth. When he heard them he said, "This time I am almost satisfied."

It was almost immediately published and in the course of several years sold about a million copies. That means, I suppose, that some four or five million people heard * what may be the most popular of all symphonies, though its moral message seems to have been put to little use by those millions. Perhaps the Ninth stands so high in popularity not only because of its music, but because of its message. At any rate, the recording became one of the milestones of the recording art. Technically that art climbed ahead, and to a new generation the sound of the Toscanini recording has become as obsolete as a kerosene lamp. What conductor, from Bernstein to Karajan to Ormandy to Solti, has not wished to show his conception of the Ninth, and to show it in sound more lifelike than was possible to achieve in 1952? Yet to many of us Toscanini's interpretation comes closer to the truth of a work in which a composer attempted to point the way toward a philosophy of communal life. One may venture to guess that Beethoven would have approved the test pressings—and to this recording one may apply a word which is too often and too carelessly used: that word is "unique."

3

In September he gave a Wagner concert in Milan, then he went to London to conduct Brahms with the Philharmonia Orchestra (September 29 and October 1). He had never conducted the Philharmonia before, though he knew the quality of the orchestra from several recordings to which he had carefully listened. It was a very fine orchestra—but could he get

* Not counting radio listeners. It was frequently played on the radio.

his ideas across to them? Would they understand him? Would they understand his English which was by now "so American"? Friends assured him that he need have no fear. Somebody there would understand him.

London displayed an enthusiasm the sincerity of which was as clear as a brook in the Highlands when the snow melts, and quite as rushing. The 3,500 tickets were gobbled up within an hour and to obtain one of the 300 standing-room places people stood for a day, the following night, and again the day of the concert. They camped before Festival Hall, while relatives and friends supplied the coffee and the sandwiches, and passers-by thought they had gone crazy. But, after all, Toscanini had not been heard in London for eleven years. Among those present at the first concert were Laurence Olivier, Vivien Leigh, and Charlie Chaplin. Walter and Wally had invited Chaplin, whom their father admired and to whom he bore a faint resemblance in his youth. (Toscanini had seen quite a number of Chaplin films, and he liked *Limelight* especially.) A festive supper at the Savoy followed the concert, at which Toscanini discussed *Othello* with Olivier, speaking of the differences between play and opera, and Chaplin mimicked Toscanini.*

A month later he was back in New York, ready for the new season of 1952–1953. He increased the number of concerts to fourteen and among the fourteen he included the second act of Gluck's *Orfeo*, an opera he had conducted at the Metropolitan at what now seemed a lifetime ago. In the first scene of the act, the Furies were as frightening as a vision by Blake; in the second scene the music sounded as paradisical as to make convincing Orfeo's exclamation, *"Che puro ciel!"* ("How pure the sky!"), and to flood the hall with the cleanest light. The pity of it was that he did not give all of the opera.

After the successful experience with the Ninth, his interest in recording grew—or his dislike of it waned—and therefore the year brought forth such things as a new *Pastoral*, Bee-

---

* Nicola Moscona, the bass, imitated Toscanini even better: he had it down pat, sighs, suffering, shouts, and all. He even managed to *look* like Toscanini when he did it. Toscanini greatly enjoyed his imitations, burst out laughing, would call friends into the room to watch Moscona, crying, "Look! Look!" and always took the caricature in good part, even when it got on the sharp side.

thoven Eighth, the *Carmen* Suite, Brahms's Second and Third, as well as once again the *Haydn Variations*, Saint-Saëns Symphony No. 3, the Strauss *Death and Transfiguration*, which caused him endless trouble (he walked out in despair at one session), three Wagner excerpts, etc. Incredulously one saw him at work, incredulously one heard him. Fourteen concerts— this octogenarian was still as eager to express himself, as keen to serve his cause, as a young Byron. How long would the oldest man in the room remain the youngest?

CHAPTER TEN

THE LAST CONCERT AND
THE LAST YEARS

═══════

T HERE is no rest for the wizard. Creative men and women, one can say almost axiomatically, keep working to the last breath. Even as they lie down on a bed from which they are never to arise, they nurse the illusion that they will be given grace to complete the incomplete and to put to new use what they have lately learned. Beethoven on his deathbed said, "I have only begun to know how to compose." Two months before he died at the age of eighty-four, Voltaire was making notes for a new edition of the French dictionary. Thomas Hardy, eighty-eight years old, was completing a collection of poems which were published posthumously under the title "Winter Words." The day before he died Wagner was sketching a few bars for an orchestral Scherzo. Bach in his last hours of consciousness dictated a chorale arrangement to his son-in-law.

Illusion lay in Toscanini's mind, though, not being a creator, that illusion, the refusal to anticipate the fall of the curtain, his belief in continuance, became diluted and was penetrated by rays of reality. I shall go on and on and become better, he thought at one moment, while in the next he realized that the time to stop was approaching. In what turned out to be his last season—1953–1954—he made plans for what he wanted to do the season after that and the season after *that*. He wished to give and record *Rigoletto* and *Trovatore* after the *Masked Ball*, to leave as full account as possible of Verdi's works.* He was thinking as well of playing with the NBC Kabalevsky's Cello Concerto and the Gershwin Piano Concerto, both of which he had recently studied, and one or two of the Rossini Overtures he had not conducted before and the Beethoven Triple Concerto, which he had not conducted for years. He was considering a Mozart cycle, including some symphonies he had never conducted, or not since his youth. He was curiously uninterested in returning to Bach. Wanda Landowska, an artist he admired but whose occasionally extravagant style of expressing herself grated on his simple manner, said to him, "*Cher Maître,* if I could but once play with you I would die happily." He answered, "*Chère Madame,* don't play with me— and live happily." As to perfecting himself, he was, as always, absolutely truthful about that. Months after he approved the recording of the Ninth, he said: "You know, I still don't understand the First Movement."

Yet while he was spinning these ambitions for the future, a contrary voice within him told him "enough." He spoke of it to Walter, to Anita Colombo, and to Wilfred Pelletier. They replied in comforting words which they but half-believed. He knew that as yet no shadow had fallen on his clear memory. When he touched his arm it was still as firm as stone. He had acquired the tiniest of paunches, in spite of his eating so little, but his legs, which used to bother him, were again youthful enough for him to run and stamp in anger. He held the score he was reading even closer to his eyes than before, and used his eyeglasses more frequently. When somebody told him, "There's a pretty woman," out came those glasses—he was still interested. When he was in a bad humor he "could not see a thing." He could hear everything, even if one of the canaries in Riverdale was twittering in a different sequence. At night he slept less than ever—"I have no time for sleep, I am eighty-seven"—but now he would nap more often in his chair for five, ten minutes at a time and Walter would turn off the telephone.

* He hoped, too, to inaugurate the new "Piccola Scala" with a performance of *Falstaff,* or to perform it again in Busseto.

That some realization of finality grew within him, much as he tried to suppress it, is indicated by his choices of music for the 1953–1954 season. Other than the *Masked Ball*, by which he would take up the sequence of Verdi operas, what he programmed was by nature of a review, a retrospective anthology of music he had played in these series of concerts. The repertoire seems like an aggregation of large stars, shining with a will before a cloud covers them.

November 22, 1953	Brahms: "Tragic" Overture R. Strauss: *Don Quixote* (Frank Miller, cellist, and Carlton Cooley, viola soloist)
November 29	Wagner: Prelude to Act III of *Tannhäuser* Berlioz: *Harold in Italy* (Carlton Cooley, viola soloist)
December 6	Beethoven: *Coriolanus* Overture Beethoven: *Eroica*
December 13	César Franck: *Les Eolides* Weber-Berlioz: *Invitation to the Dance* Mendelssohn: "Reformation" Symphony
January 17 and 24, 1954	Verdi: *A Masked Ball* (Nelli, Turner, Haskins, Peerce, Merrill) (An extra half hour was added to the January 24 concert)
February 28	Mendelssohn: "Italian" Symphony R. Strauss: *Don Juan* Weber: Overture to *Oberon*
March 7	Beethoven: Leonore Overture No. 2 Pastoral Symphony
March 14	Vivaldi: Concerto Grosso in D for strings Boito: Prologue in Heaven to *Mefistofele* (Nicola Moscona and The Columbus Boychoir)

A charming incident occurred after the *Mefistofele*. As the cheering audience recalled Toscanini again and again, he shared the applause with the orchestra, Moscona, and the two choral directors. The audience continued to cheer as Toscanini started for the wings, he having given the signal for everybody to leave. He had to come out again, just as the boys of the choir were marching off. Toscanini took hold of a boy, nine year-old Bruce Renshaw, took him by the hand, said, "Come with me," and led the child to the front of the stage, where Bruce bowed decorously. What happened to Bruce Renshaw after his moment of glory I do not know.

March 21	Rossini: Overture to *The Barber of Seville* Tchaikovsky: *Pathétique*
April 4 (An extra fifteeen minutes was added to the concert)	Wagner: Prelude to Act I of *Lohengrin* Forest Murmurs from *Siegfried* Dawn and Siegfried's Rhine Journey from *Die Götterdämmerung* Overture and Bacchanale from *Tannhäuser* Prelude to Act I, *Die Meistersinger*

German, French, Italian, Russian music, of thirteen composers, in eleven concerts: indeed, a survey of sorts.

Anyone sitting at home and listening to the first nine of these concerts would have testified that they were led by a musician at his very noon of talent, and even those privileged to sit in Carnegie Hall would have sworn that the man up there had defied augury and found an unending path of glory. Some of these performances not only were Toscanini performances, they were Toscanini performances suffused with new mellowness and pliancy, "as lissome as a hazel wand," while others sounded with prouder power than ever, and still others made one smile with happiness. To the first belong the *Don Quixote* and the *Harold in Italy*, to the second the *Eroica* and the Leonore No. 2, to the third, the *Italian Symphony* and the *Invitation to the Dance*. In Verdi's *Un Ballo in Maschera* he showed that the exceptional interpreter makes the most of the strong points of a work while sufficiently buttressing the weak points to make the structure stand. *Ballo* contains great music as well as music in which Verdi, hampered by an uneven libretto, borrows his own melodramatic early style. In Act I, Scene 2, we visit the lair of Ulrica, an old-fashioned operatic sorceress whose omniscience we doubt and whose exaltation we find it hard to accept. Nor is the episode with the sailor Silvano believable. After the heartbreakingly beautiful appeal of Amelia in the Trio and the mocking Quintet (*È scherzo od è follia*), the scene ends with a simplistic chorus. But there is not

272

a bar in the second act of the midnight visit to the gibbet and the passionate love duet, nor is there any moment of the two scenes of the third act, which cannot be placed on the highest plane of dramatic music. Toscanini presented the whole work with such all-inclusive conviction that some critics believe *Ballo* to be "his finest operatic achievement." But how can one use superlatives when one speaks of repeated and equivalent miracles? All one needs to do is to observe how the second act is shaped from its awesome beginning to the end when orchestra, chorus, conspirators, and the three principals combine to force with ironic inevitability their own ordained doom, all one needs to do is to follow this descent as Toscanini played it, to realize that one will not hear anything like it again.

He had been considering *Ballo* for several years. But just before the first rehearsal he called Chotzinoff and asked him to cancel all arrangements. He had awakened that morning, he said, and could no longer remember the words of the opera. He remembered the music, all right, but the words—and how could he face the artists not knowing the words by heart? With a heavy heart Chotzinoff set out to make the necessary re-arrangements. The next morning Toscanini phoned again. "Just think," he said, "I get up today, and I remember *all* the words. . . . Call the rehearsal."

He was pleased with the performance, entertained the artists at dinner afterwards, soared in discussions and stories, and didn't want to go home. He was equally ebullient in the three subsequent concerts. His heart beat high.

Two months after *Ballo* Toscanini did show the first signs of weakness. True, a mistake had occurred on November 22 in the *Don Quixote*, but it was a trifling error, easily condoned, especially in so complex a tangle as the Strauss score. The broadcast of March 21 was something else, a nerveless performance of the *Pathétique*, lacking pressure in the first movement, drive in the march. It was an old man's *Pathétique*. It caused those of us who loved him to wonder and to grieve. Was this the beginning of the end? Was it a passing weakness? What was happening? What had happened?

It is difficult to find the exact truth, as it consists of several truths, depending on who sees and tells them. The first and indubitable truth is that Sarnoff had become disenchanted. As most creative men, Sarnoff was passionate. And as most passionate men, he would turn *very* cold, passion spent. As I stated, from about 1949 on he concentrated his desire and energy on the development of television; to him that had become the cause for crusade. Music had little use for television, or rather vice versa. Nothing particularly worth seeing happens at a concert, and even when Toscanini was there one could not constantly concentrate the camera on that wonderful face. Nor could one subject the old man with the poor eyes to the glare of television lights. (Television then required intense lighting, which created punishing heat.) The radio concerts, Sarnoff thought, had become less useful in proportion to radio's lesser role, and now he felt the expense of the NBC Symphony to have become burdensome. Even cost-accounting is subject to emotional variance; the bills for the musicians, extra rehearsals, recordings made but not approved (at costs which rose from about $8,000 an LP to about $15,000), additional personnel, etc., now seemed excessive, or were used by the executives of NBC responsible for profits to *show* that they were excessive. Sarnoff began to lend an ear to the men who counseled, "Let's stop," the company was not getting its money's worth.

But was not the company making profits from the sale of the Toscanini recordings? To outsiders it seemed so, yet on closer analysis the matter does not appear that certain.

Statements such as those made by B. H. Haggin and others reveal a lack of knowledge of business facts. Haggin wrote in *The Toscanini Musicians Knew*, "Actually, moreover, the cost of the NBC Symphony was not money spent on a public service program, but money spent to acquire for NBC and RCA the prestige of Toscanini's name, which NBC profited by in its sale of time and programs to advertiser (as CBS profited by the prestige of the New York Philharmonic), and which RCA profited by in its sale of radios, phonographs, and records, including those Toscanini made with the NBC Symphony. It was, in other words, an investment which right from the start brought a financial return even with the broadcasts unsponsored."

It is certainly true that NBC through Toscanini earned

that rather vague benefit called "prestige." ("Prestige" is often used as a business term for a venture which loses money.) Nor would it have been intrinsically disgraceful had they made money from the Toscanini association. Why should an artistic enterprise not be a commercially successful one as well? But they didn't, and it wasn't. While the broadcasts were ultimately aided by such sponsorship as Socony's—at a special low price —NBC was not helped in the least "in its sale of time and programs to advertisers." Advertisers, trying to reach the largest possible radio-audience at the lowest possible cost, couldn't have cared less about Toscanini or about the relatively small audiences his concerts attracted, "small" that is in terms of mass communication.

RCA did not sell its "radios, phonographs" because a great artist was linked to NBC. The sale, or lack of sale, of radios and phonographs depended on quality, price, service, styling, merchandising methods, etc.

As to RCA Victor records, yes, Toscanini records sold in quantity to that relatively small part of the public (5 to 7 percent) which buys good music. A consumer research survey in the fifties showed the ten favorite "classical compositions" to have been, in order named:

> Beethoven: Symphony No. 9
> Beethoven: Symphony No. 5
> Gershwin: *Rhapsody in Blue*
> J. Strauss: Waltzes
> Rachmaninoff: Piano Concerto No. 2
> Beethoven: Symphony No. 6
> Tchaikovsky: Symphony No. 6
> Beethoven: "Moonlight" Sonata
> Tchaikovsky: Piano Concerto No. 1
> Tchaikovsky: "Nutcracker" Suite

The Toscanini recordings were the best-sellers of some of this music, about thirty million dollars' worth (wholesale price) having been sold by the end of the fifties. Their recording cost however had to be high, and if the costs of the 1950 tour as well as those of maintaining the orchestra were to be set against the income, the balance would show an inconsiderable profit, more probably an actual loss. Here again variance is possible: it depends how much "overhead" was charged against the Toscanini records. The RCA Victor Record Division did make good profits in the fifties. It could well afford and there was no question that it gladly did afford Toscanini; the money came from pop records and from such artists as Eddie Fisher, Mario Lanza, Perry Como, and the Ames Brothers.

The point is that as radio weakened and the public turned to television, NBC-RCA foresaw that it could no longer underwrite the cost of a symphony orchestra *without* a Toscanini, that cost being in the neighborhood of a million dollars a year. A firm publicly owned is not an idealistic institution and its management is responsible for making profits for its stockholders. Unfortunately, for the arts!

This is not said in defense of "The Establishment." It is said to fix the facts. The NBC Symphony *was* a public-service gesture, however personal a motive prompted its inception. Sarnoff later attempted another public-service program with the "NBC Television Opera," which, though it brought forward several fine artists, such as Leontyne Price, was a failure with the public.

Yet that does not mean that Sarnoff was ready to decide to stop, that he had decided to "dismiss" Toscanini. He was too sensitive to public reaction to act drastically in a situation where he could be made to appear as a money-grubbing Philistine. He might secretly have wished for the end, but he wanted the decision to come from Toscanini, not from him. So Sarnoff pressed him for a decision, instead of waiting patiently as he had done in the past, when Toscanini had sent him those letters of resignation which turned out to mean nothing. One version has it that Sarnoff actually had a contract prepared for the following season, took it to Riverdale, was met at the door by Walter, who said that he feared for his father's health and that under no circumstances would he let his father sign another contract, and that Sarnoff turned away and then decided to disband the orchestra. I doubt this version: it is not likely that Sarnoff would have come to Riverdale without first making sure that the visit would prove useful, or that Walter would have assumed such a responsibility. I believe what happened was that Sarnoff kept asking, "Where do we stand?," kept asking it fretfully, and that, responding to Sarnoff's obvious impatience, Toscanini finally gave him the not unexpected negative answer. Thereupon Sarnoff had a letter of resignation prepared for Toscanini to sign, and wrote one which would serve as his reply to Toscanini. Two indications are significant: first that Toscanini this time did *not* write a letter of resignation himself, but that the letter was written for him, and second, that he kept the letter for several weeks, without being able to bring himself to sign it. This is the letter—it does not sound much like Toscanini's style:

March 25, 1954

My very dear David:
At this season of the year seventeen years ago you sent me an invitation to become the Musical Director of an orchestra to be created especially for me for the purpose of broadcasting symphonic music throughout the United States.
You will remember how reluctant I was to accept your invitation because I felt at that time that I was too old to start a new venture. However, you persuaded me and all of my doubts were dispelled as soon as I began rehearsing for the first broadcast of Christmas night in 1937 with the group of fine musicians whom you had chosen.
Year after year it has been a joy for me to know that the music played by the NBC Symphony Orchestra has been acclaimed by the vast radio audiences all over the United States and abroad.
And now the sad time has come when I must reluctantly lay aside my baton and say goodbye to my orchestra, and in leaving I want you to know that I shall carry with me rich memories of these years of music making and heartfelt gratitude to you and the National Broadcasting Company for having made them possible.
I know that I can rely on you to express to everyone at the

National Broadcasting Company who has worked with me all these years my cordial and sincere thanks.

Your friend,
Arturo Toscanini

Sarnoff's reply sounds like Sarnoff. He did write it himself:

March 29, 1954

Dear Maestro:

Your letter, significantly written on your Birthday, touched me deeply. I realize that after more than sixty-five years of absolute dedication to the art of music you have fully earned the right to lay down your baton. Yet I am saddened, along with millions of people in America, indeed all over the civilized world, at the thought that we shall no longer be privileged to look forward to your broadcasts and concerts which for so many years ennobled our lives. That you have made your decision at a time that finds you at the very height of your artistic powers only adds poignancy to our deprivation.

As you know, my own life has been chiefly devoted to the development of instruments of communication. But, however important these may be, they are at best only instrumentalities. Their function is only to transmit. In the final analysis they will be judged by *what* they transmit.

For the last seventeen years radio, television and the phonograph have done their best to transmit with the utmost fidelity your self-effacing, incomparable re-creations of the great music of the past and present. And those of us who have striven to perfect these instruments feel in the highest degree rewarded for our labors. Happily, these instruments have recorded and preserved for us, and for posterity, the great music you have interpreted so faithfully and magnificently.

During these seventeen years of our intimate and happy association, I have learned from you much that is as vital in industry as it is in music. Your attitude towards your art and especially that human instrument—the orchestra —which realized your musical ideals, became an inspiration to me from the very first time I watched you at work.

You proved so convincingly that in striving to attain
perfection, the leader who seeks to obtain the maximum
from those he leads, must demand the utmost not only
from them but also from himself.

I know, dear Maestro, you will carry with you the love
and gratitude of your many friends and the great multi-
tude, unknown to you, whose lives you have enriched.

May God bless you and keep you.

Your friend,
David Sarnoff

Both these letters lay on Toscanini's desk at the time of the
broadcast of the *Pathétique*. Is the conjecture too tenuous that
here lay the cause of his weakness, the origin of his uncertainty, the source of his disturbance?

Some time after the *Pathétique*, Toscanini jumped up in
the middle of lunch, went to his room, and signed. The die had
been cast. He felt in equal measure that his resignation was
wanted—and that it was apt and just for him to tender it. The
time had come to lower the baton. Yet, as his mind came to the
conclusion, regret filled his heart. How difficult it is for any
artist to set "finis" to his work, to write the final full-stop! In
a way, it is like writing the order for your own exile. The dis-
harmony within him waxed and waned from hour to hour, and
it was in this jarring state that he came to the rehearsal of
what was to be the final concert of the season, the all-Wagner
program.

Of this tragic last concert we have the accounts of four
witnesses, Chotzinoff, Haggin, Vincent Sheehan, and Irving
Kolodin.* Their accounts differ, quite in the tradition of the
experiment in which different observers see the same event and
afterwards relate markedly different versions of it. I, too, was
present at the rehearsals and the concert and can make a fifth
witness.

At the first rehearsal on Thursday afternoon Toscanini began with the *Lohengrin* Prelude, but stopped after a few bars.
There was confusion in the orchestra because he had decided to
conduct two beats to a measure instead of the customary four,

---

* Of these accounts I believe Irving Kolodin's to be the most accurate.

trying thereby to obtain a higher level of sustained solemnity. Presently he returned to the former way of conducting the piece. He told the violins not to play the opening chords with vibrato; that he said would be appropriate for the *Inferno* but not for the *Paradiso*. He got what he wanted, a lofty simplicity, and led the piece to the end without further incident. The *Meistersinger* Prelude, however, sounded tame and lacked that marvelous contrast between gay pageantry and intimate sweetness which one was used to hear. Toscanini did nothing about this. He proceeded to the "Forest Murmurs" and the *Götterdämmerung* selections, which went fine, though he stopped several times for corrections.

On Friday morning he rehearsed the Overture and Bacchanale from *Tannhäuser*, as well as the "Rhine Journey" once again, and nothing was lacking, not power, nor excitement, nor seductiveness in the Bacchanale. It was a normal and satisfactory working session. Then came the dress rehearsal Saturday 1:00 P.M. The demand for tickets for the Wagner concert had been so overwhelming that NBC asked Toscanini if, just this time, he would allow an audience to be present in Carnegie Hall for the last rehearsal. Toscanini acquiesced—to everybody's surprise—and therefore the orchestra floor of Carnegie Hall and some of the loges were filled with people, eager and expectant. They had been told that this *was* a rehearsal and asked not to applaud. The *Lohengrin* Prelude was played without a stop, beautifully but I believe not as beautifully as on Thursday. The "Forest Murmurs" followed with all enchantment intact. No corrections. Then the *Götterdämmerung* began. At the point where Siegfried's horn call (played backstage) is heard solo for the last time, the tympanist entered too soon—or so it seemed to Toscanini—his anger and irritation rammed the wall of restraint with which he had surrounded himself in the presence of the audience, and the breach was filled with cries of *"Vergogna!"* He asked that the passage be repeated; some confusion arose as to the point at which they were to start again, further irritating Toscanini. Frank Miller, the first cellist, helped to straighten the matter out, they began again, the mistake was corrected, if mistake it was, and Toscanini exclaimed, "Finally!" Yet something else was gnawing at Toscanini's mind—he muttered "the last rehearsal," and seemed much perturbed—and suddenly, without the slightest warning, he stopped conducting, left the podium, and disappeared. A dead pause which seemed endless followed. Then the audience was told over the loudspeaker that the public portion of the rehearsal was concluded. Puzzled, they slowly left the hall while the orchestra sat waiting. After another pause the orchestra was told that they were to rehearse no more. Consequently the *Tannhäuser* selection was *not* reviewed in a dress rehearsal. And only part of the *Götterdämmerung* excerpt was rehearsed. In short, the final program was not reviewed in its entirety; that did not necessarily signal trouble, the orchestra being quite familiar with Toscanini's interpretation of these twice-told tales.

On Saturday night and Sunday morning musical New York was buzzing with rumors. There was doubt that he would conduct the final broadcast. It was known that Cia, Walter's wife, of whom he was very fond, had recently suffered a heart attack, a severe one, and that she was critically ill. She did die a few weeks later. Erich Leinsdorf had been asked to stand by; he could have taken over, knowing the Wagner repertoire by heart.

The audience assembled for the Sunday broadcast scheduled to begin at 6:30 P.M. There was Toscanini, walking toward the podium with the firm step and the look of concentration familiar to all in the hall. He nodded quickly and gave the sign for the *Lohengrin* Prelude. He went through it and the following numbers without incident, the performances being inferior only if compared to his own standards. The *Götterdämmerung* entrance was correct. Then came the *Tannhäuser* Overture, to which he gave the usual superbly judged dynamics as well as rhythmic life. But suddenly in the frenzied Bacchanale he seemed no longer in communication with the music. It broke away from him, as a rock, already weakened, is broken away by the impact of the next wave and is forced to bump crazily in the wash. The beat of his right arm became frail, he failed to give cues, and at one moment he pinched his eyes with the fingers of his left hand, like a man who is desperately searching for a lost thought. The orchestra kept on playing, knowing the

281

piece well. They arrived at the place where, after the gyrating tumult, the sirens sing (in the opera) their invitation to "approach the strand." In the concert version the sirens' song is played by a group of strings, and Toscanini always had the strings of the last desks play the passage. The harp plays an accompanying figure. At this point (the ninth bar after Letter 13 in the orchestral score), a relatively easy playing problem, the strings could not coordinate with the harp. The incredible happened: Toscanini gave up, he stopped conducting. The performance fell apart. Frank Miller quickly got up and tried to conduct. But the break-down lasted only thirteen bars, that is, twenty-eight seconds (from 7:24:10 to 7:24:38). Then (at two bars after, Letter 14) Toscanini resumed, seeming to emerge from a trance, and led the piece to the end. There was applause, and almost at once Toscanini began the *Meistersinger* Prelude. Before the final stately chords had sounded to the end, he left the podium, the baton dropped from his hand, a musician picked it up and handed it back to him, he took it indifferently and disappeared; and though the audience clamored for him, he did not show himself again. Such was the dolorous finish of seventeen joyful years.

When the breakdown occurred, Chotzinoff and Cantelli, who were in the control booth in Carnegie Hall, thought that what they had feared as the worst possibility—an enduring and perhaps final incapacity of Toscanini—had come to pass. They were prepared with a stand-by program, ready on an NBC turntable. They cut off the Carnegie Hall performance, Ben Grauer, the announcer of the broadcasts, said that "technical difficulties" had necessitated a temporary interruption, and the sounds of a Toscanini recording of Brahms's First Symphony went out to the radio audience, without an announcement of what it was or from where it came. Almost at once the men in the booth realized their mistake and switched back to Carnegie Hall. The rest of the concert, from the end of the Bacchanale through the *Meistersinger*, was broadcast. Obviously, in the nervous excitement of the moment, Cantelli and Chotzinoff had lost their heads and made a bad matter worse. Who can blame them, seeing their friend in such stress? But had they not drawn attention to Toscanini's twenty-eight-second failure, few in the hall, and certainly few of the radio audience, might have noticed.

When the journalists entered Carnegie Hall for the last concert, they were given reprints of the two letters, Sarnoff's and Toscanini's, informing them of the end. Up to then it was all kept secret. Undoubtedly Toscanini knew, as he stood there on the stage, that his artistic demise had been proclaimed that very hour, and it is reasonable to assume that this contributed to his malaise. The whole matter was handled with consummate stupidity. Even if it was necessary to come to a decision about the orchestra for the following season as early as March, there was no reason why a decision had to be publicly announced that early, no reason why the last concert of the season should have been officially stamped as the end. Anybody sensitive to Toscanini's feelings could have predicted the pain he would suffer. Why could he not have been allowed to finish the season and then, some time afterward, the announcement be released? What compelled such wanton haste?

Toscanini, incited by a meddling entourage, vented his anger on Chotzinoff. He would no longer see him or speak to him. The interruption of the broadcast had been his fault. Playing the Brahms had been his fault. Giving the news to the journalists was his fault. *Everything* was his fault, including the temporary lapse by Toscanini and the very fact that Toscanini was growing old. This was cruel and unjust punishment meted out to a man who had been devoted to him for more than twenty years. It signified the artist's revenge which strikes most determinedly and most swiftly when the revenger is in the wrong. It darkened Chotzinoff's life. To him the light which emanated from Toscanini was as "constant as the northern star,/Of whose true-fix'd and resting quality/There is no fellow in the firmament." Long before Sarnoff had invited Chotzinoff to come to NBC, when he was music critic of the New York *World*, he had expressed his admiration and declared that Toscanini had "no fellow in the firmament." Now, for him, that star was extinguished.

A few weeks passed in silence. Nothing was heard from Riverdale. Suddenly Toscanini, having listened to the off-the-air transcriptions of the *Masked Ball* broadcasts, decided that they could be released as recordings. But he wanted to improve the love duet, which seemed to him insufficiently impassioned. At the same time, he wanted to make some corrections of *Aida.* Nobody expected it, nobody at first could believe it—but early in June the notice went out to orchestra and singers of a recording session.

He appeared, proud and erect, mounting the podium like a king who had hidden his royal raiments under a black tunic. Neither doubt nor hesitation nor weakness was in him as he led Nelli and Peerce to enact once more their nocturnal scene, as he guided them to that passage, hushed and simple, when Amelia confesses, "*Ebben . . . si . . . t'amo*" and Riccardo, overcome, answers, "*M'ami, Amelia.*" For twice three hours, in two sessions, Toscanini stood there, working away, seemingly untouched by age, as he made Verdi's music sound untouched by age, with a beauty that seemed new even to us and which was, alas, only partially captured by the tape. When we, who were all deeply moved, gathered in the interval, a violinist said to me, "Has the son of a bitch made a pact with the devil?" He said it with love in his voice.

At the time, the chief engineer of the Record Division was a man named Al Pulley. He seemed to have stepped from a Grant Wood painting, gaunt and taciturn and totally unemotional. He had in the exercise of his task heard tons of music, good and bad, without taking the slightest interest in music as music. What he cared about was high and low frequencies, reverberation time, distortion, compensation, and the other electronic tricks. He didn't care much for artists, either, thinking them unreliable and presumptuous creatures. He was standing by the tape machine in the recording room, and once during the second session I happened to turn to look at him. Tears were running down his cheeks.

That was Toscanini's last "concert."

2

Fortunately a task remained for him to do, the examination of many recordings, both those made in the studio and those which were documents of performances. To the latter group belonged the Verdi *Requiem*, which RCA was eager to add to the Toscanini catalogue. Toscanini had returned to Milan in July, 1954, and one of the RCA engineers, Richard Gardner, traveled from New York to Milan carrying ninety pounds of tape, which contained all the rehearsals as well as four differently treated versions of the 1951 performance. When Gardner called at the Via Durini, an old, old man met him. Toscanini's face was sunken, he walked with effort, barely lifting his feet from the floor. He returned Gardner's greeting in a small voice, with a sigh, but he was willing to listen to the tape, though he said, "I don't think we can rescue it. *Ma*, let us see."

Gardner, as well as RCA's other technical personnel, had learned long ago how to judge Toscanini's reaction when he listened. The first few bars were the most important: during those they could divine the almost imperceptible signs of Toscanini's pleasure or dissatisfaction. A slight, slow, sidewise motion of the head—it meant No! If he sat motionless, that meant no opinion as yet. If his right hand began to move ever so little but rhythmically—hopeful. The hopeful sign became affirmed when both hands started to move. If he then began to conduct in earnest, bringing the instruments in on cue, singing with them, glancing at the players who were not there—that meant Yes, he heard something worth considering.

Usually he would give oral approvals by a single word, *Bene*. When he rejected a recording he gave a detailed and careful explanation of his reasons. He did not want to scrap the recording cost capriciously.

Gardner played what he thought the best of the four versions which had been prepared in New York. No, said the old man, it was not clear. That was not what the orchestra played. It was harsh, crude. Gardner then played another version. Worse! Perhaps there was too much artificial reverberation? he asked. Toscanini's mien indicated that he hadn't the slightest idea what Gardner was talking about. He was almost ready to give in and retire sadly. On the spur of the moment Gardner decided to throw away all the doctored tapes and to play the original transcript, just as it had come over the line from Carnegie Hall. Toscanini listened, at first impatiently, then sinking back in his chair and following with close concentration. He listened to the end of the reel. "Well," he said, his voice taking on strength, "it is far from perfect, but it is not bad." Would he listen to the rest of it tomorrow? He would.

He listened again the next day. Gardner reported:

> He listened intently throughout, indicating nothing until we had finished, when he remarked sadly that he did not see how he could give an approval. There was too much wrong with it, musically speaking. I told him that I had with me complete rehearsal tapes and that perhaps a substitution here and there might save the recording as a whole. This seemed to interest him somewhat. But he really *wanted* to go to work only after I had played for him parts of the Requiem by other artists. I felt that the expressions of amazement, anger, and contempt which swept over his face while he listened to the other recordings were indications of a dawning realization that he had an obligation to discharge to his old friend Verdi. . . .
>
> We went to work in earnest. There was not a note, not a phrase of the broadcast or any of the rehearsals that was not scrutinized many, many times. We weighed and balanced; we compared and discussed; we argued the relative merits of mechanical versus musical excellence of each portion of the Requiem. Our work was concentrated, consecrated, and often lasted far into the night. . . . Progress was slow. We went through the Requiem phrase by phrase. And then we did it again. And again. Rehearsals and broadcast. Again. [*High Fidelity*, April, 1956]

When he finally expressed "a reluctant satisfaction"—he approved the test pressing by writing "Viva Verdi" instead of the customary "OK"—he at once seemed to become well again. He opened the doors, invited friends to come, they came, champagne was served, and Toscanini touched the glass of each guest in a toast. "It almost seemed that he would dance if given the opportunity."

The stitched-together product turned out to be far from perfect; yet if we compare it today to other recordings, better sounding and with better soloists, we can feel that the imperfect representation comes closer to Verdi as he lived and breathed and thought.

3

After approving the *Requiem*, his zest for living and his curiosity once more returned. He took the liveliest interest in the fortunes of La Scala, conferred with Ghiringhelli, and he still hoped to inaugurate the little theater with *Falstaff*, to be staged by Luchino Visconti. "Do something new and fresh," he said to Visconti. After many years of not being on speaking terms with De Sabata, he decided to let bygones be bygones and went to the rehearsals De Sabata was conducting a revival of Spontini's opera *La Vestale*.

The NBC Orchestra "refused to die." Bravely they formed themselves into "The Symphony of the Air," a cooperative enterprise. They cabled Toscanini and asked him to come and conduct. Regretfully he refused. On October 27, 1954, they gave a concert at Carnegie Hall. The conductor's podium was empty. They played works they had performed with him, the concertmaster giving the tempo indications. After that they gave a series of concerts with various conductors, but all too soon the project fell apart, the best men went on to other posts, the public remained indifferent, the great NBC Symphony was no more.

Toscanini's eyes were still good enough for him to peruse scores and read books. There exists a snapshot of him, studying once again and with a smile of pleasure, the manuscript of *Falstaff*. He reread some of Wagner's prose writings, Manzoni's *I Promessi Sposi*, the poetry of Leopardi, and he read a few new books, including Carlo Levi's *Christ Stopped at Eboli*. But after a while the eyes refused to serve and reading became difficult. That was a terrible deprivation.

In February, 1955, he once more left Milan for Riverdale, partly because the Via Durini dwelling, being in the center of the city, was too accessible to the many who wanted to see him and he could not there find peace, partly because he wished to work on several as yet unreviewed recordings and that work could more easily be accomplished in Riverdale, with the machinery handy. Day after day he lived with these testimonies of his work, going back to the days of the New York Philharmonic and going forward to the *Missa Solemnis* of 1953 and the "Italian" Symphony of 1954.

In that last year of his life he was almost blind. It tore at your heart to see him try to take up a forkful of food from his plate and not be able to find it. He would refuse all help. He had a horror of being an invalid, he felt ashamed of confessing to feebleness. He would still walk down the staircase, unaided, slowly, step by step, counting the steps. One could sense that he was watching himself for the signs of dissolution. Could he still find his way to the chair in the living room? Could he still hear the chirping of the birds? There was nothing wrong with that miraculous ear. Arms and legs had aged faster than the ear. Walter had got a carpenter secretly to bore a hole in the door of the bathroom through which his father could be observed. If anything had happened to him there, he would not have called for help. Once he was so weak that he couldn't get out of the bathtub; Walter went in on some pretense and helped him.

Musicians from the NBC would come to visit him and he welcomed them. Three months before his death four of them came for dinner; after dinner they began to play the Second Rasoumovsky Quartet for him. He listened quietly. Suddenly he arose from his chair, went toward the sound, and began to show them his idea of tempo and expression of that composition which he knew as profoundly as he knew a Beethoven symphony. For the last time he conducted.

In July, 1955, he suffered a mild heart attack. He recovered. At Christmas, 1956, his heart gave another warning. But he still went about and there was a party in Riverdale on New Year's Eve at which he appeared to be more cheerful than he had been for weeks. His grandchildren were there, including Emanuela, Wally's daughter, whom he liked particularly because he recollected how pretty she was. He stayed up very late. The next night he suffered a hemorrhage, and lived on. A few nights later he had a second hemorrhage, and lived on. It took nine attacks to fell him. He lay in bed, unconscious or semiconscious, for two weeks. During the night of the fifteenth of January he awoke and sang a snatch from *Aida*. It was the return to youth, to the work he had conducted when he was nineteen years old. In the morning he was dead.

He died quietly, without pain, at 8:40 A.M., Wednesday, January 16, 1957, at the age of eighty-nine. He reached the age of Michelangelo. His wish to live as long as Verdi had been exceeded by more than a year.

At 10:07 A.M. most radio programs in the United States were interrupted with the announcement:

Arturo Toscanini, one of the immortals of our times, died this morning in his villa in Riverdale near New York.

That afternoon and evening the radio stations played his records; television stations hastily arranged commemorative programs. The newspapers all over the world carried the news on their front pages on January 17. The *New York Times* published tributes from Eisenhower, Mitropoulos, Ormandy, Monteux, Melchior, Bernstein—"The world of music will never be the same"—Lehmann, and dozens of others. The Scala was closed for the night. At the Metropolitan Opera, Mitropoulos played the Prelude to the last act of *Traviata;* the audience stood. At the Philharmonic, Bernstein conducted a memorial concert.

On Friday the coffin was on view at Campbell's Funeral Parlor. It was a bitter cold day. By 8:00 A.M., long before Campbell's opened, one hundred people had formed a line on the street, waiting to get in. By the time Campbell's closed its doors that day, five thousand had passed the bier.

The funeral service was held on Saturday at 10:00 A.M. Thirty-five hundred people crowded into St. Patrick's Cathedral. The weather had become a little milder, but the church was cold, and cold, formal, and frozen were the obsequies offered to that hot-blooded man. Cardinal Spellman officiated, and the words of the High Mass spread and blurred and lost themselves in the cavernous spaces of the church and could not be understood. The music was by Lorenzo Perosi, who had been the director of the Pontifical Choir of the Sistine Chapel and one of Toscanini's friends. It was weak music, played on an organ, weakly. The fact that the soul of Toscanini did not

289

reappear then and there in the form of an angry lion would indicate that there is not much to metempsychosis.

A month later the body was flown to Milan. The coffin was displayed in the Scala, while thirty thousand people paid homage to a compatriot who had told them, not so many years ago, that their *"Italia"* was *"tradita."* At a signal, the crowd fell silent and De Sabata and the Scala Orchestra played the *Eroica* Funeral March; after the last note had sounded, a long procession made its way to the Via Durini. People threw violets while a phonograph played the Beethoven March once again; this time it was a Toscanini recording. Then followed a ceremony at the Duomo, where the Scala chorus sang the finale of Verdi's *Requiem.* Once more the procession re-formed to proceed to the cemetery, where the Scala choristers joined the young voices of the Conservatory to sing the hymn he had so often conducted, and once after Verdi's death, the *"Va, pensiero sull' ali dorate."* Then, at last, he was laid in the earth.

4

Of the hundreds of summarizing tributes offered posthumously, perhaps the most eloquent was one by Ernest Newman which appeared in the London *Sunday Times* on January 27, 1957, under the title "Toscanini's Quest for Perfection":

> . . . Toscanini, though rarely satisfied with either himself or anyone else, must have had some sort of private scale of values, as is suggested by a not generally known but authentic anecdote concerning him.
>
> He had conducted (in America) one of the great concertos, in which an eminent instrumentalist—let us call him X—had played the solo part. The latter felt that Toscanini's inspired reading of the work had made him play better than he had ever done before or could hope to do again. But after the concert Toscanini was sunk in his customary gloom. It was a long time before he would open his mouth, and when he did it was only to say despondently, "We are not much good, you and I, X." The latter was too flabbergasted to reply. There was another long

silence; and when at last Toscanini spoke again it was only to say, "But perhaps some of the others are worse."

This, I fancy, was about as far as he was ever able to get in the way of self-approval. He sought after perfection not for his own glory but for that of the work and the composer. With each of these he tried to enter into the closest communion, and it was his desire to do this that accounted even for the virtues in his conducting that seemed on the surface to be mainly technical, professional.

The admirable clarity of his orchestral texture in complex operatic scores was not a matter of mere professional expertise; it sprang from a profound understanding of what the composer had had in his mind not merely musically but psychologically and dramatically, when he put those particular complexes of notes on paper. And this piercing insight into the composer's intentions had been the product of the complete memorising of every detail of the score and incessant brooding upon the work as a totality.

For me the outstanding feature of his performances of great works was always the impression it gave me that I was hearing the work as the composer must have heard it in the solitude and silence of his own soul. Let me, however, guard against a possible misunderstanding here. There is no such thing as a one-and-only "interpretation" of any musical masterpiece. At its lowest, but still respectable, level, musical performance is simply photography, and there can be heights of excellence and depths of badness even in that. On the higher intellectual level performance becomes a sort of re-creation; the sleeping work awakes and breathes and moves in accordance with the esoteric laws of its own being. But the re-creator, after all, can only re-create in terms of his own self. There will always be something of himself in his Beethoven or Mozart or Wagner or Verdi.

And he himself is subject to mutation. An old Greek philosopher rightly saw the universe as a complex of substances and forces always "flowing"; no man bathes twice

291

in the same river. But we can go beyond this, and say that the same man never plunges twice even into the same bathtub. . . .

And so with the true re-creative artist. The same great symphony becomes a different thing to him at different times not because it is itself a different thing but because he is a different being. So there is no conclusive finality either for him or for the rest of us in matters of this kind: there is no one and only "right" reading of any work, but several right readings. We become conscious of this when we compare a late Toscanini recording of a Beethoven symphony with one he had made some years earlier. It is not that he had changed his handling of this salient passage or that, but that his whole conception of the work had subtly changed; in each case the reading, though different, is organically, self-existently, one and indivisible.

For me this has always been the supreme feature of Toscanini's art as a conductor—that he gave me the impression, indeed, the conviction, that as a vast tonal web spun itself out upon the air I was following the actual mental process by which the music had come into being, though that long process had now been fused at high pressure into a single half-hour's or hour's consecutive organic thinking. It was the composer, rather than the conductor, whose most intimate company I had been privileged to keep for that time.

One night after some of us had been listening to a broadcast of the Beethoven Ninth my companions and I talked for a while about what we had just heard; and one of them finally remarked: "It's a funny thing, but after most musical performances one discusses the qualities of the performance, but after a Toscanini performance we talk about the work." This about sums it all up, at any rate for me.

What remains? What is his heritage?

The impression he gave that what we heard was the work

itself, that we had been bidden to the company of "the composer rather than the conductor," that invitation he wished to bequeath. And he did bequeath it to a certain extent: conductors today seek to move nearer to the text, they try to be more faithful to the composer in their fashion. Orchestral players, almost all of whom are aware of Toscanini, play the notes more punctiliously. Yet he left but a limited heritage, for his was an individual achievement, linked to his personality. Of course, about interpretation there cannot be a "conclusive finality," yet one regrets the passing of his convictions, his committed beliefs which then seemed conclusive. We have today, as we always did since the beginning of the relatively recent art of conducting, conductors who put themselves above the music. More perniciously to the cause of music, which ought to be an emotional experience if it is anything at all, we have conductors who present their programs in an unemotional, lukewarm, neutral, and "intellectual" aura. Afraid of wearing their hearts upon their sleeves, they hide the heart altogether. Or perhaps there is no heart to hide. We go to a concert and we hear technically adequate performances, and we feel something—much —is missing, we are not stirred and sometimes we are even bored by the great works. We wonder: have we lost our enthusiasm? Have we become blasé? Are we no longer able to respond to familiar sounds? No—it isn't that, it is passion we are missing. As against one Solti or one Bernstein we hear a dozen conductors who perform their office in a sanitary and objective manner. What Toscanini supplied, often to listeners who "didn't know anything about music," was the emotional thrill; he gave people a chance to respond to beauty in the ways which count: the goosepimple, the brimming eye, the beating heart.

One conductor, who in his tragically brief career was as yet little more than a disciple, might have grown to something near Toscanini's stature. That was Guido Cantelli. Toscanini loved him, counseled him, went to his rehearsals even when Cantelli conducted music the older man didn't care for (such as Bartok's *Concerto for Orchestra*), and smiled approvingly on him. Toscanini wrote Cantelli's wife, "I must tell you that for the first time in my long career as an artist I find a young man endowed with those qualities which cannot be defined, but which all the same are real and which carry an artist on high—very high . . ." *

Harris Goldsmith, the critic, observed:

Had he [Cantelli] lived longer, he would undoubtedly have been the pre-eminent conductor of the era. He began his tragically brief ascent in the Golden Age of the baton —the age of Toscanini, Walter, Klemperer, Monteux, and Furtwängler. He was born at the right time, but died too soon. His career, so brilliant and full of promise in the Fifties, was really meant for the Sixties, Seventies, and Eighties. As he himself remarked to one of his orchestral colleagues, had his reign equaled Toscanini's it would have extended to the year 2007.
In many ways, Cantelli's position was like Dinu Lipatti's in pianistic annals. He was much the same sort of artist. He too had an uncompromising mania for perfection; and like Lipatti's keyboard work, Cantelli's music-making exhibited keen sensitivity, patrician intensity, and rhythmic incisiveness. Here, plainly, was a conductor with intelligence, fire, humanity, and, most important of all, taste.
[*High Fidelity*, April, 1974]

He had these qualities but he was as yet unformed, rather he was as yet formed too firmly by his mentor. No doubt he would have expanded beyond the mold had he not been killed in the airplane crash on November 23, 1956, at Orly, en route to New York from Milan. The news of his death was kept from Toscanini, who used to ask, "Where is Guido; why doesn't he write?" and Walter, with a show of nonchalance, would answer, "Oh—he is probably too busy." I suspect that Toscanini knew the truth, that perhaps he had heard it on the radio, but that he himself refused to accept this truth: it was too horrible for him.

Toscanini did admire Leonard Bernstein and used to speak of "the fire the young man has in his heart." For a long time the two men remained strangers because, Toscanini was told,

* Quoted from Iris Cantelli, *Un Mucchio di Mani* (Rome, 1965).

"Bernstein belongs in the Koussevitzky camp." When they finally met they felt at once that they were of one mind and they got along famously. Bernstein remembers how they spent the better part of an afternoon discussing Berlioz's *Romeo and Juliet* and a hundred other topics, not alone musical.

Bernstein used as an excuse to call on Toscanini the question of a tempo in *Romeo and Juliet* which Toscanini had adopted and which in Bernstein's view did not comply with Berlioz's marking. He wanted to ask about this divergence. Toscanini jumped up, ran up the stairs, Bernstein hardly able to keep up with him, looked for the score, found it, then tried to locate his recording of the work, searched here and there, but of course had no idea where it was. Walter happened to be away that afternoon, so Toscanini finally gave up the search, after a few choice Italian expletives. When Bernstein got home, he realized that he had mistaken a Munch recording for a Toscanini recording. He immediately wrote Toscanini, apologizing. His letter crossed a letter from Toscanini which said that he had found the record, the tempo was not wrong, but neither was it good, it could be closer to what Berlioz had in mind, he, Toscanini, was stupid and thank you for pointing it out.

To this day Bernstein worships Toscanini. Just before Toscanini died, he sent Bernstein a quotation from the final fugue of *Falstaff*. Toscanini made a slight error in copying it. Bernstein looked at it and was overcome by an icy sadness. He knew the end was near.

5

During Toscanini's lifetime—and more frequently since his death—some adverse opinions were voiced. That is to be expected when an artist is extraordinary. One or two critics believed that his contrasts were occasionally exaggerated, that he artificially raised the blood pressure of music, that Mozart was conducted by him in too nervous a manner, that his fear of excessive sentimentality sometimes betrayed him into removing ease, plumpness, *Gemütlichkeit*, from certain works, that he refused to convey the kind of relaxation Bruno Walter did: Virgil Thomson, often an interesting writer, believed that Toscanini "overpowered" singers in operatic performances and obliged them "to force their volume," though the evidence clearly shows the contrary. In the performance of the *Missa Solemnis* Thomson perceived "no continuity in dynamic gamut." In a salute to Toscanini's eightieth birthday Thomson paid tribute to his "musical instinct as simple and as healthy as that of a gifted child," but as to his role in musical history Thomson made a grey prediction:

> Nobody else in our time has been so simple or so pure toward music as Toscanini. He will not loom large, I imagine, in the history books of the future, because he has mostly remained on the side lines of the creative struggle. And music's history is always the history of its composition. Toscanini has radically simplified the technique of orchestral conducting, and he has given a straightforwardness to all interpretation in our time that cannot fail to facilitate the execution problem for living composers. But his involvement with the formation of our century's musical style, with the encouragement of contemporary expression in music, with the living composers, in short, whose work will one day constitute the story of music in our time, has been less than that of any of today's other orchestral great. He has honor and glory now, but by posterity his work will probably pass unremunerated. [*The Art of Judging Music*]

Here speaks the composer, rather than the critic; one hears faintly the sound of the axe grinding. In point of fact Toscanini in youth and middle age was a champion of living composers, and not only of Bloch or Debussy or Strauss or Sibelius, who were fairly generally recognized. For example, the list of his first performances with the New York Philharmonic shows some twenty names of contemporaries, ranging from Shostakovich to Pizzetti to Hanson to Kodály to Busoni. He did not "feel," he said, Bartok, though he admired him, and he disliked the later Stravinsky and Schoenberg and Alban Berg. It is natural that in his old age he wanted to play the music he loved most, letting the light shine on it in the alembic of his thought.

While we must ruefully admit the evanescence of that thought, while we must acknowledge that like any interpreter, he was "a sculptor in snow," it is certain that his bequest is larger than the one predicted by Thomson. As I have said, his respect for the score has been handed on to modern music-making. All good interpreters have always looked at the score; fewer of them today look at it capriciously. Whimsy and waywardness are out of bounds and greater honesty distinguishes the better of today's performances.

And do we not have his recordings to remind us of his greatness? Yes—but they give only an imperfect reminder. At best they come as near as a good reproduction comes to the original painting, at worst they distort. Many of them suffer under a triple handicap. First, they were made too early, before stereo, when the skill of capturing sound was still in a beginning stage. Second, they were made in Studio 8H (before Carnegie Hall), which was a dry, unresonant studio tending to produce a shrill sound. Third, Toscanini took not the slightest interest in the problem of transmuting a concert performance into a record performance. He would never experiment as Stokowski did. To him a record needed to be a literal translation of what he heard in a live performance. He would never permit any change in the seating of the orchestra. The attempts to "enhance" the sound of the original recordings, undertaken by RCA engineers under the supervision of Walter Toscanini, ended mostly in failure.

Still, if we listen to the best of the records with an ear aided by imagination, we hear the sound of the phoenix.

If I were to choose those records I love most—a purely personal choice—I would never part with:

Beethoven: Symphony No. 3. Three versions available, 1939, 1949, 1953, all with NBC. 1953 is my choice.
Symphony No. 6. Contrast the BBC recording of 1937 with the 1952 NBC.
Symphony No. 9. NBC, 1952.

Berlioz: *Romeo and Juliet*. Orchestral Excerpt, NBC, 1947.

Brahms: Symphony No. 2. NBC, 1952.
                 Symphony No. 4. NBC, 1951.
Debussy: *La Mer*. NBC, 1950.
Moussorgsky: *Pictures at an Exhibition*. NBC, 1953.
Rossini: All the Overtures, but especially *Semir-
                 amide* and *L'Italiana in Algeri*. New
                 York Philharmonic, 1936.
                 *La Cenerentola, La Gazza Ladra, Il Si-
                 gnor Bruschino*. NBC, 1945.
R. Strauss: *Till Eulenspiegel*. NBC, 1952.
Verdi: *Requiem*. NBC, 1951.
Wagner: *Siegfried Idyll*. New York Philharmonic,
                 1936.
                 Götterdämmerung Excerpts. NBC, 1952
                 and 1949.
                 Die Meistersinger. Prelude, Act III.
                 NBC, 1951.

Of the operas I would retain all, even *Aida* and *Fidelio* with their flawed casts. Toscanini made mistakes when he chose his singers. Yet again, if you listen to the work as a whole, a concept is set before you which cannot be, or at least has not been, re-enacted. Of his operatic recordings, the most wonderful are *Otello, Falstaff*, and *Traviata*, because their casts are strongest. Vinay was a noble Otello, Valdengo a witty Falstaff, though perhaps a little too light of voice, and Albanese a lovely and passionate Violetta. In *Traviata* Toscanini did something of which I have never heard even an approximation: he made the first scene move in a continuity of tempo, febrile and frantic, never letting up, on and on, and thus not only put before us the ambience of the Parisian demi-monde, but made us understand at once that the love between Violetta and Alfredo was doomed.

In Milan a square is named after him, the Largo Toscanini. In Parma a street bears his name. In the museum of La Scala a corner is reserved for him and a bust of him (I think a poor one) decorates the theater's foyer, along with the sculptures of

Verdi and Puccini. At the Manhattan School of Music his death mask can be seen: it gives a false impression, since the face is in repose and there is even a little smile. "Perhaps only in death can a perfectionist finally smile," said the director of the school at the unveiling. The house in which he was born in Parma is turned into a museum. The Via Durini apartment is still intact, but the Riverdale villa has not been preserved. The New York Public Library contains a collection of the tapes, as does the Library of Congress. These mementoes are hardly needed by those who heard him: he gave them the only permanence in a fugacious world, the permanence of memory. Yet even those who did not hear him or see him in person, who did not fall under the spell of his magnetism, even they can feel emanate from the recordings the love he expended on every bar he conducted. He "put something" and in return we put something, such living love as has been offered to few interpreters. I conclude with the theme with which the biography began: he caused love for music to swell in us. It is the life-giving force, it is the animating impulse. Samuel Johnson, speaking of Pope, defined genius as "that energy which collects, combines, amplifies, and animates." Toscanini animated music.

CHRONOLOGY OF TOSCANINI'S CAREER

<table>
<tr><td></td><td></td><td align="right">His age</td></tr>
<tr><td>1867</td><td>March 25, born in Parma.</td><td></td></tr>
<tr><td>1876</td><td>Enters the Parma Conservatory.</td><td>9</td></tr>
<tr><td>1885</td><td>Graduates from the Conservatory.</td><td>18</td></tr>
<tr><td>1886</td><td>June 26, unexpected debut as conductor in Rio.
In November leads Catalani's Edmea in Turin.</td><td>19</td></tr>
<tr><td>1887</td><td>Plays as cellist in La Scala Orchestra at premiere
of Verdi's Otello.</td><td>20</td></tr>
<tr><td>1888 to
1895</td><td>Conducts in many Italian houses.</td><td>21 to
28</td></tr>
<tr><td>1896</td><td>Engaged by Turin. Conducts Götterdämmerung and
premiere of La Bohème.</td><td>29</td></tr>
<tr><td>1898</td><td>Conducts series of orchestral concerts in Italy.
Is summoned to La Scala.</td><td>31</td></tr>
<tr><td>1899 to
1908</td><td>At La Scala. Gives first performances in Italy of
Siegfried, Eugen Onegin, Salome (public rehearsal),
Pelléas et Mélisande, Louise.</td><td>32 to
41</td></tr>
<tr><td>1908</td><td>Goes to Metropolitan Opera.</td><td>41</td></tr>
<tr><td>1908 to
1915</td><td>At the Metropolitan; principal conductor from
1910 on.</td><td>41 to
48</td></tr>
<tr><td>1910</td><td>World premiere of La Fanciulla del West.</td><td>43</td></tr>
<tr><td>1913</td><td>New York debut as symphonic conductor,
Beethoven's Ninth.</td><td>46</td></tr>
<tr><td>1915</td><td>Breaks with Metropolitan. Returns to Italy.
Refuses regular engagements but gives performances
for soldiers and war benefits.</td><td>48</td></tr>
<tr><td>1920</td><td>Recalled to La Scala, forms orchestra and takes it
on Italian and American tour. Makes recordings
in Camden, New Jersey.</td><td>53</td></tr>
<tr><td>1921</td><td>La Scala reopens with him as musical director.</td><td>54</td></tr>
<tr><td>1926</td><td>Gives premiere of Turandot.</td><td>59</td></tr>
<tr><td>1926 to
1928</td><td>Dual role at La Scala and as conductor of
New York Philharmonic.</td><td>59 to
61</td></tr>
<tr><td>1929</td><td>Takes La Scala Ensemble to Berlin and Vienna. Is
appointed principal conductor of New York
Philharmonic.</td><td>62</td></tr>
</table>

BIBLIOGRAPHY

(Books only are mentioned. References to newspaper articles, magazine articles, letters, and other documents are given within the text.)

Albrecht-Carrié, René. *Italy, from Napoleon to Mussolini.* New York, 1950.

Aldrich, Richard. *Concert Life in New York, 1902–1923.* New York, 1941.

d'Amico, Fedele, and Paumgartner, Rosanna, editors. *La Lezione di Toscanini.* Florence, 1970.

Anonymous. *La Scala, Cronache, 1778–1960.* Milan, 1960.

Antek, Samuel. *This Was Toscanini.* New York, 1963.

Barblan, Guglielmo, and others. *Toscanini e La Scala.* Milan, 1972.

Blaukopf, Kurt. *Great Conductors.* London, 1955.

Bonardi, Dino. *Toscanini.* Milan, 1929.

Carse, Adam. *The Orchestra from Beethoven to Berlioz.* New York, 1948.

Chotzinoff, Samuel. *Toscanini, An Intimate Portrait.* New York, 1956.

Ciampelli, G. M. *Toscanini.* Milan, 1946.

della Corte, Andrea. *Toscanini visto da un critico.* Turin, 1958.

Dorian, Frederick. *The History of Music in Performance.* New York, 1942.

Downes, Olin. *On Music.* New York, 1957.

Erskine, John. *The Philharmonic-Symphony Society of New York. Its First Hundred Years.* New York, 1943.

Ewen, David. *Dictators of the Baton.* Chicago, 1943.

——. *The Man with the Baton.* New York, 1936.

——. *The Story of Arturo Toscanini.* New York, 1951.

Frassati, Luciana. *Il Maestro.* Turin, 1967.

[*Bibliography*]

Gatti-Casazza, Giulio. *Memories of Opera*. New York, 1941.

Gilman, Lawrence. *Toscanini and Great Music*. New York, 1938.

Haggin, B. H. *Conversations with Toscanini*. Garden City, 1959.
———. *The Toscanini Musicians Knew*. New York, 1967.

Hughes, Spike. *The Toscanini Legacy*. London, 1959. Revised Edition, New York, 1969.

Kolodin, Irving. *The Metropolitan Opera*. New York, 1966.
. *The Musical Life*. New York, 1958.

Kralik, Heinrich. *The Vienna Opera*. Vienna, 1963.

Krebs, Carl. *Meister des Taktstocks*. Berlin, 1919.

Labrocca, Mario, and Boccardi, Virgilio. *Arte di Toscanini*. Turin, 1966.

Lehmann, Lotte. *Midway in My Song*. Indianapolis, 1938.

Lyons, Eugene. *David Sarnoff*. New York, 1966.

Mahler, Alma. *Gustav Mahler, Memories and Letters*. London, 1946.

Marsh, Robert Charles. *Toscanini and the Art of Orchestral Performance*. Philadelphia, 1956.

The National Broadcasting Company. *The NBC Symphony Orchestra*. New York, 1938.

Newman, Ernest. *More Essays from the World of Music*. London, 1958.

Nicotra, Tobia. *Arturo Toscanini*. New York, 1929.

Sacchi, Filippo. *The Magic Baton*. London, 1957.

Sargeant, Winthrop. *Geniuses, Goddesses and People*. New York, 1949.

Sarnoff, David. *Looking Ahead*. New York, 1968.

Schliessmann, Hans. *Dirigenten von Gestern und Heute*. Vienna, 1928.

Schonberg, Harold C. *The Great Conductors*. New York, 1967.

Selden-Goth, Gisella, editor. *Toscanini* (in pictures). Vienna, 1937.

Seltsam, William N. *Metropolitan Opera Annals*. New York, 1947.

Sheehan, Vincent. *First and Last Love*. New York, 1956.

Stefan, Paul. *Toscanini*. Vienna, 1935; New York, 1936.

Storr, Anthony. *The Dynamics of Creation*. New York, 1972.

Strauss, Franz, and Strauss, Alice, editors. *Die Welt um Richard Strauss in Briefen*. Tutzing, 1967.

Taubman, Howard. *The Maestro*. New York, 1951.

Thomson, Virgil. *The Art of Judging Music.* New York, 1948.

Vergani, Orio. *Toscanini nella Pittura di Caselli.* Bergamo, 1950.

Wagner, Friedelind, and Cooper, Page. *Heritage of Fire.* New York, 1945.

Walter, Bruno. *Theme and Variations.* New York, 1946.

Weigel, Hans. *Das Buch der Wiener Philharmoniker.* Salzburg, 1967.

Wooldridge, David. *Conductor's World.* London, 1970.

INDEX

GEORGE R. MAREK

George R. Marek was born in Vienna, came to New York in 1920, and has lived here ever since. He joined RCA Records in 1950 and in due course became vice president and general manager. He worked with such musical personalities as Toscanini, Reiner, Heifetz, Rubinstein, Horowitz, Van Cliburn, Ormandy and such actors as Laurence Olivier and John Gielgud. On the Broadway scene, he recorded the original casts of *Hello Dolly, Fiddler on the Roof, Hair,* etc. He is interested in many kinds of music and has worked with Harry Belafonte on an anthology of Negro music.

He has written eight books on musical subjects, including biographies of Puccini, Richard Strauss, Mendelsshon and Beethoven. Of the last, Clifton Fadiman wrote that it "provides a reading experience of high value." His latest book is a biography of Franz Joseph and Elisabeth of Austria, *The Eagles Die.*

He is an enthusiastic traveler and a pretty good bridge-player.

1064